THE

# ORIGINAL CANADIAN CITY DWELLER'S ALMANAC

FACTS, RANTS, ANECDOTES *and*
UNSUPPORTED ASSERTIONS
*for* URBAN RESIDENTS

*by* HAL NIEDZVIECKI
*and* DARREN WERSHLER-HENRY

*illustrations by Marc Ngui*

VIKING
CANADA

VIKING CANADA

Published by the Penguin Group

Penguin Books, a division of Pearson Canada, 10 Alcorn Avenue, Toronto, Ontario, Canada M4V 3B2

Penguin Books Ltd, 80 Strand, London WC2R 0RL, England

Penguin Putnam Inc., 375 Hudson Street, New York, New York 10014, U.S.A.

Penguin Books Australia Ltd, 250 Camberwell Road, Camberwell, Victoria 3124, Australia

Penguin Books India (P) Ltd, 11, Community Centre, Panchsheel Park, New Delhi—110 017, India

Penguin Books (NZ) Ltd, cnr Rosedale and Airborne Roads, Albany, Auckland 1310, New Zealand

Penguin Books (South Africa) (Pty) Ltd, 24 Sturdee Avenue, Rosebank 2196, South Africa

Penguin Books Ltd, Registered Offices: 80 Strand, London WC2R 0RL, England

First published 2002

10 9 8 7 6 5 4 3 2 1

Text copyright © Hal Niedzviecki and Darren Wershler-Henry, 2002
Illustrations © Marc Ngui, 2002

Julie Doucet comic is reprinted by permission of *Drawn & Quarterly* Publications; "World-Class Vancouver" chart is reprinted by permission of Paul Razzell and Dominic Ali and *Geist* magazine; "Story of Anita's Missing Bike" is reprinted by permission of Sharon Wilson and *C.U.N.T.* zine; excerpts from *A Drifting Year* by Dany Laferriere is reprinted by permission of Douglas and McIntyre Publishing; "Montreal Break Down" is reprinted by permission of Valerie Joy Kalynchuk and Conundrum Press; "Milgaard and Me" by David Collier is reprinted by permission of David Collier and *Drawn & Quarterly* Publications; "Baroque a Nova" by Kevin Chong is reprinted by permission of Kevin Chong and Penguin Canada; *Lie With Me* excerpt by Tamara Faith Berger is reprinted by permission of Berger and Gutter Press; "Save Our Winnipeg Jets" comic is reprinted by permission of Bruce Coyston and Nicholas Burns; and "Sunburn Bathhouse" by Simona Chiose from *Good Girls Do* is reprinted by permission of Chiose and ECW Press.

Printed and bound in Canada on acid free paper.

NATIONAL LIBRARY OF CANADA CATALOGUING IN PUBLICATION

Niedzviecki, Hal, 1971–
    The original Canadian city dweller's almanac: facts, rants, anecdotes and unsupported assertions for urban residents /
    Hal Niedzviecki and Darren Wershler-Henry.

Includes bibliographical references and index.

ISBN 0-670-04338-9

1. City and town life—Canada.  I. Wershler-Henry, Darren S. (Darren Sean), 1966–  II. Title

HT127.N54 2002          307.76'0971          904614-9

Visit Penguin Books' website at **www.penguin.ca**

*To the remaining 20%*
*(Rural Canadians: Resistance is futile. You will be assimilated.)*

# Acknowledgments

Thanks to all of the editors and production people at Viking Canada for putting up with us, especially Susan Folkins, Tracy Bordian, Karen Alliston, Ed Carson, and Andrea Crozier. Thanks also to Jennifer MacTaggart, who suggested this project to us in the first place.

Special shout-outs to our design guy Kyle Gell for letting us drop by his studio at random moments; to photographer Paul Fairweather; to Jason Dunda, tastemaker extraordinaire, for the use of his lists (and to *Lola* magazine for letting us reprint them); and to all of the zinesters, authors, musicians, thinkers, and artists who let us write about them, interview them, and reprint their work in these pages.

Gigantic gratitude to Marc Ngui, essentially the third author of the *Almanac*, for his amazing, vertiginous illustrations.

Thanks also to Rachel and Liz for tolerance and understanding beyond the call of duty during the writing and assembly of this book.

Props to cousin Bradley for braving yet another mish-mash on our behalf.

Bits and pieces of this book originally appeared in various forms and mutations in fine Canadian periodicals, so thanks to *The Globe and Mail, Outpost, Geist, This, Broken Pencil, Masthead,* and *Azure* for finding room in their pages to ruminate on the urban Canadian environment.

*Hal Niedzviecki and Darren Wershler-Henry*

# Contents

**T**HE CANADIAN CITY STINKS.

It stinks of exhaust, fried eggs, heaped garbage, stale beer, urine, grey slush, pot smoke, perfume, sweat, sex, and wet pavement.

The Canadian city reeks.

It reeks of dreams, laughter, misery, promises, lies, births, deaths, failures, fuck-ups, families, friends, the lonely, the ugly, the beautiful, the lost, the found, and the in-between.

In other words, the city smells of life, and there's no other smell like it.

This book is an exploration of the Canadian city's unique stench. Part smarmy survival guide packed with disingenuous advice (the best place to get shit-faced, how to break into a bank machine), part obnoxious and hopelessly biased urban Canadian cultural primer (bands, books, publishers), part haphazard sociological study of the 21st century Canopolitan zeitgeist (goths, hockey players, squeegees), these pages are imbued with the scent of Canadian city life, just like the pages of *Cosmo* smell of Calvin Klein (well, no, *just as*, because our publishers didn't want to shell out for the Scratch-n-Sniff card we wanted so desperately to include).

### WHAT IS A CITY?

*In the old days, it was relatively easy to define the differences between urban and rural settlements, because cities were surrounded by walls. When the walls came down and the children of the nation began to roam the burbs freely in their parents' Ford Pintos, the distinction between the cities and the surrounding areas began.*

*Today, urban settlements are defined by legal boundaries, or, from a common-sense perspective, the limits of a contiguous built-up area. The legal definition of city varies around the world; as with most other aspects of postmodern life, confusion reigns.*

*As one Human Geography class's course outline put it so succinctly, "These definitions are arbitrary and significant class time should not be spent on them."*

Canada is no longer a nation of trappers, lumberjacks, farmers, and assorted benevolent small-town caricatures. We are accountants, computer programmers, retail clerks, dentists, poets, punk activists, plumbers, slackers, bus drivers, and students. We are every possible profession, race, creed, and religion. The sole thing that binds us together is that we live in Canadian cities.

In fact, *almost 80% of all Canadians today* live in urban communities. Yet many of us do not fully grasp the full implications of this new environment. We cling, as we did in 1957, to the notion of a Canada replete with clear streams dammed by pesky but adorable beavers, watched over by caribou and grizzlies being stalked by the burly, plaid-shirted outdoorsy types the media would like us to think are the real Canadians.

This book is, in many respects, a kind of dysfunctional family photo album, full of snapshots of the good, bad, and ugly sides of our urban clan, along with their various and sundry places of residence. Sometimes we've caught people with their eyes half-closed, or their pants down, or have inadvertently chopped off the tops of their heads. Some of the images herein are blurry, or underexposed, or missing from their frame on the page altogether (as cultural anthropologists, we are avowed amateurs). The brief and hopelessly superficial remarks we have scrawled in the margins reference everything from pollution to sprawl to rising rents and the invasion of the cookie-cutter box store … but it's not like we have a lot of answers to the ills affecting our cities, or even a thesis, really. A family album doesn't really have a plot or a conclusion, just lots of weird characters and scenery of sporadic interest. And be warned: the imagery can sometimes be graphic—or dangerous. A cautionary parable follows.

While inching our way up Toronto's Don Valley Parkway, aka "The Don Valley Parking Lot"—an auto-engorged ribbon of concrete that parallels the polluted trickle of what used to be a major river—to meet with the bigwigs at our publisher's corporate HQ, traffic begins to slow below even the normal crawl. Just before the Bloor Street Viaduct we pass several police cars and an ambulance. On the span of concrete railway bridge looming overhead, an agitated figure mimes a bobbing up-and-down motion for a yellow rain-slickered police officer. Ambulance attendants in the ditch far below are just pulling a sheet over a crumpled mass. "Jumper," your quick-witted editors pronounce in unison. (With its plethora of dizzying bridges and hard pointy landing surfaces, the Don Valley is Toronto's dry-dive central.)

A macabre event that, while not exactly representative of the entire zeitgeist of the Canadian city, is not exactly without resonance, either.

While the official myth of Canada as a great unspoiled northland replicates and perpetuates itself, the other unofficial myth—of a Canada of clean, friendly, safe, and fun cities with nicknames like Toronto the Good—has become a bad joke. Both myths leave us unprepared for our inevitable confrontations with the raw reality that lies beneath the crinkly cellophane—and unable to address the problems that our cities are facing.

*Canadians have flocked to the cities, but their institutions, their habits of mind, and especially, perhaps, their mythology, have lagged behind. The jut-jawed outdoorsman, still vivid against a prairie sky, a rocky coastline or a stand of black spruce, still works long hours as a national symbol. To a degree, this is very well: such people exist, and their race will, we profoundly trust, endure, providing a flesh-and-blood link with the pioneer past. But the unromantic fact is that most Canadians today are not like this at all. They live and work in cities and towns; their environment, for most of the year at least, is an urban and largely man made one.*

—The Royal Commission on Canada's Economic Prospects (The Gordon Commission), Final Report, 1957

*In sprawling urban areas such as Toronto, Vancouver and Montreal, gridlock plagues commuters and companies that ship goods by truck, but there's not enough money for mass transit or road improvements. Smog-related asthma among urban children has been rising dramatically. Homelessness in economically vibrant cities such as Calgary and Mississauga, Ontario, once unknown, is now endemic. Garbage on the streets is no longer swept away promptly, public parks fall into disrepair, and untreated municipal sewage pours into city harbours from one end of the country to the other.*

—John Lorinc, "Decline and Fall of the Great Canadian Cities," Saturday Night, 2001

Look, don't get us wrong. Even as we were trying to portray the Canadian city in all its unique and dubious glory (while having a little fun in the process), we realized something: we love our cities. Mockery, sarcasm, and irony—our generation's birthright—only go so far. To

write about the Canadian city is to celebrate it. We are 100% *for* the Canadian city, and wouldn't live anywhere else. We want you to come away from this book enthused, amazed, and surprised at the possibilities of urban life. But if this book also leaves you concerned about the problems our cities are facing, and how little both their denizens and politicians seem to care, well, so be it. We're just trying to tell it like it is. Lingering anxiety is now just as recognizable a feature of our cities as the CN Tower, Mount Royal, the Citadel, or Stanley Park.

Forget everything you thought you knew. Abandon your myths, your dreams, your pretensions. For the next couple of hundred pages, give in and chill out. We'll show you desires you didn't know you had, places you didn't know you needed to go, and we'll introduce you to the Canadian city's most delectable treats and fascinating personalities. We are your tour guides. Grab your stun guns, flasks, cameras, raincoats, rappelling equipment, condoms, cheap sunglasses, phones, smokes, bus tickets, and (most importantly) your noseplugs.

It's time to enter the city.

*Hal Niedzviecki*
*Darren Wershler-Henry*

**"It's so clean and bland! I'm home!"**
    —*Marge Simpson, on visiting Toronto*

# Zeitgeist

SOME PEOPLE BELIEVE that every time and place has a spirit, an essence, a bouillon that can be distilled from the aesthetics, politics, passions, and prejudices of the moment. Germans and tedious academics call this spirit a *zeitgeist*, and frankly, who are we to argue? This first chapter presents a Coles Notes–style summary (with all the reductiveness, overgeneralization, and general obtuseness the designation implies) of the bathtub brew that is the zeitgeist of the 21st-century Canadian city. Drink deep, as long as you're not driving.

# Beginnings

We all have to start somewhere.

Most of Canada's cities began as either trading posts, territorial pronouncements, or a combination of both. Way back in 1608, Samuel de Champlain founded a fur outlet near present-day Quebec City. Montreal had a similar start. In 1795 Edmonton began as Edmonton House, built by the Hudson's Bay Company to better facilitate fur trading in the region. It was a log building, 60 feet by 24 feet, roofed with sod—a long-ass way from the glory of West Edmonton Mall.

On the east coast, St. John's and other Atlantic cities were founded primarily as fishing outposts or military bases. In 1739 British Admiral Peter Warren had the following to say about the founding of Halifax: "The form and situation of the islands of Canso seems calculated by nature for the use of the fishery and nothing else, for which reason a small fortification there for the protection of the fishery would be necessary."

Although Montreal, Quebec City, and St John's are among the oldest communities in North America, like most Canadian cities, they weren't actually incorporated as such until the second half of the 1800s, when their populations were already in the thousands.

At least two of our greatest cities were founded pretty much by accident. York—later renamed Toronto because there were already too many towns named York—was founded when the Upper Canada brain trust decided that Kingston (the capital of the day) was too vulnerable in the event of an American attack. So they moved the government types and the lawyers farther west (though arguably not far west enough … Hawaii would have been sufficient) down Lake Ontario, where they've been sitting ever since. The place wasn't exactly a roaring success, however. Says Frances Stewart, a pioneer, in 1822:

> *The Town or village of York looked pretty from the lake as we sailed up in a schooner, but on our landing we found it not a pleasant place, as it sunk down in a little amphitheatre cut out of the great bleak forest. The lake*

---

*At 8 o'clock this morning 21 guns were fired from the Citadel. This salute was in response to the salute fired on Saturday by the Austrian war-ship Novaro. The military authorities at the Citadel, on Saturday, it is said, failed to comply with the regulations, by not firing gun for gun with the Novaro, having only returned 11 guns to 21 by the latter. Explanations were called for and the matter was arranged satisfactorily. At 9 o'clock this morning the American flagship Constellation saluted the Citadel with 21 guns, which was promptly returned by the latter. The Constellation then saluted the flag of Vice Admiral Fanshawe, with 15 guns which was returned with an equal number for the Royal Alfred. The Novaro then saluted with 15 guns, duly acknowledged by the latter.*

—Newspaper report of "very brisk" saluting at the Halifax Citadel, July 10, 1871

---

Calgary from the Elbow River on the Canadian Pacific Railway, 1885

*in front is full of rushes which have been caught and left to decay in the shallow water, causing it to be very unhealthy. It is not a healthy town (fever and ague are common) and it is said to be much fallen off within the last 2 years; a deadness hangs over everything, Kingston is much preferred as a place of residence.*

In a similar vein, when Lord Selkirk toured Yonge Street in 1803 he noted that it was well settled, but remarked, "No trade passes this way."

Out West, things weren't much different. George Young's *Manitoba Memories* (1897) describes Winnipeg, originally part of the Red River Colony and founded by the Hudson's Bay Company to develop fur trading with the natives. In 1868, two years before Manitoba entered the Dominion, Young wrote: "What a sorry sight was presented by that long-thought-of town of Winnipeg on the day we entered it! What a mass of sticky Red River mud was everywhere spread out before

us!" (The wide streets that persist there to this day were a result of oxcarts moving ever outward in an attempt to avoid becoming trapped where others had previously passed.)

Calgary was founded in 1875 by an order to establish a fort on the Bow River, which was intended to discourage fur smugglers from across the US border. A police officer and his guide staked out a buffalo robe marking the spot where the fort was to be built, in the vicinity of present-day Holy Cross Hospital. It was named Fort Calgary—thought to mean "clear-running water" in Gaelic—because of its location on the crux of the two rivers. Later, academics would argue that Calgary actually means something like "big pasture"—which is more like it, because as the example of Winnipeg had already established, what mixing two rivers together produces, mostly, is mud.

In keeping with this tradition of inauspicious beginnings, Vancouver was somewhat arbitrarily established by Sir William Cornelius Van Horne, head of the

BEGINNINGS

National Archives of Canada

Canadian Pacific Railway, who decided that the railway would end at that particular harbour. He wrote to his trusty aide in 1885: "Hamilton, this eventually is destined to be a great city in Canada. We must see that it has a name that will designate its place on the map of Canada. Vancouver it shall be, if I have the ultimate decision." As it happened, Vancouver started up with the less grand but much more accurate appellation of Gastown. Then, when it was more than a cluster of shacks but still basically a sawmill, it was christened Granville. Finally it was renamed Vancouver, after the English explorer-captain who proved once and for all that there was no such thing as the Northwest Passage. Official centennial historian Margaret Ormsby provides this account of Vancouver in 1929:

> *The spirit of the city was still, as it had been at the beginning, predominantly materialistic. An eager, grasping, acquisitive community, it squandered its own resources of natural beauty, all the time extending its economic power until it held most of the province in fee.*

Ouch. But keep in mind that much the same could be said for most of Canada's cities. Founded with economics and politics in mind, Canadian cities have their roots in hardscrabble realpolitik that kept concerns like conservation pretty far down on the list. As historian J.G. MacGregor puts it, "Great cities grow only where resources abound and only when men are ready to use them."

No account of our unpromising beginnings would be complete without a discussion of July 1st, on which we celebrate Dominion Day, aka the beginning of Canada— always a contentious occasion for anyone with a bone to pick with the federation, such as the Maritimers, the Québécois, the Westerners, the Torontonians, and the Northerners. Halifax's reaction to dominion demonstrates the Canadian city's typical positivism. When Nova Scotia joined Canada in 1867, parades, celebrations, and fireworks ensued on July 1st to mark the occasion. But Haligonians were not impressed. The *Nova Scotian* reported that half the stores "were doing business: showing unmistakably that it requires something more than a proclamation to compel men to rejoice … over the destruction of the liberties of their country."

# Ottawa:
# The Nation's Capital

Like most Canadian cities, Ottawa (a) has an ignoble history and (b) came into being through a combination of paranoia, chance, and the tedious but nearly unstoppable machinations of bureaucracy.

In the interest of creating a stopping point between Kingston and Montreal so that Upper and Lower Canada could communicate in the heady, dangerous days after

Timber raft on the Ottawa River, 1899

the war of 1812, the Powers That Be sent one Lieutenant-Colonel By to build a canal between those aforementioned major cities. By planned out a canal and town around the waterway, which he called, with the kind of flair and modesty all too frequently demonstrated by military officers at the time, Bytown.

With a canal, a river, and plenty of trees to cut down, Bytown grew like a cold sore. By 1855 the place was too large to retain such a lame name, so it was incorporated and christened Ottawa. Twenty years later, on the other side of the river, Wright's Town would follow Ottawa's example and become the city of Hull. (To this very day, Hull remains Ottawa's id, sustained largely by pork-barrelling, greasy spoons, late-night boozecans, strip joints, and the various and sundry other services necessary to sustain a population of civil servants; hence the expression, "I'll see you in Hull, you bastard.")

But the fun and games of establishing a seat of government was far from over. In 1857, Quebec, Montreal,

Ottawa Parliament Buildings, 1912

BEGINNINGS

Kingston, and Toronto all vied to be named capital of what was then the Province of Canada. In typically bold Canadian fashion, we invited Queen Victoria to make the final choice. For reasons that are either lost in the mists of time or obscured by indifference, she picked Ottawa (who said she didn't have a sense of humour? Maybe it was all those marijuana seeds that her physician prescribed for her menstrual cramps).

Work on the Parliament buildings began immediately. As if to test the country's resolve, Ottawa was almost burned to the ground in 1900, then the Parliament itself was razed by fire in 1916. Rather than come to our senses and move the government to a balmier spot, we sucked it up and rebuilt. As a result, Ottawa now has a thriving industrial climate based on museum revenues, skate rentals, and the sale of "beaver tails," a sort of greasy, deep-fried pancake topped with a yummy assortment of fats and sugars.

For better or worse, these are the defining characteristics of our immediate past: egotism, piss-poor urban planning, and the bumblings of timid bureaucrats. But hey, self-awareness is half the battle, right? Knowing these things now ("An Important Part of Our Cultural Heritage") makes it much, much easier to take a long hard look at the contemporary Canadian urban zeitgeist.

# Angst and Alienation

*Now that Toronto is becoming a world-class city we need more than ever to be conscious of our relationships to others and the community at large. Making small talk with slight acquaintances and strangers is by no means a solution to the problems of anxiousness and alienation that accompany our growing urbanism, but it can, as they say, "grease the pig."*

—Lorne Foster, City Magazine, *1988*

"The city is a fraud," proclaimed William Teron in a prominent 1970s screed. "For it beckons people to it on the premise that it offers a diverse life, but, because of the city's inefficiency and the resulting high cost in time and money of every human transaction within the city, the individual has been alienated from it."

Well and good, but here at Almanac headquarters, we take a different tack on the matter. The city is not a fraud at all—what you see is what you get.

With its intimidating press of tall buildings, subways rushing to nowhere at unthinkable speeds, and omnipresent crowds of sneering, glamorous hipsters, the city promises alienation and angst, and delivers exactly that—by the busload. No matter who you are, or how successful and well adjusted you might be, if you live in

FELLOW CITIZENS

the city, you've felt its power to set people against each other, alienate friends and neighbours, and leave each and every one of its millions of denizens feeling totally and absolutely alone.

So why fight it? *Embrace* the big-city mystique. Learn to cultivate your alienation and angst—building blocks in the construction of a better you—alone and embittered on the dim streets of the dirty metropolis. Here are some quick tips and techniques that'll help you enhance your alienation from "every human transaction within the city":

- Refuse to talk to anyone in public. When people talk to you, shake your head and stare at them blankly. If someone asks you for directions, point randomly and keep on walking. If necessary, communicate with a pad and pencil. Dark sunglasses and a portable MP3 player are also helpful in creating that all-important bubble of "personal space."

- Stand perilously close to the subway platform with your head down and your arms slack at your sides. When a train comes, appear agonized, like you can't decide about something. If someone asks you if you're all right, alternate between bursting into tears and laughing in their face.

- Order an expensive coffee replete with all manner of flavours, sprinkles, syrups, and whipped creams. As the "baristas" (shouldn't that be "Maquiladoristas"?) pass it to you over the counter, drop the coffee. Apologize profusely and accept their offer to make you another free of charge. Repeat.

- Taking a page from the 80s "straight edge" movement, proclaim yourself booze-, cigarette-, and drug-free. Go to bars, shows, and raves with your pals. Mock them constantly for their inability to follow your example of purity. Ingest illegal substances alone in the clear pure light of dawn.

ANGST AND ALIENATION

- Go into the local co-op women-friendly sex shop and ask in a loud voice if you can sign up for the cunnilingus class.
- Never answer your door. People come around with their causes, looking for your dollars and your sympathy. It's best to ignore them.
- Get call display. Sometimes people you don't know will call with their causes, especially if they can't get in the front door.
- Every time you think about, say, clearing the snow off the stretch of sidewalk belonging to the 90-year-old grandma next door, ask yourself: Am I getting paid for this?
- Don't frequent the same bars and restaurants every week. The staff and other patrons might become familiar and try to talk to you.
- You know that great idea you had about solving the problem of traffic congestion in your neighbourhood? Forget about it.
- Jane Jacobs is always popping up somewhere, telling us how to fix our cities. Whenever you encounter a Jacobs tome, the quickest cure is to immediately watch several episodes of *Entertainment Tonight*, back to back. (See *Denizens, Intellectuals* for something on Jacobs that's less snotty.)
- Buy a wheelchair, dye your hair grey, and call Meals on Wheels. Tell them you're a broke, crippled shut-in. Arrange for delivery. You deserve a treat today.

# Mental Illness

It's no surprise that, for reasons ranging from the insane climate to the uncertain economy to the high cost of renting a crumbling downtown shack, a considerable number of Canadians are stressed, depressed, or downright bone crazy. Problem is, no one knows how many of us are a few beers short of a two-four.

In May 2002 Statistics Canada launched its first-ever major survey of Canadian mental health. Lorna Bailie, Statscan's assistant director of health statistics, says that despite not knowing the number of mentally ill Canadians, they do know that five of the ten leading causes of disability are related to mental disorders.

Meanwhile, Phil Upshall, president of the Mood Disorders Society of Canada, says that one in five Canadians will suffer depression at some point, and that an increasing number of people suffer from eating disorders, panic attacks, and other psychological concerns.

National Archives of Canada

Incline railway, Mount Royal Park, Montreal, 1875

# Your *Mental Breakdown* in *Montreal* Will Require Careful *Planning*

**by Valerie Joy Kalynchuk, from *All Day Breakfast***

Your mental breakdown in Montreal will require a year or more of careful planning. Here are a few tips to get you started:

1. If you don't speak French well enough to talk about what the matter is, make sure your apartment is in a postal code served by an English hospital. (The system is sectorized in Montreal so that, as one doctor put it, "Folks can't go shoppin' around for psychiatrists.")

   Or

   Spend an extra year learning to speak French fluently BEFORE organizing your major depressive episode, or other mental illness.

2. If you can't afford ninety-dollar-an-hour psychotherapy, put yourself on a list to see a psychologist for free through your CLSC, hospital or clinic. The waiting period will be three to six months. Buy an agenda notebook and pencil in your breakdowns, breakups, job losses and all the other events to occur around the time someone will be calling you back about therapy.

3. If, in planning all this, you find yourself getting depressed long before it is feasible to do so, head for the office of any GP and leave any cynicism you may have regarding medication in whatever overcrowded waiting room you are waiting in. You can be in and out of the office in under 15 minutes with a handy dandy SSRI script in your pocket. Pick one of your fave colours!

Remember, pharmaceutical companies have one motivation only: helping you to function.

4. If you are getting impatient and want to have a psychotic episode, say this coming Thursday, you would do best to plan it between 8 AM and 5 PM, when psychiatrists are on emergency duty. The advice of overnight residents in the ER can be quite enlightening, however. My own life was changed by these two pearls uttered by two different med students not much older than myself.

"Well just—don't cry so much, ok? Eh?" and "When I can't sleep sometimes I like to have a cup of warm milk." •

# *Montreal*

**by David McGimpsey**

"Montreal winter is like a hundred funerals,"
I said to my new best friend in the world,
"if by a hundred one means a thousand."
My new best friend, a sophomore at Dartmouth,
in town to fete Quebec's sweet liquor laws,
took my insight philosophically:
"Whoa, dude," he said, "you should love your city
more." Weekend trips for students languishing
in their worlds of 21 or Over

continued

MENTAL ILLNESS

are as Montreal as a two-cheeked kiss
or a fist fight in the grand parking lot
of the Place Versailles Mall. Do I not love?
Have I not defended this city right down
to not being able to turn right on red?
Did I not suggest local personalities
Ron Reusch, Mitsou and The Great Antonio,
have their faces carved in Mount Royal?
And just this past Saint Patrick's Day Parade,
the oldest such parade in North America,
did I not welcome the Grand Marshall
to splendid Sainte Catherine Street by yelling
"Hey! Sparky! I'm a helicopter! Whoo!"?
It's been a bad year.
Despite the best efforts of Britney Spears
and Katie Couric to keep us all perky,
despite assurances from know-it-alls
who say Silken Laumann and Catriona LeMay Doan
are actually two different people,
Montreal has limped along with its limp:
Pierre Trudeau and Mordecai Richler are gone
and somebody said they saw Leonard Cohen
in the Gap, berating a clerk, saying
"You call this snug-fit?" I've been staying clear
of The Smoked Meat Hut and Chez Rosbif alike,
and the east winds that push refinery smoke
away from the island, turn warm with Spring:
I've been anticipating the last season
of the cursed but cute Montreal Expos,
who've now been contracted to be patsies,
baseball's answer to the Washington Generals;
by September our star outfielder
will be traded to the Yankees or Sox
for an astigmatic shortstop and a can
of diet soda; in the grandstand of the Big O
I will read O Magazine and I will have
a Dr. Phil Moment with the sucker

who sits beside me; I'll make up homespun
sayings that make no sense: "As mad as
a june bug with a cotton flyswatter,"
"Tired as a hen in a peach orchard
with a junebug sitting in the choir."
With Nos Amours in last place for the last time,
(the Winston-Salem Expos #1!)
I will not wait for the July moving day
to sing the simple songs of POM bread
and the pain du POM festival de poesie
to say "O the poutine O the bagels;
O bagels stuffed full of poutine!" I will
even finish my stinging reply to
the Toronto writer who suggested
Montreal should be renamed "Loserton."
Sophisticated in both cappuccino AND latte,
I will say we deserve something classier
something along the lines of "Loserton Heights."
After all, there's a place just up the street
which claims to have invented "hot chicken"
and a place called "verres sterilises"
(sterilized glasses) where, coincidentally,
I met my new best friend in the whole world.
His girlfriend, Taffy-Jane, was there with him
and she was just as philosophical.
A sports therapist who really believes
glue pots can be motivated toward the roses,
she said "you should really just try to love
yourself a little more." I left for home,
through the Plateau streets towards
pigeon-gray downtown. The chesterfield.
I should love myself a little more
God, I hope she means that in a sexual way. ●

Though we at the Almanac are hardly qualified quacks, we can't resist noting that as Canada has become increasingly urbanized, suburbanized, and generally paved over, more and more of us have gone nuts. Now why would that be?

Making matters worse, mental illness affects more than just the individuals who are suffering from it. Epidemiologist Tom Stephens estimated in 2001 that mental illness costs the Canadian economy $13.4 billion a year through lost productivity or sick days.

The Statscan results will be released in fall 2003. Until then, we here at the Almanac are pleased to offer you this book, which is filled with important advice about hanging on to your marbles.

# Crime

Despite media histrionics, right-wing whining, and the steady demands of urban police forces across the country for more cops, copters, and cash, crime in our cities has been on a steady decline for the last decade. In general, the denizens of urban Canada are on pretty good behaviour. It's entirely possible that you're more likely to be mugged wandering the empty late-night streets of Stratford, Ontario, or Merritt, British Columbia, than you are taking a 2 a.m. stroll through downtown Winnipeg or Windsor. The same thing that makes a city dangerous—the fact that it's filled with people—is what keeps it safe.

In fact, the vast majority of crime in the city is not particularly violent. Some of it's even relatively amusing—though not necessarily for the guilty party (see *Arts & Entertainment, Elvis Impersonators*). Consider the case of Ann Nagle, arrested in Halifax in 1870 for stealing. After police confronted her, they discovered that she had large quantities of stolen dry goods, dresses, spices, sugar, coffee, and tea hidden in various caches. Apparently, she was about to be married and had taken to stealing to expand her trousseau. She got 18 months in the pen instead.

Fast-forward to the year 2001 and we come to the story of the Toronto Emergency Task Force rescuing a 42-year-old female hostage in a motel room ... *after* her abductor fell asleep from gorging on the two orders of Kentucky Fried Chicken he'd demanded the police deliver.

Our KFC-loving friend would have been in real trouble if the year had been 1649 and the place Quebec City. The first executioner in Canada, a pardoned criminal, performed his inaugural assignment that year on a 16-year-old girl found guilty of theft. (The last executions in Canada took place in 1962—two murderers just after midnight in Toronto's Don Jail.)

Of course when something serious does go down, it tends to be in a city, sending shock waves across Canada that carry the invisible—and totally fraudulent—vibe of a violent cityscape. Every time such a crime occurs, the media wring their hands and say "Look at how violent our cities are!" Rural types around the country watch on satellite TV and make smug "told you so" noises.

That was certainly the case when, in an incident of appalling urban desensitization, a badly beaten half-naked teenager was left lying next to a Montreal office building for several hours before any one of the several workers who saw her bothered to call the cops. Workers arrived and saw her at 7:25 a.m., but nobody did anything about it until nearly three hours later.

CRIME

# ORGANIZED CRIME IN CANADA: A Meteorological Survey

## ❧ LEGEND ❧

### Genres of Criminal Organizations

- (T) Traditional (Mafia)
- (A) Asian-Based
- (EE) Eastern European
- (MG) Outlaw Motorcycle Gangs

### Types of Criminal Activities

 Cocaine (trafficking)

Heroin (trafficking)

 Marijuana (production and trafficking)

Extortion

Prostitution

 Gambling

 Smuggling

Methamphetamine (production and trafficking)

 Fraud

 Gang Warfare

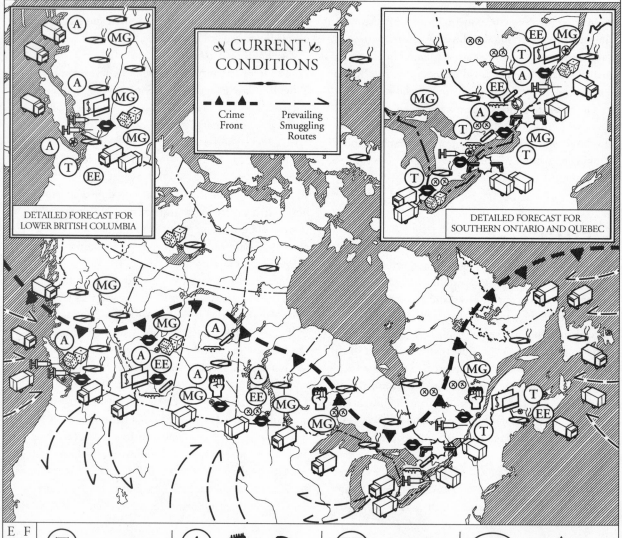

## ❧ CURRENT CONDITIONS ❧

▲▲ Crime Front

- - → Prevailing Smuggling Routes

DETAILED FORECAST FOR LOWER BRITISH COLUMBIA

DETAILED FORECAST FOR SOUTHERN ONTARIO AND QUEBEC

## EXTENDED FORECAST

(T)  Drug trafficking and money laundering and illegal gaming will continue to be essential activities.

(A)  Alliances with youth gangs will be used as a means to build a labour pool and protect senior members.

(EE)  Increase in the use of legitimate businesses to conceal and launder criminal profits.

(MG)  Continued growth of the Hell's Angels will exacerbate tension with rival U.S. expansionist OMG, the Bandidos.

of coming to Canada's cities. Though the *People's Daily* of Beijing once described Canada as a "land of ice and snow" and discouraged Chinese from emigrating here by claiming that a recent survey of Chinese emigrants found them jobless and destitute, Canada receives immigration applications from China in the tens of thousands every year.

For the most part, urban Canadians do their best to welcome those who continue to flock to our cities—75% of immigrants who came to Canada between 1981 and 1996 settled in Canada's three largest cities. The Canadian people even received an award in 1986 in appreciation for the country's efforts to welcome refugees.

But despite all anecdotal and statistical evidence that immigrants are a boon to Canadian cities, the cliché of the dirty, resource-sucking immigrant continues to be trotted out by reactionary right-wing proles. In the 21st century, we can only hope that a newer, truer cliché can take root: that of a country of cities populated and made what they are today through the industry and inherent humanity of immigrants and their ancestors.

# Nostalgia: Dare to Get Drunk Where Your Father Did

When the seedy, veteran Toronto rock and roll club the El Mocambo (best recognized by the garish palm tree adorning its exterior) announced that it was closing its famed upstairs stage, the local and even the national media made it sound as though Can-rock had finally died. Lengthy articles and reports lavished attention on its supposedly celebrated past and bemoaned its fate at the hands of its callous new ownership.

The ElMo's reputation was truly international—this was the home of many legendary shows, including the 1978 Elvis Costello gig that was first broadcast on FM radio, then bootlegged and later turned into an actual CD. (*Darren's personal ElMo nostalgia note:* When I first moved to Toronto over a decade ago, this album alone inspired a visit to the ElMo's shrine; I was convinced all through junior high that Elvis was the only person on the planet more cynical, ungainly, and pissed off than I was … though a thousand other future record store employees evidently felt the same way. Killing a cockroach on top of the bar with the bottom of my beer mug was the only omen I needed to convince me that I had truly arrived in the big city.)

But was the latest of the ElMo's closings really nigh for Toronto tunage? A lengthy CBC Radio report on the ElMo failed to mention that its heart and soul—booker Dan Burke—was relocating, following the lead of such classic ElMo events as monthly glam-queer dance party Vazaleen, now held at a Bloor Street location. The reports focused on the past and ignored the future. (Sadly, the Burke relocation never got off the ground, but the media didn't know that at the time…)

So why the feeding frenzy of doom? The answer can be boiled down to one word: nostalgia.

Like a tapeworm in the colon, nostalgia feeds off our desires. The enemy of artistic and cultural production, nostalgia is the sense we have that our present day is empty, our creative urges pointless, our aesthetic redundant, our dreams displaced by those who did it faster, harder, better—all before we were out of diapers. Nostalgia lodges deep inside, attaches itself to our every

# NOSTALGIA: A Symptomatic Guide

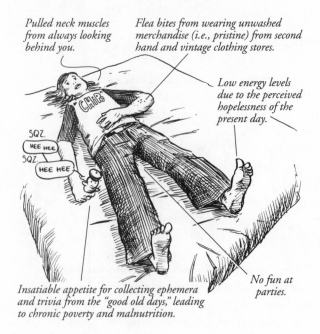

Pulled neck muscles from always looking behind you.

Flea bites from wearing unwashed merchandise (i.e., pristine) from second hand and vintage clothing stores.

Low energy levels due to the perceived hopelessness of the present day.

*Insatiable appetite for collecting ephemera and trivia from the "good old days," leading to chronic poverty and malnutrition.*

*No fun at parties.*

effort, leaves us perpetually hungry no matter how much we consume.

In the urban environment, nostalgia is particularly corrosive. It provides a mythical alternative city, a chimera by which we can compare our deflated present to a pumped-up past. Nostalgia tells us that things will never again be as good as when the Rolling Stones smelled like teen spirit, not corporate ooze. As the legend goes, long before Jagger et al. were the geriatric gentlemen of arena rock, they spontaneously and completely rocked our world by staging a surprise takeover of the vaunted El Mocambo, in the process securing the club's status through the ages, despite the horrible sightlines, lack of ventilation, and reek of stale beer. Pointing the way to a vibrant past (that never really was) at the expense of a (supposedly) lousy present, nostalgia gnaws away at our cultural confidence.

In its guise as fuel for "tourist attractions," nostalgia also consigns significant segments of our urban centres to the status of third-rate theme parks. Downtown Calgary, for example, is choked with gimcrack "Western" stores, most of which sell the same raggedy assortment of stale maple sugar candy, cute Mountie figurines, Western shirts, beef jerky, beer mugs silk-screened with pictures of moose, cheap cowboy hats, and "dreamcatchers" made somewhere in Asia. This farrago of crap isn't representative of past, present, or (keep your fingers crossed) future culture in Calgary or anywhere else. Rather, such objects stand in for culture and history in a generic way, offering contempt to both the culture they supposedly represent *and* the people who so gladly purchase them.

But urban nostalgia can also serve as a signpost pointing the way toward inspiration.

When the city of Edmonton finally demolished what used to be called "the Rathole," a 169-metre-long blind tunnel built in 1927 to accommodate the CN tracks crossing Edmonton's 109th Street, Edmontonians naturally wanted to pay homage to this long-time traffic blight. A procession of cars, led by a 1924 Buick, took one final journey through the aging structure just prior to its demolition. But let us tell you, nobody got all teary-eyed for its demise. Benevolent nostalgia speaks to us of another era, even idealizes that era, but does so in a way that nevertheless recognizes the primacy of our own living, breathing struggles. Urban nostalgia should be about making things better and moving forward—not becoming mired in a celebrated past.

A great example of this can be found in the ongoing legacy of Mae Brown, who in 1972 graduated from the University of Toronto as Canada's first deaf-blind university degree holder. With the committed help of her "tutor" Joan Mactavish—who patiently guided Mae through, among other things, a psychology multiple

So yes, we feel obliged to admit that, generally, the most shocking crimes *do* seem to occur in urban areas. Though this is by no means the place for a comprehensive list of urban Canadian crimes, following are a few dramatic incidents that will forever blight the urban environments where they occurred.

On March 16, 1946, a group of children playing just outside of Hamilton discovered something nasty: a mutilated male torso, with the head and limbs missing. It turned out to be the body of the late John Dick, a poor, salt-of-the-earth-type streetcar driver who had been unhappily married to a much less solid citizen, a woman named Evelyn.

Born Evelyn MacLean to a thieving drunkard of a father and a mother who prostituted her to rich older men inclined to give expensive gifts (such as gold jewellery, a car, several diamond rings, expensive clothes from Eaton's—all of which Evelyn managed to have during WWI without holding down a job), Evelyn had several strikes against her out of the gate. The last of Evelyn's three illegitimate pregnancies, a baby boy named Peter, "disappeared" after Evelyn's discharge from the hospital.

Evelyn married John Dick in October of 1945. He was 16 years older than her, and lived a very basic lifestyle because he was supporting his mother and grandmother. Depending on whom you believe, Evelyn either spent her wedding night with Bill Bohozuk, her lover, or in bed beside her mother. For about five months, the newlyweds fought like cats and dogs, occasionally sharing residences. Then John Dick disappeared.

When the police searched Evelyn's house, they found John's streetcar driver uniform with blood on it, human teeth and bone particles in the coal furnace … and, in a locked suitcase, a dead male infant wrapped in a Red Cross uniform. On the uniform was a tag with the name "Evelyn MacLean." The baby had been strangled to death with a piece of cord. In Evelyn's parents' house, there were bullet casings and bullet holes in the basement walls. Her father, Donald, tried to bribe the police with $10,000; evidence suggested he had been embezzling cash from his employer for years.

Evelyn and Bill were charged with the murder of the infant, and the two of them, plus Evelyn's parents, were charged with the murder of John Dick (Canada still had the death penalty at the time). A long series of trials began in October 1946, attracting thousands of spectators. And it was quite a show: Evelyn dressed to the nines the entire time and admitted to sleeping with at least 150 men. She was initially found guilty of the murder of her husband and sentenced to hang, only to have the verdict overturned as her father's involvement in the crime became more evident. In the end, Evelyn got life for the murder of her son (but served only 11 years), Bill Bohozuk walked, and Donald MacLean got five years after entering a guilty plea for his role in the murder of John Dick.

All the players have long since died or disappeared, but a dirty children's rhyme from the time lives on in the punk lyrics of the Forgotten Rebels, an infamous Hamilton band:

> *She cut off his arms!*
> *She cut off his legs!*
> *She cut off his head!*
> *Oh how could you, Mrs. Dick?*
> *How could you*
> *Miss his dick?*

Don't you just *love* kids?

CRIME

THAT FIRST TIME, IN '84, I *FLED* SASKATOON, BUYING A TRAIN TICKET HOME WITH THE *LAST* OF MY MONEY.

BUT SIX YEARS LATER, WITH A LUMP SUM PENSION PAYMENT FROM THE ARMY, I WAS READY TO *TRY AGAIN!*

ALTHOUGH I WAS NOW MARRIED AND WELL PREPARED, FRIENDS NEVERTHELESS SHOWERED US WITH CRITICISM!

ARE YOU *NUTS?* DON'T YOU KNOW THAT SASKATCHEWAN HAS THE HIGHEST RATE OF OUT-MIGRATION IN THE *COUNTRY??*

EVERYONE WANTS TO *LEAVE* THE PRAIRIES!

THE RENTAL VACANCY RATE IN SASKATOON WAS OVER 10% IN 1990 AND THE RESULT WAS AN ABUNDANCE OF AFFORDABLE HOUSING!

I SHOULDN'T PAY MORE 'N $250.00/MO.

...OR TAKE ANYTHING SMALLER THAN A 3 BEDROOM...

50% OFF EVENINGS & WEEKENDS SaskTel long distance

I'LL NEVER FORGET THE FIRST TIME I MET THE OLD LANDLADY AT THIS ODD, 1912 TRIPLEX THAT I NOW LIVE IN. IT WAS BACK ON A WARM DAY IN AUGUST...

ARE YOU THE LANDLADY?

YAH, OK 'S ME!

THE LANDLADY, MRS ENG, MOVED HERE FROM CHINA IN ORDER TO ESCAPE THE COMMUNISTS, BUT FOR A CAPITALIST SHE WAS PRETTY UNUSUAL...

YOU LIVE HERE, I TAKE $20.00/MO. OFF!

WHEN I FIRST REGISTERED MY CAR IN SASKATCHEWAN, I CHECKED THE BOX MARKED "SETTLER'S EFFECTS", WHICH MADE IT SOUND AS THOUGH WE GOT HERE BY COVERED WAGON WHEN REALLY, IT WAS SOMEWHAT EASIER...

SASKATOON'S CLEAR ACROSS TH' COUNTRY, CORPORAL... I CAN'T FIND A PLACE *NOW*, BUT WHEN I DO, CAN YOU SEND ME MY STUFF?

LOGISTIQUE LOGISTICS

OK.

BAT 513

IT'S BEEN A *WEEK* SINCE YOU CALLED—WE'RE *NEVER* GONNA GET OUR FURNITURE

HE *SAID* OK!

TO AVOID BACK PAIN KEEP AWAY FROM T.V. TRAYS-AS-A-SUBSTITUTE FOR *TABLES*.

# Racism:
# Some Ugly Truths

Along with the US, Australia, and New Zealand, Canada is a country that was "founded" by massive groups of settlers and their descendants, who quickly outnumbered and marginalized the indigenous peoples.

One of the problems of that beginning—and there are many—is that those indigenous peoples are still being denied their rights. The small parcels of land they've been allowed to keep are regularly expropriated by the government whenever they become of economic importance. To name just a few ongoing problems, the Dene of the Mackenzie Valley are losing territory for oil pipelines; the James Bay Cree are being displaced to make way for massive hydro-electric projects; the First Nations peoples of British Columbia are continually battling with the forest products multinationals; and the Mi'kmaq of Nova Scotia and New Brunswick are continually beleaguered by the forestry and fishing companies.

But it's not like the majority of the settlers themselves have fared much better. Employers always need large sources of cheap labour for the shitty jobs that more established, earlier waves of settlers refuse to do, so each new wave of immigrants has been subject to new racist attacks designed to strip them of any rights, render them docile, and keep their wages low. The truly sad thing is that former victims of racism eventually swallow the propaganda that the newest immigrants represent a threat to their livelihood and become willing but sometimes unwitting propagators of the same horrible cycle. Everybody's taken a hit in turn—the Chinese labourers who built the railways, the Eastern Europeans who settled the prairies, the East Indians who worked in the mills of BC, and the current groups of immigrants from Europe, Asia, and the Caribbean.

Canada was officially a racist society up until the 1960s. In 1911 the federal government drafted an order-in-council allowing cabinet members to prohibit the entry of "any immigrant belonging to the Negro race." The order was quietly shelved due to its explicit language; Canada has always preferred a model of racism that's as slick and subtle as a thrown-back hood. Truth was, the Immigration Act of 1910 still stood, and it basically said the same thing as the 1911 law, only with much more finesse. That act empowered federal officials to bar the entry of "immigrants belonging to any race deemed unsuited to the climate or requirements of Canada."

Our shame doesn't end there. When Halifax beautician Viola Desmond wanted to see a movie in New

> *Thomas Jefferson notwithstanding, "All men," and I'd better be careful here, "or women, are not created equal." Far from it. We are born unequal in intelligence, talent, beauty and economic privileges. So we should enjoy, in so far as it is possible, equal rights. That is to say whether our ancestors came here three hundred years ago or last week, once we are Canadian citizens there should be no self-serving nonsense about founding races.*
>
> *—Mordecai Richler*

RACISM

Africville street scene, Halifax, 1965

Ted Grant, National Archives of Canada

Glasgow, Nova Scotia, in 1946, she was told she could only sit in the balcony. She made Canadian history by taking a seat downstairs. She was promptly arrested. When the case made it to court, she won on a technicality, though the judge's prevailing opinion remained that business owners could discriminate as they pleased.

Ninety-one-year-old Ray Lewis, who won a bronze medal for Canada in the 1932 Los Angeles Olympics, remembers those days from his home in Hamilton. He sums them up succinctly: "It was worse than the States, because it wasn't supposed to happen here." Unlike his white counterparts, Lewis did not find a hero's welcome and offers of coaching and teaching jobs waiting for him back home. At the time, most blacks in Canada worked as labourers, shoe shiners, and domestics.

In the early half of the 20th century, when immigration to Canada really took off, immigrants were even more ghettoized than they are today, consigned to living in communities like Halifax's Africville. Founded in the 1850s, it was a horribly neglected area with no plumbing or road maintenance, located next to a city dump.

Nevertheless, the decision to clear out the 70 families still living in Africville in the 1960s left many bitter feelings and memories. The few surviving residents are old and dying off, but they won't forget their forced removal. Eddie Carvery, born in Africville in 1946, continues to live in a trailer on the former site (now a sparse-looking park). He bemoans the loss of community he remembers as a child, and told the CBC in 2000: "When they took Africville and killed it, they created a genocide. As a people, we've been destroyed. I think they should be held responsible."

Not unlike Africville, Toronto's "The Ward" was a sprawling downtown ghetto-home in the early to mid-20th century to 79% of Toronto's Jews, 78% of its blacks, 75% of its Italians, and 62% of its Chinese. The Ward was not looked on favourably by the British-born upper class. It was, as one historian put it, "a blemish whose foreign contagion was best kept from the sanctity of the suburbs."

Even the few well-meaning types who sought improvement for the lives of immigrants were hard-pressed to keep their disdain from overcoming their "kindness." Says one Bryce M. Stewart in a 1913 address to the Canadian Political Science Association entitled "Housing our Immigrant Workers":

> *"In Hamilton the ... houses inhabited by Italian and Slavic immigrants are dotted along the streets which ... extend well up into the main business portion of the city. Many of the former residents have left because of this immigrant invasion and the newcomers occupy their houses, keeping the Health Department busy to maintain even lower standards of cleanliness."*

Despite harsh conditions and a legacy of sly racism, many people from all over the world continue to dream choice test that took 15 hours over three days to complete—Brown got her BA. But, sadly, she had only a brief time to pass on what she had learned—she died the next year at age 38. Rather than wallow in nostalgia over Brown's achievements, Mactavish pressed for a formal training program for "intervenors" assisting the deaf-blind. She was also involved in the opening of a Toronto apartment building designed especially for the deaf-blind, the only such building in North America. The Brown-Mactavish legacy led to the founding in 2001 of the Canadian Helen Keller Centre, a Toronto institution focusing on the needs of the deaf-blind. Here, what could have been just another sappy nostalgic tale complete with a plaque for tourists to gawk at became just the beginning of a legacy that continues to make the city a better place for everyone.

# Community (And How to Find It)

"**A**re the people … doing their full duty as citizens to themselves, the community, and the men they elect to office to administer community affairs?" So asked R.D. Waugh, mayor of Winnipeg in 1916. "The citizen does not, as a rule, take any of the blame or responsibility for mismanagement on himself. It is almost invariably 'the system' or 'the council' that is wrong."

Well, you have to admit it—the guy had a point. We city dwellers are notorious for blaming others, be they the members of city council, the urban sanitation professional who leaves half the garbage lying on the sidewalk, the ever-popular teenage hoodlums, or, of course,

## COMMUNITY: Signs and Symptoms

*Buzzing in ear and general warmth from talking too much on the telephone.*

*Sharpened memory from having to keep track of names, phone numbers, birthdays, relationships, etc.*

*Clarity and perspective; no time for self-involvement or solipsism.*

*Confidence and optimism based on a general sense of security.*

*Belly developed from a regular schedule of eating and drinking with friends.*

*Nice tan.*

local politicians of all varieties. But what about us? What are our responsibilities to the city, the community, the block where we live? How many times can we swerve around the dog poop nobody bothered to pick up, the heap of garbage somebody dumped in a front lawn, the drunk in the alley?

The hard truth is that most of us are either unwilling or uninterested. We're out to get laid, party, advance our careers, and make cash. If the scene outside our windows is ugly, we'll pull down the shades, maybe put bars on the windows. If the smell seeps in, we'll burn incense. (See *Angst and Alienation*.)

The city is overrun with cynicism, self-obsession, and guys in cars specially modified to be really really loud as they cruise down your street at 3 a.m. And yet, despite everything, it's in the city where you find out the true meaning of the word "community." For some people, community means you have to do gross things

COMMUNITY

like volunteer, pick up the trash on the street, or attend a planning committee developing a new park. Now, we're not saying you *shouldn't* do those kinds of things, but community can be simpler than that. (As one of our uncles once noted, once the people find your ass, they'll never stop kicking it—clearly, philanthropy isn't for everyone.) Community can also be stopping for a few minutes to chat with your neighbour. Such seemingly meaningless acts can lead to lifelong friendships and, well, better cities.

When we talked to people about their relationship to the urban communities they live in, many cited simple things. One story we were told concerned a couple who had recently moved into a primarily Portuguese downtown neighbourhood. The entire block was Portuguese except for a middle-aged man who lived with his elderly mother (a Scottish immigrant) next door. (Incidentally, many Canadian cities have developed these kind of loose, unstated immigrant communities—Chinatowns, Koreatowns, Caribbean villages, Little Italys—the sense of ownership and care these communities display for their neighbourhoods make them great places to live, regardless of your ethnic background.) When, a few weeks after they moved in, the man's mother passed away, the couple was surprised to find that the block was circulating a sympathy card, which they were asked to sign. Later, their neighbour explained that even though his mother didn't speak the language of the ladies her age in the neighbourhood, in the 30-plus years she lived there she made friends with many of the local children, who would often visit her. The card was a simple way of acknowledging that neighbourly connection.

Another story we heard was about dog parks. In many urban communities in Canada, taking the dog for a walk (and a bowel movement) has become a community experience. As the animals sniff each other's asses and relish their brief moment of freedom at the local square of grass, neighbours get to know one another. One friend of ours said that in his neighbourhood people would often bring cocktails and hors d'oeuvres to these open-to-anyone-with-a-poodle gatherings. What better way to get to know the folks on your block than sharing poop-scoop tips over a glass of Chablis? (Our informant did point out, though, that in many cases he knows the names of the dogs, but not the names of the dog owners he chats with almost every evening.)

If you don't have a dog and want to meet your community, we recommend you pray for a natural disaster. When ice storms knocked out the power in Montreal and when rivers threatened to drown prairie cities, the doors in apartment buildings opened up and people made quick friends with strangers living across the hall. After a few days sharing heat sources and bailing techniques, people knew something they'd never otherwise thought to find out—the names of their neighbours.

Sure, it's dog-eat-dog out there. Everybody knows that. And for most of us, just surviving in the big city is plenty enough work, without even thinking about doing our "full duty as citizens," as Mayor Waugh once put it. But if you start with the little things, you'll soon find yourself actually interested in what's going on in the city around you. Next thing you know, you'll be circulating a petition, planning the block barbecue and (shudder) volunteering at the old-age home down the street.

# TRANSPORTATION

**P**ART OF THE REASON FOR LIVING in a city is that it's actually possible to get wherever you want to go on foot. And this is a good thing—fewer cars mean less pollution, fewer deaths, and fewer idiots in from the suburbs for a night on the town. (We have a theory that the megabass in contemporary car audio systems works like whalesong, allowing stupid people with loud cars to locate one another from many blocks away for the purpose of mating.)

The tradition of *flânerie* as practised by the French poet Charles Baudelaire—the alienated, mocking stroll of the writer around the city, surrounded by the world of commerce but separated from it by intelligence and aesthetics—is in desperate need of revival. Before we were an urban nation, being a *flâneur* didn't make a lot of sense. It's hard to stroll ironically along a dirt road separating two quarter sections of wheat, especially when there's no one for miles to witness you doing it. But times have changed.

*Flânerie* transforms the most mundane of activities (getting from point A to point B) into an aesthetic act that involves seeing and being seen. The Italians have always understood this notion intuitively; hell, they get dressed up to go down to the corner. Now that Canadians are trading in their parkas and Sorels for leather jackets, PVC, baby tees, baggy pants, high heels, and Fluevogs, slowing down and taking a look at the people who surround you is becoming a whole lot more interesting.

A leisurely pace and complete absence of visible perspiration are crucial to the notion of *flânerie*; you can't be fast *and* be a *flâneur*. (Bike couriers and people on Rollerblades are cool in a whole different way—see *Bikes*. Razor scooters are only cool if you're under 12 years of age, and even then it's touch and go.) The point? To separate oneself from the hustle and bustle of the business world. What could be more perverse—and therefore more interesting—than moving through the city *slowly*?

We can also thank the French for another interesting, and slightly more macho variation on *flânerie*—the action that Guy Debord and the Situationists referred to as the *dérive* or "drift." Drifting is basically drunken, deranged *flânerie*; the trick is to get shitfaced beyond belief and then stagger for hours or even days in search of "situations"—novel ways to experience the city that might point to a renewed, more engaged mode of daily life. Unfortunately, it's often difficult to distinguish between neo-Situationist drifters and garden-variety drunken assholes, so we cannot recommend drifting as wholeheartedly as we can *flânerie*.

However, there will always be occasions when the distance to be covered is too great for walking, or you're too drunk, or (horrors) you even have to *leave* the city. When such situations arise, we recommend the following:

# Bikes

There is nothing, we mean *nothing*, like the feeling of hurtling down a busy street, weaving in and out of traffic, pumping, working those legs, breaking a sweat, skidding to a halt when you can't beat the yellow, and otherwise biking like you *mean* it through the urban environs. We've fallen off our bikes, been ticketed on our bikes, had our bikes stolen, and had our tires stolen and/or punctured—but nothing has deterred us from biking in the city. In case you haven't gotten the message, we love the taste of grit on our tongue, the scent of exhaust in our nose, and the rush in our veins as we

Paul Fairweather

outmanoeuvre cars full of jerks and look way cool in the process.

Naturally, the city does not always accommodate us—bike lanes are scarce and not respected, and when a biker and a vehicle collide, it's the biker who gets hurt and, a lot of the time, it's the biker who takes the blame. But don't get the wrong idea—biking in the city is safe and getting safer. A report on biking statistics in Vancouver shows that accidents involving bikes are down sharply since 1996, when 472 incidents were tallied. In 1997 there were only 253 accidents, and, in 1998, Vancouver was heading toward something like 220. In those three years, there were only two biking-related deaths. The more people bike, the more aware drivers are of bikes on the road, and the safer we are. If you look at those numbers, you'd probably have to conclude that it's safer to bike than it is to drive or even walk.

But biking isn't about safety or convenience or the environment or fitness or any of the things people say it has to do with. Biking is about two things only: fun and freedom. If you aren't having fun when you bike, by all means, give it up. But trust us, you will have fun! You will! You just can't help yourself. It's freezing or scorching and you've got a huge backpack of groceries slamming into your spine and you're halfway up a steep incline and about to be cut off by a tractor trailer making a blind right turn. But you're still having fun. Why is that?

Because of the freedom. When you bike, you can stop any time you want, go through parks and shortcuts, and you don't have to pay a cent in insurance or gas. So don't start biking 'cause you're on some kind of wacky health fad. Bike because you want to have fun, and you'll quickly become an advocate and even an addict.

BIKES

# The Story of Anita's Missing Bike

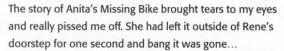

by Sharon Wilson, from C.U.N.T. (Chicks United by Non-noxious Transportation), a now-defunct Toronto zine that had a great run celebrating girls and biking

The story of Anita's Missing Bike brought tears to my eyes and really pissed me off. She had left it outside of Rene's doorstep for one second and bang it was gone…

The mission was clear: we put out an all-points bulletin to all our friends, who are many. I became obsessed riding my bike across Bloor, College, Queen scouting for Anita's bike. I even ran through traffic once to confront a guy with

a light blue bike which wasn't even close to her bike. Then Rene heard that a woman had been spotted in the area riding a baby blue bike. Rene found out where she lived and we staked out her place. We sat on the patio of Pizza Delic sipping ice tea when out of the corner of our eye we spotted Anita's bike locked out in front of Inti Crafts. I couldn't believe the nerve of this person to actually park the bike on our turf. Before I knew it I was locking my bike lock to the bike. Then we spotted the chick taking a back alley … we went up to the apartment and confronted the woman's

boyfriend who told us that he felt really bad, he gave us a whole long story how he had acquired the bike.

The next day we felt it was time to confront the girlfriend who was eating at Dooney's with her parents. Her story contradicted her boyfriend's. Then the police arrived and this wrestler-looking bald sturdy cop was overwhelmed by three brujas who had done their own legwork. Anita told her story and proved it was her bike. The cop then decided it was time to step in. He questioned the accused woman who said she bought the bike at Value Village for a measly nine dollars. Yeah, right. The cop ordered the woman to unlock the bike. The woman pulled off the tassles to "her" bike, signifying to us that that was the only property she actually owned.

Victoriously, Las Brujas rode off into the sunset feeling empowered riding beside the baby blue bike down the road of loyalty, honesty, and integrity. •

Paul Fairweather

## Critical Mass

A popular event for bikers in the Canadian city that captures the essence of the fun freedom ethos is the Critical Mass Ride. There are Critical Mass events in many cities including Halifax, Ottawa, Toronto, Vancouver, and Montreal.

Critical Mass occurs when a group of bikers get together at a designated time and place and take over the street. It apparently got its name from a Chinese phenomenon. When a biker in China comes to a busy intersection, there are often no traffic lights and no chance of cars ever stopping. So the biker waits for more bikers. When there are enough of them, they surge forward, forcing cars to stop and let them through. Yeah, baby!

With groups of 50 to over 100 riders cruising down a busy downtown street, Critical Mass events in Canadian cities not only garner notice, but give you a chance to check out the other cyclists, piss off commuters, and otherwise have a great time. Look for Critical Mass announcements on the web or at community bike stores.

Whether you're biking on your own or with 70 of your cycling compatriots, there's never a good excuse not to bike. (Don't even think about whining about the weather. You can expect our ode to winter biking in the silver anniversary edition of the Almanac …)

## Public Transit

*Have you ever thought of the fact that there are eight different street car fares in the city? There is the 5 cent fare, the 10 cent night fare, the 3 cent children's fare; there are tickets at 25 for the dollar, blue tickets at 6 for quarter, red tickets at 8 for a quarter, white tickets at 7 for a quarter and children's tickets at 10 for a quarter. The result is that no man who has not a lot of change at his disposal can equip himself at once with a supply of yellow, red, white and children's tickets.*

—F.S. Spence, Toronto controller, 1908, "Some Suggestions as to Toronto Street Railway Problems"

"On the bus," writes Grant Buday, Vancouver novelist and editor of *Exact Fare Only*, an anthology of public transit literature, "we're nose-to-nose and hip-to-hip, and like it or not we examine each other's scalps, inhale each other's breath, hear each other talk, and watch the mad talk to themselves. And if we're standing we watch for free seats."

Buday gets it exactly right: the bus isn't for misanthropes, hypochondriacs, or all-of-the-above suburbanites. Public transit—subway, bus, or streetcar—is for urban denizens who love and hate getting their hands dirty, who can't resist listening in on the conversation one seat up, who don't mind chatting about the weather with a man wearing mostly garbage bags. After biking, public transit is *the* way to get around in the city. It tests the functionality of your immune system, gives you many a story to tell, and is a good place to learn important city techniques like squeezing into incredibly small spaces without ever abandoning your rictuslike apologetic grin. Plus, there's an equanimity, a kind of serene beauty, that

PUBLIC TRANSIT

comes with waiting for the bus that cannot be matched by any other urban activity.

Sadly, according to the Canadian Urban Transit Association, overall funding for public transit has declined 18% in the last five years, resulting in service cuts and fare increases. Despite the growth of the cities, ridership is increasing at a meagre 1.5% annually. And all this at a time when traffic is out of control.

Still, it doesn't matter what you do to our public transit. We'll keep riding. We'll brave fare increases, arbitrary cuts in service, surly drivers, and anything else you throw at us. We say we do it because we don't really have a choice. But in some deep smog-scorched cranny of our urban heart, we ride because we really really love it.

(See also *Bikes*.)

Some Canadian transit facts:

- Annual transit ridership in Canada has been increasing since 1998, reaching 1.5 billion in 2000, with service available to approximately 95% of urban residents and 61% of the 30 million residents of Canada.

Laying the tracks on Bathurst Street, Toronto, 1890s

City of Toronto Archives

Paul Fairweather

Ride the rocket, baby!

- Transit usage (passenger trips per capita) has not kept pace with population growth over the years.
- On average, 10% of work trips in Canada are made on public transit. In some larger Canadian cities, 50% of work trips to downtown are made on transit, but the growing suburban market is more difficult to serve effectively.
- There are 14,335 active transit vehicles in operation in Canada, averaging 10.7 years of age (roughly three years more than desirable).

## Excellent Reasons to Take the Bus That the Bus Company Sometimes Forgets to Mention

- You can get drunk anywhere, any time.
- You can close your eyes and pretend you're floating on a raft in the Caribbean Sea.

- You can read other people's discarded newspapers.
- You can peep, eavesdrop, and otherwise surreptitiously invade people's privacy.
- You can act morally superior to drivers even though if you had a car you'd probably drive too.
- You can cruise parts of the city you've never seen before without having to figure out where you are and where you're going.
- You can have erotic fantasies about the driver and passengers.
- You're guaranteed to see something you've never seen before.
- You can make friends and influence people you will never meet again.

Pack a sandwich. Make a day of it. Our favourite transit game: keep your head down. Look at people's shoes. Imagine the appearance of the shoes' wearers completely before you look up. (This game has the added advantage of convincing those around you that you might well vomit at any moment, so the seats around you will remain clear.)

# Fare Evasion

by Nev Gibson, from *Bosevus Mega Zine*, Victoria

**The mission:** *See Choke in Vancouver*
**The problem:** *Extortionate ferry rates too high for our budgets*
**The solution:** *FARE EVASION!*

At 8:00 in the morning I got onto the #70 bus bound for the ferry terminal. On board already were Jesse, Leigh and the rest of the Choke-going party who did not attempt fare evasion and thus are not involved in this story other than this brief mention. Using a ridiculously large knife borrowed from a friendly fellow commuter we set to work preparing the cardboard for the eventuality that we would need to use "Plan B." We arrived at the terminal 20 minutes before 9:00, stashed our cardboard and proceeded to attempt "Plan A."

Plan A: Upon entering the foot passenger terminal we avoided the ticket lineup and instead took the elevator down to the bus loading zone with a group of lacrosse players. We then left the loading zone and proceeded to the lineup of cars just getting ready to board the ferry. The plan: Find sympathetic kids with extra seats and sneak on the ferry for free in their car. The flaw of this plan: Kids don't take early ferries and old people want nothing to do with 3 teenagers trying to get on the ferry for free.

Plan C: The time now was 10 to nine and over the loudspeaker a cheery voice informed us that it was our last chance to get tickets for the ferry. We began to run

---

*"That looks more like a body than anything I've seen before."*

---

back to the elevator when a "Plan C" formed in our minds. We told the BC ferries worker, who was skilfully directing cars onto the ferry, that we had missed our bus and that we needed to get on the ferry. He pointed us towards an area near the terminal and told us to wait there. At this point we realized there was a good chance "Plan C" would not work and we would miss the ferry and the show so we instead ran up a flight of stairs not knowing where it would take us. We found ourselves in the terminal again and proceeded to "Plan B."

Plan B: Leigh and myself bought tickets at the last possible second and ran for the ferry with Jesse close at our heels. Me and Jesse stepped into an alcove and I proceeded to insert her completely into two large plastic garbage bags. The aforementioned bags were two out of hundreds I have stashed in my room from a heist completed years ago at my jr. high but that is another story for another issue. I threw Jesse, completely concealed in the garbage bags and looking far more like a body than I had hoped, over my shoulder and began my trek up the ramp with all possible haste. In our rush to get tickets we hadn't had time to get our carefully stashed cardboard which would have helped disguise the human features of my load. In the planning phase I never realized how long the loading ramp truly is and also how steep. Needless to say by the time I got to the ramp I was feeling the effects of fatigue very strongly and Jesse had begun to slip off my shoulder.

Despite these factors I made it past the ticket taker with no questions asked. And made it aboard the ferry. Unfortunately the loading of a BC ferry is overseen by two people, one at the terminal side, and

# The Crisis Girl Guide to CHEATING TRANSIT

**BASIC RULES FOR CHEATING**

1. The maximum safe fare cheat is 20–30% less than the listed fare.
2. Use smallish change with a maximum of 10 pennies.
3. Always keep some change so you can fake a mistake if you are busted.
4. Always take a transfer.
5. Never admit to guilt.
6. Always sit/stand within flirting distance of any hotties on your bus/train.
7. Always remember to BE the 3 CONS: CONfident, CONvincing, CONgenial.

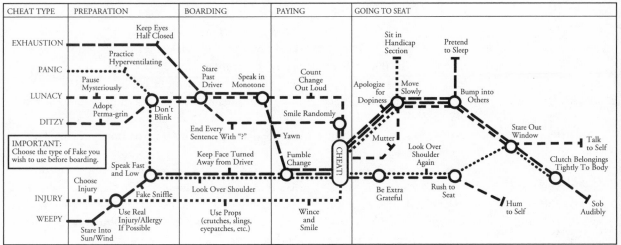

another on the boat. I managed to make it onto the boat, past the second ferry worker and inside. Sadly, that was as far as I got. The fatigue I mentioned earlier had entered advanced stages and Jesse was slipping further off my shoulder so I had to put her down on the floor just inside the door. In front of me were about 50 people waiting in line for the buffet who were all staring at me and my mysterious package. Behind me was the ferry worker who supervised the loading. "That looks more like a body than anything I've seen before," he informed me. I made up some half-assed story or laughed it off or something and he proceeded to lock the doors, much to my relief, although I was sure that he knew exactly what was going on. "What's in the bag man?" asked one of the people in the lineup. I explained to her I was moving to Vancouver and I had most of the stuff I own crammed into that bag. "It's breathing" was her response. This was followed by an awkward period of silence in which I had the undivided attention of everyone in the lineup. Finally Jesse broke the

silence with a feeble "I can't breathe." At this point I decided it was time to make our move so I pulled the bags off her and told her to run … Jesse, Leigh and I took off leaving behind a sea of startled passengers and the loading supervisor who was walking after us.

We split up and laid low for a while but we got cocky and got back together fairly quickly. The loading supervisor cornered us on the top deck and took me and Jesse down to the chief steward's office. The worker who busted us was a good natured guy and we all had a number of laughs about the situation on the way down. The chief steward and security staff did not find it as amusing. Jesse had to pay and now we are on permanent BC ferries record for "fare evasion" but at least we got an amusing story for the zine. As a footnote, the Choke show was nothing short of the best show I have ever seen. Go see Choke. If you haven't heard them before listen to them. You won't like it at first—I know I didn't—but you will grow to love it, then go see them live and you will be blown away. •

# UFOs

If you're one of those city slicker types who think they're too sophisticated and world-weary to have an unidentified flying object experience, think again. Canadian cities are rife with UFO sightings and other unexplained, potentially extraterrestrial experiences. No, we're not talking about your creepy neighbour or that guy on the street corner who says he's hearing voices from Mars (though you never know).

We're talking about real live UFO sightings in, above, and all around the Canadian city. The 2001 annual Canadian survey of UFO reports indicates that there was a staggering 42% rise in UFO sightings that year. Apparently Vancouver and Ottawa had the most sightings, with 17 and 15 reports respectively. (We're not surprised by this—Vancouver is home to some far-out people and Ottawa is home to … well … politicians and bureaucrats driven crazy by their own ineffectuality—not that UFO sightings and insanity have even the slightest correlation.)

1937 - Photo Taken of UFO Over Vancouver City Hall.

Sightings included "a luminous object that hung in the sky over Hull, Quebec, for two consecutive nights before appearing to explode" and "three dots of white light that 'played tag' with each other over Richmond, BC." Says Chris Rutkowski, one of the authors of the report: "There were a number of odd cases. There's a mixture of things that we're seeing from one end of the country to another."

Indeed, similarities are frightening and surely more than coincidence! A January 2000 triangular sighting over southeast Edmonton had a witness who was driving his car attempt to follow a UFO that was moving slowly and was illuminated with yellow lights set out in a triangular shape. He turned a corner, and the mysterious shape was gone! Similarly, in 1993 there were several reports of a black triangle UFO sighted over Lethbridge, Alberta.

Then there's the story of Ryan and Terry, two young men from West Vancouver who, in November 1996 at 6 p.m., got the scare of their lives. This account from Canada's premier UFO monitoring organization, <ufobc.ca>, tells us the story: "They thought they were in big trouble as what looked like a plane was very close overhead and appeared to be coming down. It was however evident that no sound was accompanying this craft and also apparent it indeed was no plane at all as it appeared to both witnesses." Ryan tells his parents, who think he's a nut job, but two weeks later a local paper reports that a bus driver saw a triangular object near Ryan's street. So what became of Terry and Ryan? Terry never said a word about the encounter again. Ryan "later left to join an Ashram in London."

For today's modern cynical urban dweller, it's easy to make fun of these incidents. But UFO sightings in Canadian cities are serious business. What if one landed in downtown Vancouver, crushing a Starbucks? Where would the people buy their extra-large skinny lattes with chocolate-shaving topping? Is Mel Lastman really an alien? It's more than possible! Seeing is believing for today's jaded, world-weary hipster, so we refer you to the stunning 1937 photo at the start of this section—taken long before photo doctoring was conceivable—that clearly shows a UFO skimming over Vancouver city hall. One look at this ominous photo and you'll agree that UFOs are stalking Canadian cities with consequences we can only imagine!

# A Brief Note on Scooters, Rollerblades, and Skateboarding

While walking and biking are our recommended ways of getting around the Canadian city, we've also noted that some urban residents seem to think that every stroll could be an opportunity for reclaiming youth via any number of wheeled contrivances, most notably the scooter, in-line skates, and the skateboard. Officially, the Almanac sees the value of these modes of transportation—like bikes, they allow for greater speed and distance, keep residents connected to their city, and do not necessitate insurance payouts and pollution spewage. Unofficially, however, the Almanac is skeptical. The only thing sadder than an office worker barrelling his way down the sidewalk outfitted in spandex, knee/elbow pads, and a

bright red pair of boots-with-wheels is watching this sad specimen trying to figure out how to stop.

Really, what are the protocols for these intermediary transportation devices? They block up bike lanes, streets, and sidewalks, and are a danger to pedestrians and storefront windows alike. Worst of all, these methods of locomotion look ridiculous attempted by anyone over 20 years of age. Should you *really* be skateboarding? At *your* age?

# Traffic

Traffic is bad. Let's be clear on this point: Traffic sucks. It's not just bad for people trying to get from one place to another; it's bad for every aspect of city life: the air we breathe, the cost of goods and services, the din to which we are subjected (especially during World Cup—instead of 12 hours of honking horns and driving up and down busy streets, why can't people just strap flags to

 *Official admonition from 1800 reads:*

Whereas the streets in the town of York are frequently obstructed and made dangerous to passengers, by piles of WOOD and STONES placed in them, and PITS dug in several places, It is notified by the order of the magistrates in quarter sessions assembled, that whomever shall leave any wood or stone, or suffer any nuisance to remain in the said street, opposite their respective premises, after the 12th day of May next will be prosecuted as the law directs.

TRAFFIC

Streetcar strike, Toronto, 1919

Not much has changed ... Toronto, 2002

their heads or paint themselves gaily in the national colours of their choice and stroll around leisurely on foot?), and the roads that cut cities in halves and quarters. Believe it or not, traffic—more than crime and taxes—is the biggest problem facing the city.

Consider this: University of Toronto professor Eric Miller did a study showing that automobile ownership rates, the number of daily car trips, and the number of people living outside Toronto's core have all increased substantially over the last 30 or so years. The CAA estimates that Canadians waste 236 million litres of gasoline annually because of congestion. Car emissions rise dramatically at slow speeds or in stop-and-go traffic.

The Goods Movement Study of 1991 concluded that delays in moving goods through Toronto were costing consumers more than $1 billion annually. The average travel time for a Vancouver commuter has increased 20% in the past decade. Traffic in Vancouver is so bad that an "increase in general congestion" lost the city the number one spot in the William M. Mercer annual ranking of 215 cities with the best quality of life. In Montreal, an informal study by a city councillor revealed that only 5% of motorists bother to stop at crosswalks. When the Quebec government finally amended provincial laws to allow right on red starting August 2002, they exempted Montreal. Said the transport minister: "Maybe it will never apply to Montreal." The government estimates that in 11 major Canadians cities alone, air pollution is responsible for 5,000 premature deaths a year. That's a greater toll than that caused by breast cancer, prostate cancer, and highway accidents.

Meanwhile, our frustration shows in the staggering number of traffic tickets we accumulate. In Calgary, almost 300,000 tickets are issued by the city police traffic section each year. In Ontario, more than a million tickets are given out every year. "Something has to give," Professor Miller told the Greater Toronto Services Board. "We either have to build our cities differently or change

TRAFFIC

our expectations or invest in transit. I just don't see the current trend being sustainable."

Yet the problem continues to get worse, and it's fair to say that the measures the three levels of government have taken to deal with the issue are half-assed at best. Driving around in their limousines with their laptops and cell phones, traffic really isn't that much of an issue for our politicians and upper-crust bigwigs. If they want to get somewhere quick, they'll climb into the cockpit of a private jet. The rest of us are stuck on the street, sucking up exhaust, twiddling our thumbs and listening to the inanity of talk radio (the other day: an hour-long discussion regarding the relative merits of the circumcised penis).

Even as the problem gets worse and worse, the so-called experts wrangle about what causes the problem and what we should do about it. German physicists did a study and decided that traffic is caused by … traffic. "The components of [a] system and their interactions themselves—rather than any external cause—give rise to the non-linear behaviour of the system as a whole." Thanks guys. Very helpful.

Truth is, there is probably no one dramatic explanation except that there are too many cars on the road. Next time you're sitting in gridlock, think to yourself: am I part of the solution, or the problem? Too much of our traffic is taken up with suburban commuters who spend half their day in a slow crawl to and from their fenced-in low-tax mansion in some outlying area where you have to drive 15 minutes to get to the closest corner store. Yeah, we blame them for just about everything. But seriously. If you live in the city, you have many options that are superior to sitting in traffic. Bike, walk, take transit. The air will be cleaner, you'll be thinner, and the Canadian city will be a better place. If you don't live in the city, well, then, we hope you're enjoying your bland, pasteurized life. (See *Bikes, Public Transit*.)

**B**EING A CONTEMPORARY URBAN HIPSTER requires a complex and frequently bewildering array of accessories: phones, bikes, computers, makeup kits, coffee makers, drugs, vibrators, audio systems, personal digital assistants, sunglasses … the list recedes into the distance. Thus, in the following pages, we're more than happy to offer some assistance in what to use and where and how to use it.

Before getting into the minutiae of several of the more important tools at your disposal, we at Almanac central would like to offer one sterling piece of advice: avoid the Batman Utility Belt look at all costs. Clipping a phone to your belt is dorky enough, but adding Leatherman multitools, Palm Pilots, iPods, Mag Lites, etc. is permissible only for roadies and other superheroes.

… and speaking of superheroes, in our search for sage advice pertaining to the equipage of urban Canada (and not wanting to do too much of the work ourselves), we hit on young Canadian art star Jason Dunda, whose list of must-have equipment for the urban student is just the first of several handy Dunda lists to appear throughout this book. When not ranking things for *Lola* magazine, Jason teaches at the School of the Art Institute of Chicago; runs Modest Contemporary Art Projects, a negligible exhibition space dedicated to small art with medium-sized ideas; and shows in Toronto and Chicago at the Katharine Mulherin Gallery and Fassbender Gallery. Jason also wants you to know that "top ten suggestions and piquant hate mail are most welcome" <jdunda@artic.edu>.

# ATMs

We love them, we hate them. In the name of instant access to our money (in English, French, Spanish, Italian, Chinese, Portuguese, and Braille) we've invented yet another way for banks to squeeze more money out of us through transaction fees while simultaneously eliminating the need to pay an actual person to handle the transaction. The rash of new "third-party" banking machines only compounds the damage by adding a second service charge on top of the first.

Meanwhile, bank machine interfaces keep changing … why? Surely it's possible to add new features without

## THE HISTORY OF CANADIAN BANKING
# CANADA'S FIRST ATM

"The Perpetual Accounting and Transacting Machine" was unveiled on the 27th of October, 1879, in the ante-chamber of the Royal Haligonian Trust Company. It was the invention of Milton Quigley, amateur accountant and rodent keeper at the Halifax Zoological Gardens. It was powered by three generations of grey squirrels, specially trained to do rudimentary banking procedures utilizing an ingenious lever and bead system devised by Mr. Quigley. Here, Mr. Quigley is shown assisting a patron of the bank in the use of the machine's piano-like fingerboard.

having to change the key sequence of every single frigging function the machine already performs … It's enough to drive one to … crime.

Difficulty seems to be translating into resentment, as the number of ingenious ways to rob an ATM keeps growing. A BAI Global study estimates that one ATM crime is committed for every 2 million transactions, or about 5,500 crimes a year. There are many colourful ways to rob an ATM, including driving a backhoe through the wall of the bank and simply hauling the machine away, or plugging all visible cracks with bubble gum, pumping the machine full of liquid nitrogen, and then smashing it open with a sledgehammer (for all the gory details, visit TOTSE—The Temple of the Screaming Electron <www.totse.com/en/bad_ideas/scams_and_rip_offs/atm_92.html>).

# Jason Dunda's
# Top 10 School Supplies

1. *Sharpie Marker* Smudgeproof, waterproof, fade-proof, and bulletproof. Ideal for writing your name on your underwear (or on someone else's). Available in seven colours and three sizes, but the best is basic bullet-tip black. $1.46

2. *Crayola Glitter Glue* The perfect thing for writing Corey Hart's name on your science binder. Bonus: It's acid free, so you can use it to restore turn-of-the-century fine art and antique furniture, too. $3.48

3. *Pilot Dr. Grip Pen* With a special space age silicone grip, Dr. Grip is the cushiest pen on the market. Pilot's self-professed "Revolutionary" ink is ideal for writing those edgy, against-the-grain manifestoes. $9.16

4. *Three-inch Duct Tape* Duct tape as wide as your fist. $15.96

5. *Honda S2000 VTEC Convertible* The perfect accessory. Fully loaded with leather seats, power top, AM/FM CD player. It's shiny and brand new. $28,000 and counting on eBay. Hold your breath until Mom and Dad buy it for you.

6. *UHU Glue Stick* Not the stickiest or smelliest glue on the market, but I just love saying UHU. Yoo hoo! Various sizes, the 9 gram is best for on-the-go gluing. 93¢

7. *Crayola Crayons 96-Pack* The fully loaded model. Complete with a built-in sharpener, and sans the non-PC Indian Red and Flesh colours, you can colour in style. Crayola recently denied reports of asbestos in its crayons, so it must be a coincidence that I experienced memory loss, dizziness, bone rot, explosive diarrhea, night sweats, dry mouth, sleeplessness, liver spots, muscle spasms, flaking skin, and hyper-obesity while using this product. I still managed to stay inside the lines though. $4.69

8. *Pokémon Pencil Case* The label says "carry-all pouch," but you and I know it's a pencil case. $2.99 for the real thing, $1 knock-offs available on the street.

9. *Bristol Board* Available in a wide selection of crappy colours, you can't beat it for the all-important science fair or geography project. Accept no substitutes. 99¢ a sheet

10. *Pink-N-Ink* The more versatile yet equally lousy cousin of the infamous Pink Pearl. This handsome two-tone number will erase both pencil and ink, badly. 96¢ ●

ATMs

But theft isn't the only sign of our cultural antipathy toward ATMs. There was a rash of "urban legend" e-mails making the rounds in Ontario in 1999 suggesting that "whenever you go to an automatic teller machine to make deposits, make sure you don't lick the deposit envelopes (spit on it). A customer died after licking an envelope at a teller machine at Yonge & Eglinton."

Perhaps the best thing that can be said for ATMs is that their lobbies provide snuggly shelters for the homeless during the long Canadian winters.

# Cell Phones

The British have a rule: never use a cell phone anywhere that you wouldn't feel comfortable farting.

To clarify, this means don't take or make calls in movie theatres, plays, concerts, sports events, churches, funerals (it happens), restaurants, and other public spaces. If you're going to leave your phone on in such environments, learn to use your voice mail, call display, and silent ring/vibrate functions, and return crucial calls in hallways, lobbies, or other private spaces.

Yuppies: Taking calls during meetings will only make people wonder about your priorities. Answering your phone while working out at the gym will only convince the person on the other end that you're a mouth-breathing pervert. Elevators, by the way, drop calls, so avoid looking any dumber than you have to and end the call before you get in. And don't shout. The people around you don't want to be part of your conversation, because you're just not that interesting.

Suburban Britney clones: Phones are tools, not accessories. Don't stack your phone and cigarettes on the table

## FIRST AID FOR EXTREME CELLULAR PHONE EXPOSURE

**1** Identify yourself as a first aider and offer to help.

**2** Sit or lay the casualty down. Tilt head back and turn slightly to injured side. Check circulation.

**3** Shave hair surrounding the injured area.

**4** Apply liberal amounts of butter, unsalted.

**5** Hold casualty down firmly by the shoulders. Smash cellular phone to small pieces with a rubber first aid mallet (or any appropriately heavy object).

**6** Cover the injured area with clean, lint free dressings and give ongoing casualty care until medical help takes over.

in front of you; it not only limits the amount of space that the server has to put your Crantini on, but also confirms the suspicion the rest of us are harbouring that your teeny-tiny little backpacks really aren't good for anything other than strapping to a garden gnome. (An online survey of diners by the publishers of Zagat Restaurant Guides found that 95% of respondents wanted a separate section in the restaurant for phoners and smokers.)

Teenage boys and geeks of all ages: No dumb-ass downloaded ring tones. We do not need to hear the theme from the Cantina Band scene in *Star Wars* any more. Ever. Especially in bleep-boop-bleep form.

Couples: Grocery store use of cell phones is permissible only in giant supermarkets and other forms of box stores as a walkie-talkie system with your significant other. As box stores are already irredeemably repugnant, a cell phone call or two can't make matters worse for anyone. (See *Shopping, Box Stores.*)

Drivers: There are over 9 million wireless phones in Canada that are used regularly in motor vehicles. Some of these uses are legitimate; Canadians use wireless phones to call 911 or emergency numbers over 3 million times a year. But don't phone and drive. According to a report by Dr. Don Redelmeier of the University of Toronto in the 1997 *New England Journal of Medicine*, talking on a cell phone while driving quadruples your risk of an accident. At least 14 countries have banned drivers from using cell phones, and British Columbia, Alberta, Newfoundland, Nova Scotia, and Ontario have all considered bans or restrictions on their use.

Violations of these rules will result in the commissioning of a Canadian national force of phonebashers. The existing practitioners are two guys who had a friend working on a video shoot for an anti–mobile phone song. The main characters in the video wore full-length cell phone suits. The nascent phonebashers simply waited till the last day of the shoot, hung around the set drinking coffee, then nabbed the suits out of the wardrobe truck.

Since then they've been roaming the urban landscape like guardian angels (only covered in foam rubber and giant pushbuttons), locating people committing gross breaches of cell phone etiquette. The offenders are taunted, then their phones are seized and smashed … and while the incredulous rude person tries to overcome the shock of having two men dressed in cell phone suits and black leotards destroy their precious toy, the perpetrators flee to fight another day. For videos of the phonebashers in action, see <www.phonebashing.com>.

# Drugs:
# Mainline and Online

Vancouver's downtown East Side—with an estimated 7,000 heroin users wandering the streets—is the drug capital of Canada. In the East Side, you can't walk down a block without being offered smack, crack, or some other dubious substance. Most Canadian cities have a less-obvious drug acquisition zone, but it isn't hard to get the illegal substance of your choice.

Street drugs are a problem for the big city. Even if you don't care about the fate of the addicts, consider that, according to the *Canadian Medical Association Journal*, an estimated 7,000 injection drug users in Vancouver's skid row will cost at least $150,000 each to treat when

DRUGS

**Jones of Kelowna**
*Abridged Manual of Cigarette Rolling*

*with Descriptions of Instruments Adapted for Use in Learning the Art of Rolling*

Three-time British Columbian cigarette rolling champion and author T. Roland Jones with his patented hand-rolled Devil's Fork cigarette.

Learn to construct wonderful and varied fumigatory contrivances, such as:

*The Tulip,*     *The Hog Pen,*     *The Whirly Gig,*     *...and Many Others!*

*For all levels of dexterity and intelligence.*

**Jones of Kelowna Co.**
No 34. Hemp Creek Way, Kelowna, British Columbia
*Send for free booklet*

they invariably contract HIV. These same users are then 40% likely to infect someone else. Healthcare costs due to drug abuse—not to mention costs of criminal activity and jail time as a result of that activity—are all spiralling up, up, up.

So, what's the solution? Certainly methadone clinics, needle exchanges, and adequate programs to help people quit the habit are crucial. At the same time, our entire thinking about drugs has to change—we've got a pharmacy on every block hawking any number of mind-altering substances, and now it's possible to get just about any damn thing you like over the Net.

There are well over 15,000 online sites selling prescription drugs worldwide. While a few are above-board and associated with brand-name pharmacies, many are offshore or considerably more casual about whom they'll prescribe drugs to ("Hi Doctor Nick!"). So naturally,

people are taking advantage of the situation. Earl Berger, managing director of the respected *Berger Population Health Monitor*, believes that as many as 240,000 Canadians a month are buying prescription drugs online.

Of course, drug buying on the Net focuses on the burgeoning ultra-urban interest in "lifestyle drugs" like Viagra, Xenical, Zyban, and Propecia. As our cities get ever more crowded with wrinkled boomer types finding that a giant SUV and a tiny sports car aren't enough to stave off those old-in-the-big-city blues, they're turning to steroids, human growth hormone, cancer treatments, narcotic painkillers, sleeping pills, antidepressants, birth control pills, antibiotics, acne medication, and even drugs that have been withdrawn from Canada after a number of deaths, such as Prepulsid (a heartburn medication). Zyban is a drug that helps people stop smoking; Propecia helps to fight hair loss. If it's potentially embarrassing or inconvenient to obtain, people are buying it online.

There's also a brisk online trade in Xenical. The drug inhibits an enzyme in our digestive tract that normally breaks fat down so that the body can absorb it. This property has made it extremely popular with diet freaks, bulimics, and anorexics—exactly the wrong people to be taking it, because it's recommended only for obese patients. It could make anyone else very sick by preventing essential nutrients from entering the bloodstream.

Even though it's illegal to write an online prescription in Canada, it's dead easy to order drugs online and have them delivered right to your door. There seems to be some confusion about whether or not doing so is illegal: *The Straight Goods* asserts that it's "illegal to bring schedule F drugs or prescription drugs into the country," but the *Globe and Mail* says "There are virtually no restrictions on consumers buying drugs on-line from offshore suppliers, as long as they are for personal use." For a consultation fee of $40 to $75 Yankee dollars, online pharmacies will evaluate an online questionnaire to determine if the drug is right for you. They arrive in anonymous-looking packages from companies with generic names, usually marked "gift" on the declaration form or disguised as dietary supplements so that they'll sail right through Customs. Two hundred and four such packages were seized in Canada last year—a relatively small number of the estimated total—most of them large shipments of steroids or growth hormone. Sorry, muscleboys.

Meanwhile, these lifestyle drugs are also finding favour with those who don't yet worry about receding hairlines. We all know about Viagra and the wonders it's done for some of our droopier elders. But some yuppies and rave kids have started using it as a party drug. After the highly publicized case of a 16-year-old Kansas boy who bought some online without lying about his age, the authorities began to sit up and take notice, which means it may be a bit harder to get your urban pharmaceutical accessories online in the future.

Still, contemporary urban life has other options for the jaded. One of the wonders of living in the global village is that new intoxicating substances are pouring into the Canadian city at a phenomenal rate. Substances like … khat. Khat? Yes, khat.

Khat is the young buds and fresh leaves of the *catha edulis*, a large shrub native to Ethiopia. Used throughout Africa and the Middle East as a mild social drug (not as a street drug), khat is usually grown in the vicinity of coffee bushes. Its use produces effects similar to coffee—but much stronger. Chewing on khat sticks results in feelings of bliss, clarity of thought, loquacity, and euphoria (and eventually, if you chew too much of it, semi-coma).

Because one of its psychoactive ingredients fades 48 hours after the plants are harvested, khat is smuggled into the country in large suitcases by "khat mules," usually in time for weekend use. According to the RCMP, khat arrives in Canada primarily at Pearson International Airport in Toronto, on planes from the UK, Netherlands, Germany, and Kenya. Canada Customs seized nearly 11 tonnes of khat in 2001, an increase from 8.6 tonnes in 2000, 6.3 tonnes in 1999, and 7.3 tonnes in 1998.

Khat users claim that it's a relatively innocuous substance, no worse than having a whiskey after dinner. But for beleaguered khat users everywhere, science is coming to the rescue. Apparently, illegal labs have been creating a synthetic form of khat's most active ingredient (cathinione), known on the street as "Cat."

Of course, most of us will be more familiar with the possibly insidious and certainly media-friendly Ecstasy. This amphetamine-related hallucinogen is the fave drug for younger generations of urbanites looking for a good time. Why is Ecstasy so popular in the Canadian city? Well, it makes the city not only bearable but desirable. Think about it: on Ecstasy you cram into a hot sweaty space and subject yourself to incredibly loud noises and overpriced beverages—and you love it. On Ecstasy, strangers press against you, grope you, and generally share their sweat—and you love it. For many, it's the perfect drug: comparatively inexpensive, it can last up to six hours and make you feel relaxed, energetic, and very very friendly. In her zine *Jook Sing Mui*, Tifanny Wong

DRUGS

## Drugs Seized in Canada, 1993–2001
*(Weights in kilograms; Ecstasy in dosage units)*

| | 1993 | 1994 | 1995 | 1996 | 1997 | 1998 | 1999 | 2000 | 2001 |
|---|---|---|---|---|---|---|---|---|---|
| heroin | 153 | 85 | 128 | 83 | 95 | 105 | 88 | 168 | 74 |
| cocaine | 2,731 | 7,915 | 1,544 | 3,110 | 2,090 | 2,604 | 1,116 | 1,851 | 1,783 |
| Ecstasy | | | | 1,221 | 10,222 | 68,496 | 400,000 | 2,069,709 | 1,871,627 |
| marijuana (kg) | 7,314 | 6,472 | 5,500 | 17,234 | 50,624 | 29,598 | 23,829 | 21,703 | 28,746 |
| marijuana (plants) | 238,601 | 288,578 | 295,999 | 675,863 | 689,239 | 1,025,808 | 954,781 | 1,102,198 | 1,367,321 |
| hashish | 56,721 | 36,614 | 21,504 | 25,155 | 6,118 | 15,924 | 6,477 | 21,973 | 6,677 |
| liquid hashish | 669 | 659 | 663 | 805 | 824 | 852 | 434 | 1,240 | 397 |

describes taking "E" for the first time while attending a rave at a downtown Toronto club:

> *I think this was where I started to get really communicative. I couldn't stop commenting on my arms! It was so demented. It's like the E went straight into them. Long and thin, they seemed to float when I moved them. I pulled my pants up to my knees to cool down and this girl next to me, who was totally mashed, ran her fingers lightly on my shins. It was like she was touching a new shimmery skin on top of my own. It tickled. Tori then demonstrated the "good-feeling-when-people-touch-you" thing by giving me a back massage. This time, I could feel my back being pushed and moulded like a pile of wet sand. I just felt like flying. Now doesn't that sound nice?"*

Of course, things don't always work out so wonderfully. At a massive rave in Edmonton, six teens on Ecstasy suddenly dropped to the dance floor with seizures. Why? To this day no one is sure. It gets worse: Jamie Britten died at a Halifax rave after taking Ecstasy and Allan Ho died after taking it at a rave in an abandoned Toronto building. In 1999–2000, 14 deaths were linked to the drug. Considering that more than half a million pills were seized by police in 2000, it seems you're more likely to die of air pollution than taking E, but at least in this case, you can do something about it by just saying no. The day after her rave (E)xperience, Wong reported in her zine that she felt odd and uncomfortable—just what exactly do they put in those pills? she wondered. Well, no one really knows. All we do know is that in big, relatively affluent cities that are literally awash with drugs from the pharmacy to the corner pusher to the high school dope dealer to the online Viagra merchant, what we need isn't bigger and better jails, but better education and a serious commitment to explore why our cities are turning so many of us into drug fiends. From Vancouver's seedy East Side to upscale neighbourhoods in cities across Canada, we're replete with drugs, legal and illegal. So ask yourself this: Is there something about our urban environments that encourages the use of mind-altering substances? (See also *Attractions, Watering Holes, Mental Illness.*)

# Coffee

## Tim Has a Second Cup and Sees Stars: Some Brief Ruminations on the Elixir of Life

While most people agree that coffee was introduced to the New World in 1607 by Captain John Smith, founder of Virginia at Jamestown, some Canadian historians claim that it arrived in Canada first. Here at Almanac HQ, our sources tell us that fragments of disposable birchbark coffee cups containing coffee residue and hand-rolled, filterless, lipstick-marked cigarette butts have been found around the archaeological sites of early 17th-century hockey arenas, indicating the presence of the first "hockey moms" … which would mean that we've been pounding coffee to keep the chills away for 400 years now.

Even if the doughnuts were disappearing from our diet (fat chance), Canadians still swill over 15 billion cups of coffee a year. Sixty-seven percent of adults drink coffee every day, and most people have three cups if they have any. Eighteen percent of all the beverages we consume are coffee-based. Is it any wonder that the city is full of agitated people desperate to get where they're going even when they aren't quite sure where they're going?

This massive consumption of caffeine has led to an obscene profusion of choices, complicating the former Zen-like simplicity of pouring yourself a cup of joe. Until recently, even our coffee franchises were straightforward—what else could a chain of stores opened by the man who invented the slapshot (Tim Horton) possibly be? Caf or decaf, cream or sugar, to stay or to go, end of story. But times have changed. These days, buying a coffee has to say something about who you are as a person, an individual, a potential scriptwriter, sculptor, and safe-sex instructor with a penchant for the anti-globalization movement and a weakness for crullers. Such an individual cannot be caught dead at a Second Cup or Starbucks, though will very occasionally enter a Tim Hortons or Coffee Time for something maple frosted to dip, ironically, in a white mug. Generally, though, such artistic aspirations require that you find a smoke-filled café offering organic beans picked by workers with a pension plan (see *Fair Trade*) with a heavy-rotation soundtrack of Sarah McLachlan and the wailing, uh, *singing* of Alanis Morissette.

Of course, times have changed and the once ever-present hippie coffee house is harder and harder to find. Why, you wonder? Well, for one thing, our cities are effectively occupied by an insidious invading force from the West. The streets have been colonized by the pseudo-bohemian-yuppie-positive mega-latte-smoothy-skinny mocha-espressso offerings found in multifarious Starbucks franchises from sea to polluted sea. We at the Almanac hate everything about Starbucks: the soothing jazz, the complicated coffees, and, most of all, the ubiquity.

COFFEE

Believe it or not, you young 'uns, there was once a time before Starbucks, when noble Hortons, Coffee Times, Second Cups, and even non-chain-affiliated coffee shops freely roamed the paved streets without a care in the world. But today all that has changed—neighbourhood stores have disappeared, and even some of the venerable chains have lost outposts to the ravenous beast that won't stop till our minds are turned into a frappaccino mush.

Let's use Toronto as an example. Starbucks opened its first store in Canada's largest city in January 1996. By the end of that year, they planned to have roughly 100 stores up and running. That's a lot of coffee shops, even to serve an urban community admittedly obsessed with getting that daily caffeine jolt. Things went along swimmingly for the hungry chain until Starbucks set out to take over a local café in the downtown Annex area of the city. Dooney's had been operating for 15 years until its landlord, smelling the scent of Seattle beans and knowing the lease was up, signed a long-term rental deal with the upstart invaders. Poor Starbucks didn't know what they were getting into. News of the demise of the local fave hangout spread like a double espresso through the twitchy veins of the neighbourhood. Next thing you know, more than 1,500 people had signed a pro-Dooney's petition. "Friends of Dooney's" demonstrated. Media across the country carried the story, lattes and slabs of chocolate cake were consumed, and Starbucks beat a hasty retreat down to trendy neighbourhood-lite Queen Street.

Of course, it's coffee-shop-saturated Vancouver where Starbucks is at its most frighteningly pervasive. But even there, Starbucks faces rejection. A transplanted small-town boy from Ontario who had taken up residence in the trendy beachfront suburb of Kitsilano, where there's a Starbucks *and* a local coffee shop on almost every block, recently told the Almanac yet another cautionary tale. Seems his parents had come to visit from small-town Ontario. Mom got a bit homesick and wanted a coffee. No problem, he said. We have about 30 places to choose from. No, Mom said. I want a coffee like back home. What kind of coffee is that, Mom? A Tim Hortons, Mom said adamantly. He tried to tempt her with foamy chilled shakes, soothing new age soundtracks, flaky pastries, but to no avail. Mom had to have Tim Hortons. Desperately, our small-town escapee consulted a phone book—there *was* a Tim Hortons. In Burnaby, an hour's drive if they were lucky. Did his mom really want to spend half the day in beautiful Vancouver driving to a distant suburb just to replicate her hometown coffee? Yup, she nodded. And away they went.

# Webcams

orry, no naked people here … only the essential scenery of the urban landscape.

### Victoria

**http://pullmancanada.net/cam.html** Unidentified intersection with provincial legislature in the background.

**http://rbcm1.rbcm.gov.bc.ca/visit-museum/web-cam.html** View of the harbour from the Royal BC Museum.

### Vancouver

**www.portvancouver.com/the_port/web_cams.html** A staggering 18 views of the port area.

**www.jericho.bc.ca/webcam/webcam.htm** North from Jericho Beach in Vancouver … soothing.

**www.parking.ubc.ca/gsab.htm** UBC parking lot north. Lame.

**vancouverview.com/cameras/index.html** Seven views including a cruise ship panorama of downtown from the north shore and West Vancouver traffic.

### Calgary

**http://gumbo.adv.ualberta.ca/webcams/quad** It was minus 19 when we dropped by this site showing the University of Alberta's central quad.

View of the Victoria harbour from the Royal B.C. Museum

### Edmonton

**www.chiaweb.net/webcam/chiacow.html** Several cams showing views in and outside of this Edmonton guy's house.

### Regina

**www.yqr.ca/cam.htm** Empty patch of concrete; has something to do with the airport.

### Winnipeg

**www.tnewmedia.com/forkscam** Camera controlled live by visitors to the Forks!

### Toronto

**www.buzzardpress.com/cam** Spadina and Sussex plus changing tunage; Sarah McLachlan's "Song for a Winter's Night" when we were there. Actually, most of it's the empty roof of a building; you can barely make out the street and just see the occasional car. (Although we did like the trashing of the Spiderman on the building wall …)

WEBCAMS

**www.tsn.ca/shows/webcam.asp** TSN sportsdesk newsroom, but too high up; you can't really see anything. Stuck at October 1999 when we stopped by!

**www.toronto.com/feature/238** Skyline from the Toronto city centre airport, view of City Hall and Nathan Phillips Square.

## Hamilton
**http://members.tripod.com/~HamCam/index.html** Grainy view of downtown.

## Ottawa
**http://parliamenthill.gc.ca/text/index-e.html** Live Hill cam! Watch our lawmakers ignore the plight of the Canadian city!

## Montreal
**www.montrealcam.com/en-tour-bourse.html** Downtown corner of Peel and Ste. Catherine.

**www.montrealcam.com/en-placecartier.html** Quaint view of old Montreal with a superb view of Place Jacques-Cartier from the famous restaurant Chez Queux.

**www.montrealcam.com/en-biodome.html** Polar World at the Biodome. Frolicking penguins last time we checked.

**www.techbull.com/techbull/tourisme/quebec/webcam/cam60.html** Sixty traffic cams.

## Quebec City
**http://pages.infinit.net/rvief/camera.htm** Enormous view of the entire city; cheesy soundtrack.

Two views of downtown Charlottetown

## Fredericton
**www.mycityweb.com/pans.asp?Section=Community &CityID=1&LID=6** A view of Fredericton from the rooftops! With do-it-yourself panoramics.

## Charlottetown
**www.gov.pe.ca/islandcam/index.php3** Grafton and Queen Street, downtown, and the view overlooking St. Peter's Cathedral.

## Halifax
**www.chebucto.ns.ca/Webcam/index.cgi** View of the water from Fenwick Place, student dorm and the tallest building in metropolitan Halifax.

## St John's
**www.ozfm.net/skycam.htm** Panning cam overlooking the harbour and southeastern part of the city.

**www.cfog.net/snow.htm** Flavin Street. Saw a car go by.

"**F**UN" IS A RELATIVELY NEW CONCEPT for Canadians. Historically, our culture has been all about mind-numbing, unpleasant, backbreaking work. Farming is not fun. Fishing for cod or salmon is not fun. Mining coal is not fun. Running a trapline is not fun. Harvesting trees is not fun. And being an accountant is *definitely* not fun.

There are still plenty of shitty, thankless jobs to go round, of course. But since we're now doing them all together in relatively cramped quarters instead of being strung out in tiny hamlets scattered across thousands and thousands of square kilometres of empty wilderness, it's much easier to find someone to bump uglies or lose a few brain cells with at the end of the day.

In the brief period that we Canadians have managed to be social (please, don't waste our time with the barn-raising and quilting-bee stories—now that we have digital cable [see *Arts & Entertainment, Moses and MuchMusic*] you can always catch a *Little House on the Prairie* rerun), we've developed some relatively ingenious ways to enjoy ourselves. Filed notes on a few of our favourites follow.

# Parties

The house party is an urban institution. You get the invite, the e-mail, the voice message and you spread the word around, making sure every friend, acquaintance, and known felon on the block is aware of the fact that some fool is opening up their domicile and refrigerator to total strangers.

The result? A packed house or apartment hot as an elephant's ass despite the frigid snowy weather. There's slush on the carpet and piles of ski jackets cover the various drunks passed out in the corners. If it's a metal party, there are black leather scuff marks on the drywall (see *Arts & Entertainment, Heavy Metal*). An indecipherable mush of dance music wails over the shouts of pals as they shove their way over to an already-stripped-bare cheese plate meant for 25, not 125. Whether it's being hosted by people under the legal drinking age or old enough to be there because they're draft dodgers from the Vietnam War, there will be drugs (see *Tools, Drugs*), but you will

not be offered any. Unless you brought the drugs. Then everyone is your friend.

There's a definite skill set required for surviving these parties. We have it. You don't. (Our credentials: we once survived a summer toga party crammed full of Winnipeg punk rockers that was so successful it only ended because of the arrival of six cop cars, a paddy wagon, and a drug-sniffing dog unit.) So listen up. Here are the essential House Party Survival Tips:

- Never bring your own booze. Why bother? There's always some other sucker's beer in the fridge. Grab a generic brand like Ex or Blue so you don't get discovered. (The flipside of this is: if you must bring your own, buy a weird micro-brewery flavour that nobody else will have. That way, if some buttwad borrows one of your brewskis, you can be like, "Excuse me, I believe that is *my* Mountain Ox Genuine Belgian Dry Ice Draft Pilsner Cream Ale you're knocking back, asshole ...") You may also want to consider hiding your beer in the washing machine, unless you expect someone to vomit in it (which is always a possibility).
- All the action is either (a) in the kitchen or (b) out back with the smokers.
- Go directly for the food. If the meagre snacks are already gone, don't hesitate to poke into fridges, cupboards, and stoves (sometimes, the panicked host forgets the tray of President's Choice cheese baubles in the oven). If you're feeling really desperate, raid the deep-freeze while you're hiding your beer in the

# HOUSE PARTY BASICS

washing machine. You may find frozen desserts, waffles, or other edible things that don't require venturing into the kitchen to consume.

- The safest place to pass out is under the pool table.
- Stay away from the stereo. It will be surrounded by Music Nazis—guys who work in record stores or write for campus newspapers and underground zines (see *Arts & Entertainment, Zines*) but lack anything resembling normal social skills or basic hygiene. They will not only control the stereo for the duration of the party, but will attempt to draw you into an impassioned discussion of bands that you've neither heard of nor care about. If cornered, pretend to use American Sign Language and they will immediately lose interest.
- Don't be afraid to explore; you never know what you'll find. If there's a book, CD, or pair of panties you discover, don't hesitate to borrow it. You'll return it next time you come around.
- Don't get the dog drunk.
- Watch carefully for anomalous behaviour, such as generosity. At one event from our booze-soaked teenage years, we dimly recall a particularly rodent-like individual lounging against the wall, proffering a handful of salty snacks to passersby. After careful observation, we determined that he wasn't eating any of the snacks himself, though they were being glommed rapidly from his outstretched palm by drunken partyers. Our suspicions were confirmed when we caught him dipping into the cat kibble for a refill.
- It's generally considered poor form to nail someone on the same bed that holds all the coats.

**1** Never bring your own booze.

**2** Don't be afraid to explore.

**3** Always dress semi-normal.

**4** If the host or a pal of the host asks who you are, be general.

**5** Be wary of generosity.

**6** Do not give the pets alcohol.

# Festivals (a Few of Them, Anyway)

Our cities are host to a stunning list of excuses to gather, cavort, and waste money. We generally call these festivals, and they run the gamut from tiny and relatively bizarre to huge and celebrity top-heavy. For a small country we have some pretty impressive gatherings. The Ottawa blues festival is second biggest in North America after Chicago's. The Montreal Just for Laughs comedy festival has been known to launch sitcom careers and the Toronto International Film Festival is on the calendar of every sleazy film producer in the world. But there's also something to be said about the more obscure events. Drop in at Regina's annual Louis Riel trial fest and who knows what kind of fun you'll have? What weird wonders wait to be discovered at Toronto's Canzine festival of underground culture, or the Vancouver queer film festival? Good times await, and here's a list of just some of the events to which our festive cities play host.

Artessential—the ultimate art show (Calgary)
Ashkenaz Festival of New Yiddish Culture (Toronto)
Atlantic Film Festival (Halifax)
Calgary Folk Music Festival
Canadian Tulip and Music Festival (Ottawa)
Canzine Festival of Underground Culture (Toronto)
Celebration of Nations Festival (Edmonton)
Cisco Systems Bluesfest (Ottawa)
CKCU Ottawa Folk Festival
Edmonton Heritage Festival
Edmonton Folk Festival
Enbridge Symphony Under the Sky (Edmonton)

Festival of Art and Social Change (Vancouver)
Festival Internationale de Jazz Montreal
Festival 500 Sharing the Voices (St. John's)
Festival of Friends (Hamilton)
Festival by the Sea (Saint John)
Festival Vancouver
First Ontario International Youth Fair and Culture Festival (Ottawa)
Folkorama (Winnipeg)
Forever Young Folk Festival (Oakville, Ontario)
Halifax International Busker Festival
Harvestfest (Toronto)
Hot and Spicy Food Festival (Toronto)
Hot Docs Documentary Film Festival (Toronto)
Images Independent Film and Video Festival (Toronto)
International Organ Festival and Competition (Calgary)
International Festival of Authors (Toronto)
Jazz City International Music Festival (Edmonton)
Just for Laughs Comedy Festival (Montreal)
Les Fêtes de la Nouvelle France (Quebec City)
Mariposa in Parkdale (Toronto)
Maritime Fall Fair (Halifax)
Masala! Mehndi! Masti! (Toronto)
Montreal First People's Festival
Montreal World Film Festival
Montreal Jazz Festival
Montreal International Celtic Festival
Montreal Bike Fest
New Brunswick Summer Music Festival (Fredericton)
Newfoundland and Labrador Folk Festival (St. John's)

Northern Lights Festival Boreal (Sudbury)
Ottawa Fringe Festival
Ottawa Greek Festival
Ottawa International Animation Festival
Ottawa International Chamber Music Festival
PEI International Shellfish Festival (Charlottetown)
Philippine and Asia Pacific Arts Festival (Toronto)
Regina Folk Festival
Ritmo y Color (Toronto)
Rootsfest Music Festival (Victoria)
Royal Red Arabian Horse Show (Regina)
Saskatoon International Fringe Festival
Shakespeare on the Saskatchewan Festival (Saskatoon)
Shakespeare by the Sea Festival (St. John's)
Sprockets Toronto International Film Festival for Children

The Cabbagetown Film Festival (Toronto)
The Festival of Fathers (Charlottetown)
Toronto International Film Festival
Toronto Festival of Beer
Toronto Jazz Festival
Toronto Jewish Film Festival
Toronto International Choral Festival
Trial of Louis Riel (Regina)
Unisong Music Festival for Canadian Choirs (Ottawa)
Vancouver Folk Music Festival
Vancouver Fringe Festival
Vancouver International Comedy Festival
Vancouver International Dance Festival
Vancouver Queer Film and Video Festival
Victoria Summer Music Festival
Windsor Theatre Festival

National Archives of Canada

Arch in Chinatown, Vancouver, 1901

FESTIVALS

CNE garbage collection, Toronto, 1951

# Hangout Spots

Even though it's not always possible to find the place where the fun is happening, you can always simply go where it's statistically likely that fun will erupt and just *hang out* there.

Whether or not fun actually occurs as a result of hanging out is another question entirely. Still, we are a hopeful people, as attested by the abundance of urban Canucks hanging out in all manner of spots, from the time-honoured and humble (the 7-Eleven parking lot, the outdoor hockey rink penalty box in mid-July, the mall food court [see *Shopping, Malls*], the wrinkly-old-man bar [see *How to Choose a Bar*]) to the posh and elite (Asian fusion restaurants, Bally Fitness Centres, preschools for gifted toddlers). And, at any rate, hanging out in the city is an attraction all on its own, largely because you never know who you're going to meet or what strange wondrous moment might occur (wild animals loping by as you roll a joint in an urban ravine; a lengthy sidewalk conversation about underwear with Don McKellar). To help you whittle down your hangout possibilities, we've provided this handy list of one young woman's fave spots. So pick your poison: something's bound to happen sooner or later…

*Once upon a time the Old Town Clock on Citadel Hill was a quaint gathering point where the locals of Halifax "gathered to talk things over in the summer evenings." My, how times change. The citadel is now a cruising spot for late night gay pick-ups.*

# Candace's Top Fredericton Hangout Spots of All Time

by **Candace**, from *Maggot Zine*, **Fredericton**

The Jam Shack (Church St.):  I mention this place mainly because it's soon going to be torn down to accommodate a new 96-unit apartment building and parking lot, courtesy of Alfred and Robert Brown Rentals, local owners and operators of Bellboy Dry Cleaning. Not only do some downtown residents oppose the housing construction for environmental/wildlife and green space preservation, but some kids used to skate at one of the abandoned warehouses and dammit, where are bands gonna jam now? I've been to some pretty rockin' hoe-downs in the shack, and I'd hate to see it go. Also, there's a little bit of a "music scene history" on the walls, with all the graffiti in there. I mean, it's the closest thing Fredericton's got to a "music centre" or "music museum."

The Regent Mall Food Court:  I know, I know, I'm hurtin' for admitting it: I used to be a mall rat. I mean, there used to be a cool arcade in there, though, with pool tables 'n prizes 'n all. And who hasn't done a bit of shoplifting in their day? It's fun sometimes to pretend everything in the mall is yours (ever see *Dawn of the Dead*?), and besides, yah used to be able to smoke anywhere you wanted. Getting chased by security guards was the best.

The Old Train Bridge:  Now it's a walking bridge, but it was way cooler as a rotting old train bridge. Only true rebels ever used to risk their lives, drinking and jumping from beam to beam. Actually, it's not cool to joke about—some kids *have* died goofing around.

Officer's Square:  Ah the classics … I couldn't even begin to recall the countless days spent in this downtown park: many stoned afternoons and drunken evenings. Heck, even a whole lot of drunken afternoons. Yup, I don't even know where to begin. Lots and lots of "freaks" hung out there. Everyone used to "oil" along with the changing of the guards. Now who can forget that?

Rooftop Across from Barracks (Queen St.):  You can't get up there any more cuz someone caught on to all the trespassing and put up one great big hunk of metal covering the ladder. Dang. Good spot to get away, though, if the people in the square were getting annoying. (Geez, them damn drunks … Get a job, eh?) My gal pals & I used to sing on the rooftops at ridiculous hours in the morning, in ridiculous states. We believed the entire city belonged to us. It was rad.

Paul Fairweather

# Watering Holes

*Mostly all offences are due directly or indirectly to intemperance. What is the cause of almost all larcenies?—drink! Of assaults—drink! Disorderly conduct?—drink! Fights, furious driving, interference with the police, foul language, blasphemies?—drink, drink, drink!*

—*Montreal chief of police, 1873*

When it comes to bars and pubs, city life kicks ass and takes names over suburban and rural living. Proximity means you can walk, bus, or cab to and from your chosen watering hole. Population density means there are many such watering holes to choose from. Relatively high employment means there's always a sucker running a tab. Extreme levels of stress and anxiety mean that drinking is an urban survival necessity, not a sickness or addiction as teetotalling villagers sometimes suggest. Finally, an Anglo-Franco culture means that both predominant strands of Canadian heritage like to get pissed! (There's no place better than Montreal to get drunk, period. As the graffiti over the urinal in one Anglo Montreal watering hole used to read, "A Bad Thursday in Montreal is Like a Good Friday in Toronto.") So what are you waiting for? Get your coat and your Almanac and head for the bar!

Urban Canada is a drinking culture and at night we do what we do best: we engage in convivial boozology with pals, acquaintances, and best friends we met five minutes ago. There are people who tell you that they don't drink. There is something wrong with those people and they do not belong in the Canadian city. The appropriate attitude to drinking is an essential survival skill in the big city. What is the appropriate attitude to drinking? Simple. You're always available for a quick one, or a slow one, or an entire night of heavy drinking. You're particularly available if someone else is buying, though you never hesitate to pull your weight if necessary—no one wants to drink with a cheapskate who can't cover a round.

The fact is, any true urban Canadian should take his or her bar scene very, very seriously. Canadians aren't actually very evil, on the whole, but for reasons of street credibility we like to *think* we're evil, and sitting in dark, smelly bars helps to foster that illusion. It can even turn you into a folk hero. Vancouver, for instance, was practically founded by one "Gassy Jack Deighton," described by a 19th-century pioneer as an innkeeper "of broad ready humour, spicy, crisp and ever flowing. He was of grotesque, Falstaffian proportions and green-muddy,

---

**I strongly suggest that the number of licensed liquor selling places be reduced in this city. Certain sections of the city are literally infested with restaurants and bars. Let us not forget that, for young men especially, the saloon, where fire-water is imbibed, not to say the worst of poisons, is truly the ante room to the accursed house; with passions inflamed and their reason distracted.**

—*Hon. Justice Henri Taschereau, Superior Court of Montreal, "Report on the Police Investigation and Its Results," early 1900s*

---

Five bartenders, Saint Charles Hotel Bar, Toronto, 1911

purplish complexion, with the gift of grouping words and throwing them with the volubility of a fakir. A man who shot at random, but always hit the mark." Now *that's* an innkeeper!

Halifax in the 1800s was as overrun by British navy men as it is now by students from the prairies. Both have led to the same results: one helluva hectic night life. Describes a disapproving doctor:

> The upper streets were full of brothels; grog ships and dancing houses were to be seen in almost every part of the town. A portion of Grafton street was known under the appellation of Hogg street from a house of ill-fame kept by a person of that name. The upper street along the base of citadel hill between the north and south barracks was known as "'knock him down" street, in consequence of the numbers of affrays and even murders committed there. No person of any character ventured to reside there.

Now *that's* a neighbourhood with plenty of watering holes to choose from!

More recently, Calgary has been a proud supporter of the dubious "bikini bar" phenomenon. As one newspaper noted in 1998, "There are now six bikini bars in the city, and it seems to be a perfect bikini climate, in Calgary at least: It does seem as though bikini bars have been particularly popular in Calgary compared with other cities such as Toronto and Vancouver." Cowboys, one of the most famous of such establishments, is rumoured to pay for the boob jobs and tooth cappings of its best-beloved waitresses. A Calgary alderman had police look into the doings of Fantasia Bikini Bar, which installed bikini-clad dancers in their front window during rush hour—he was apparently concerned that drivers would get dangerously distracted. "'Is this bikini thing a fad?' asked one proud bikini bar entrepreneur. 'I don't know. Business is still strong…'" Now *that's* a city with, uh, class!

WATERING HOLES

# How to Choose a Bar: Do's and Don'ts

As the bikini bar fad suggests, the pubs and bars of today's city are fraught with danger. Following are some tips on how to locate excellent venues for your next piss-up. And remember, have a little class—if you're gonna be sick, do it in a bathroom or an alley. This isn't your farming community; this is the big city and the rest of us shouldn't be put off our pints by your inability to go the distance!

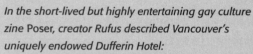

### THE DUFF

*In the short-lived but highly entertaining gay culture zine* Poser, *creator Rufus described Vancouver's uniquely endowed Dufferin Hotel:*

An honest-to-God dirty-old-man bar, 1970s decor, and patrons and staff who proudly display beer bellies and hockey hair. Operating like a speakeasy during this time of societal prohibition, the Duff offers sanctuary to its loyal clientele, most of who exist on the fringes of polite society. Tucked away behind the disco, in the back bar, is a tiny stage, a filthy mirror and some of the wildest erotic entertainment in the country. I've heard some remarks that the strippers at the Duff are homeless men trying to make a quick buck and/or they are hustlers advertising their wares. Although it's true that the men who get up to take it all off at the Duff tend to be a bit rough and unpolished, there are ARTISTS in this house.

• *Look for:* Regulars. Any bar worth its beer will have regulars. Regulars are the ruddy-faced gals and guys who warm the stools and know the names of all the barkeeps and waitresses. Regulars will look at you rudely the first few times you appear in THEIR bar, but if you act respectably (no moonwalking to the lite rock or asking the waitress to put on the cartoon channel) and keep dropping in, you'll quickly find yourself on a first-name basis with those tippling toadstools. (You might even find yourself becoming one of them.) A special category of regular is the Wrinkly Old Guy; you know you've found a saloon worth patronizing if there are more than two but fewer than six in a given establishment. They don't move a lot or say much, but it's usually entertaining when they do. To engage a Wrinkly Old Guy in conversation, simply utter this phrase: "George Chuvalo … now *there* was a boxer!"

• *Avoid:* Chains. Like most of the world, our urban environs are awash with lame name-brand chains offering a cookie-cutter experience of everything from book buying to thirst quenching. Why support the bland and boring when there's so much else to choose from? Chains are easily recognized; the pubs always have faux Olde English signs featuring names that include words like "Firkin" or "Elephant." Their menus all offer the same selection of brown, greasy fries, wings and burgers, and their pints are all several dollars more expensive than they should be. Chain bars offer American-style "entertainment" such as girls in skimpy outfits, distracting you from your primary goal: getting ripped. Evil American chain Hooters is one particularly offensive

culprit, and is a blight on any landscape—overlit, incessantly cheerful, and oddly asexual in the way that all T&A joints are—to be avoided at all costs. The least offensive chains are the sports bars which, if nothing else, offer the comforts of wide-screen televisions methodically showing whatever obscure hockey game can be pulled off satellite. (Note: Canadian city bars with televisions must always be showing hockey. If a drinking establishment is not showing hockey, turn around and walk out.)

- *Look for:* Seediness. A seedy bar is a good bar, because it means low prices and people who aren't too uppity when it comes to talking to a stranger. Telltale signs of seedy bars: yellowed clippings in the windows (no dates more recent than 1979 are acceptable); sections of flocked wallpaper, preferably red and/or gold; vinyl surfaces; and handicrafts made by the employees—one of our faves used to prominently display a rack of model wooden shotguns made by one of the waitresses. Don't be tempted by the platter of "bar sandwiches" gathering mould on a shelf next to the scorched coffee pot and you'll be all right. (Bars aren't for eating, they're for drinking.)

- *Avoid:* Hotel Bars, Restaurant Bars, Clubs with a View. These are over-priced scenester-oriented hell-holes where you'll pay eight bucks for a bottle of beer and the privilege of mixing with tourists and the hoity-toity. They may also try to inflict jazz on you, a fate too horrible to contemplate. The only

reason you should ever be in that kind of bar is if someone else is buying or if you're heading to a gourmet meal and they're making you wait so they can work an extra 30 bucks onto the tab with a force-fed advance round of drinking.

- *Look for:* Laughter. A good bar is a fun bar, where people aren't afraid that they're not looking cool if they crack up out loud. People like to express themselves when they're drunk, and the establishment that gets them drunk has an obligation to provide an environment where the bellicose, the morose, and the hysterical all have their place. Not necessarily a place where everybody knows your name (which could potentially lead to legal difficulties later), but rather where no one cares what it is.

- *Avoid:* Entertainment. Piano players hawking their schmaltzy Billy Joel stylings, pint-waving poets who think they're the next Milton Acorn (see *Poetry*), eclectic jazz combos that play the cheese grater and the synthesized clarinet—these have no place in a bar. A bar should be about drinking, not "entertainment," "dining," "meeting singles," or "bikini waitresses." There are venues and times and places for all that other stuff—that's why we live in the big city, and not some rural outpost. Thus, all these things should be kept separate from the bona fide dark, slightly scummy but not necessarily overtly threatening, reasonably priced (relatively speaking), urban Canadian drinking emporium.

WATERING HOLES

# Sex

At a book launch held in the upstairs of a trendy Toronto Italian café, Gutter Press publisher Sam Hiyate introduced his latest discovery, the writer Tamara Faith Berger. Instead of extolling her novella's spectacular prose and poignant insights into the human condition, he informed the crowd that he published the book because it turned him on. As he explains: "I told them that as a publisher you want to get a mental hard-on, but in the case of Tamara's book, it was great, because it came with the physical accompaniment." Where once such frankness might have shocked and horrified staid Upper Canada, Hiyate's lewd public pronouncement was met with applause and appreciative chuckles.

So it goes in cities across the country: attitudes are relaxing, prudes are pouting, and sex is on every billboard, movie, TV and computer screen, magazine cover, and mind. The city has always been a venue for challenging sexual mores and pushing a sex-positive agenda. Whether it's the rise of queer-positive environments and gigantic gay pride days (see *Denizens, Queer Culture*),

the publishing of groundbreaking texts like Berger's, the "reluctant" pornography of a filmmaker like Toronto's Bruce LaBruce, or the increasing prominence of sex shops meant to make women, queers, and couples comfortable searching for dildos or seeking counselling on cunnilingus, sex is out in the open in the city now more than ever before. Remember, the big city is the place to explore your sexual ambitions, but it can also be a place of frustration, danger, and loneliness. So play safe, respect your partner (if you're lucky enough to find one), and don't do anything we wouldn't do. Or if you do, do us the courtesy of writing it down and publishing it.

## Great Moments of Urban Canadian Sexual Liberation

- A Toronto woman launches a $225,000 lawsuit against her ex-boyfriend, claiming he two-timed her with his wife and took her off the "singles market" during a four-year relationship.
- Dominatrix Terri-Jean Bedford, convicted of running a bawdy house in the Toronto suburbs, opens Madame's House, a bondage bed-and-breakfast for fetishists.
- A modern-day Lady Godiva protesting a logging operation on Salt Spring Island stops traffic in downtown Vancouver. Accompanied by an escort of police and bare-breasted protesters, Brioni Penn rides her horse down busy Howe Street to the offices of Texada Land Corp. The protesters were mounting a last-ditch effort to stop Texada from

logging forests on private land on the island off the BC coast known for its idyllic scenery, small farms, and eclectic lifestyles. Penn, who hedged her bets on the sunny but crisp January day by wearing flesh-coloured bottoms, was also among several women who posed nude for a calendar that raised $100,000 toward their conservation efforts last year.

- Kids in the Hall troupe comic Scott Thompson is booed off the stage during the Griffin Prize gala ceremony for Canadian and international poets after performing a raunchy skit and wagging a sex toy. "I've never been fired in the middle of a gig before," Thompson told reporters. "They said, 'You're not going back on' and booted me out through the kitchen."

## Sex Stores

Used to be your average sex store was a seedy emporium of peep booths, glory holes, and dusty dildos. Paint was peeling off the walls, the clerk was slovenly and about as sexual as someone offering to share their gum, and other than desperate dirty old men, only roaches braved the xxx threshold.

But times have changed. These days, the city has discovered the joys of the sex-positive, woman-friendly erotic emporium. Here couples browse dildos organically designed for maximum pleasure. Classes on the joys of anal exploration are led by staff experts who regularly try out the wares. Seedy gawkers are politely shown the door. Stores like Womyn's Ware in Vancouver, Venus Envy in Halifax, and Good For Her in Toronto have changed the face of the sex store forever. Sex, in fact, has become disturbingly like aerobics: something that we *should* be doing because it's good for us (see *Arts & Entertainment, Poetry*).

Come As You Are, also in Toronto, opened in 1996 as Canada's only co-op-run sex shop. Co-founder Sandra Haar had this to say when talking to *Broken Pencil* magazine about the emergence in the mid to late 90s of the urban Canadian pro-sex sex shop:

> *I'm not sure exactly what happened. I have certain theories. It seemed to happen concurrently with a mainstreaming or a breakthrough of queer politics. There seemed to be more visibility and acceptance. All the [new] stores are fairly queer positive. Things*

Paul Fairweather

SEX

*that had been known within and had been accepted within sex-positive feminist and queer communities stepped out of the confines of the small communities in which they were maintained. Certain kinds of knowledge, like a standard acceptance of dildos or the pervasive knowledge of the use of strap-ons, suddenly just popped up in more general environments.*

Changes in the sex shop environment have put pressure even on traditionally cheesy and seedy chains like Adults Only Video, Canada's biggest porn video outlet based in Mississauga. Squeezed between the Internet and the new sex shops, they've been trying to remake themselves as a destination for couples looking to liven up the sex life. They've added the kinds of items that a Good For Her might sell: aromatherapy, sex toys, and literature. One question: where are the seedy old men going to go now?

## The CanSex Library

**Passion Lost: Public Sex, Private Desire in the Twentieth Century, Patricia Anderson**  Vancouver writer Patricia Anderson takes great pains to point out that *Passion Lost* is not trying to suggest that society should or could move back to more stringent control over matters sexual. "My book isn't about sex," she told the *Globe and Mail*. "It's about unhappiness as it relates to the representation of sex and the interaction of that in private lives." Regardless, as she charts the history of sexual representation to the present day, Anderson has

a lot to say about the pressures of a hyped-up urban erotic environment on our inevitably more banal sex lives.

**Lie with Me, Tamara Faith Berger**  Bridging the gap between diary, porn, confession, erotica, and literature, this surreal psychological thriller operates with the assumption that there are no boundaries left to break down. The plot consists of a series of seemingly random and often violent sex acts recounted from the point of view of a nameless nymphomaniac, constantly reminding us that we aren't supposed to be shocked any more. With its pink cover and crude cartoon drawings, it's even packaged to look as though it belongs in the children's section, further reinforcing both its provocative nature and our ambivalent reaction to it.

*We both straightened our backs,
like we were bracing ourselves. All
my flesh pulled towards his flesh.
I gulped my drink and banged for
more. "More!" I shouted.* More! More! More! *I
started rubbing that guy with my fist up and down
under the bar.*

—*Tamara Faith Berger,* Lie with Me

**A Very Lonely Planet: Love, Sex and the Single Guy, Ryan Bigge**  Vancouver/Toronto freelance writer Ryan Bigge does not hold back the personal details in this manifesto/biography/how-not-to text. Let's see, there's the old single friend who confides during a walk on an abandoned beach that she "had" a crush on him in high school. Bigge screws up his opportunity. Then there's the woman in New York who invites him on a sleep-over blind date. It's ambivalence at first sight; she kicks him out of her guest room and he ends up taking the bus to Toronto just to kill time until his flight back to Vancouver. Ouch. Bigge perfectly captures the essence of single guy life, and in doing so seems to have forever consigned himself to the lonely planet he has so adroitly colonized.

***Carnal Nation, Brave New Sex Fictions,* eds. Carellin Brooks and Brett Josef Grubisic** This anthology of sex stories includes some of the best young urban sex-obsessed writers and creators, including Derek McCormack, Sonja Ahlers, Marc Macdonald, and Larissa Lai.

***Sex Carnival,* Bill Brownstein** *Montreal Gazette* columnist Bill Brownstein interviews various sex workers and sex enthusiasts and tries to make sense of the changing cultural landscape that gives us naked news and naked car washes.

*Our front window featured two female mannequins. On the left side, we would dress the mannequin in leather gear and chaps, and on the right side, we would dress her in something more befitting a 50's housewife. We even had those pink slippers with feathers above the toes.*

*Every so often, this deranged madman would stop and talk to the mannequins through the plate glass windows. To the leather goddess he'd scream and shout, "You fucking whore! You dirty, dirty bitch! Fucking bitchpig!" Then he'd turn to the faithful housewife, touch his hands ever so gently to the window and*

*whisper lovingly, "Hello sweetie! I've been missing you. Did you miss me? You look sooo beautiful."*

*Now, despite the fact that what he was doing was completely weird, we never bothered him or shooed him away. He was completely harmless. Or at least we thought so.*

*When we changed our mannequins' clothing, we usually took them out of the window and into the back room because we had to pull their arms and legs off to put the clothes on, and it was cumbersome to leave their limbs lying on the floor while we served customers.*

*One day, one of my co-workers arrived at work early and decided to change the mannequins in the window while she had the chance. Of course, as fate would have it, lover boy walked past just as she was yanking his fair lady's arms off.*

*He went nuts. I mean, he was ALREADY nuts, but he went nuttier. He was even frothing at the mouth. He started throwing himself bodily at the plate glass window, shrieking: "What are you doing? You fucking animal! Look at what you've done to her! Don't worry, baby, I'm coming to save you!"*

*Terrified, my co-worker tried desperately to put the mannequin's arms back on. In her hurry, she broke the finger off one of the hands. This, of course, sent our Romeo into a renewed frenzy.*

*Fortunately, two police officers happened to witness the whole thing and promptly carried Casanova away kicking and screaming.*

*We never saw him again after that, but we still made sure to change our mannequins out of public view—just in case.*

—Renata Ramunda, Sex Shoppe Tales

SEX

### Good Girls Do: Sex Chronicles of a Shameless Generation, Simona Chiose

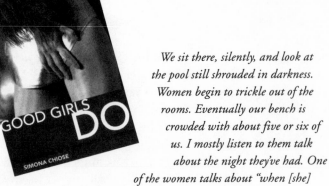

Toronto's Chiose ponders her sexual psychology while visiting lesbian bathhouses, dominatrixes, high-end call girls, and strip clubs. She also mixes genres, incorporating memoir, diary, and journalism into her narrative. But at the crux of this book is Chiose's quest for her own sexual self in an age of permeable, permissible sexual identity. She both revels in and blames the seemingly endless proliferation of sexual options she recounts in the book: "We're not giving up much by loosening our sexual mores. Or are we? Does losing the thrill of the forbidden, the suggestion, and the flirtation, count as a loss? Does not knowing the feel of leather that's been used against your body count as a loss?"

*4:00 a.m.: Anna and Jennifer and Andrea have all gone home after not scoring. Exhausted, I would also like to head out except that Rosalee has given me her room keys while she is visiting another woman in her room. And now, Rosalee is missing somewhere behind the closed doors. The bathhouse is supposed to close now, but the organizers aren't going to kick anyone out until 5. I go and sit outside on a bench by the pool. A woman in a short kilt and a leather vest comes over with her friend and asks me if I had a good time.*

*"Yeah, it was great," I tell her.*

*We talk for a while and I tell her who I'm waiting for.*

*"Oh, she was a dancer, wasn't she?" her friend says.*

*"Yeah, she was great too," I say.*

*"I really like her. I think I'll wait with you," the woman says.*

*We sit there, silently, and look at the pool still shrouded in darkness. Women begin to trickle out of the rooms. Eventually our bench is crowded with about five or six of us. I mostly listen to them talk about the night they've had. One of the women talks about "when [she] used to like boys."*

*"I used to go for these loser guys," she says, shaking her head.*

*"Remember how crazy I was about that guy?" she asks the friend sitting next to her. The friend looks heavenwards.*

*"That girl tonight, she's just like that guy," she says and frowns to herself.*

—Simona Chiose, Good Girls Do

## Sports

**S**ports are serious business in the Canadian city. And we do mean business, since all too often that's what it comes down to—not our love for our teams and heroes, not our commitment to long-standing sports legacies, but some absentee owner's cash flow. And so the Winnipeg Jets are gone, the Quebec Nordiques are no more, and NHL teams in Edmonton, Calgary, and Ottawa are perpetually threatening to head south. Vancouver had a basketball team just long enough for the franchise and the NBA to decide they weren't making enough money and pull out. Long-standing storied baseball franchise the Montreal Expos aren't cutting the

From *Sunburn*, comic anthology, Winnipeg

*B*ALANCED COVERAGE BY THE CITY'S UNBIASED MEDIA OUTLETS KEPT THE ISSUE IN PERSPECTIVE.

THOSE RESPONSIBLE FOR LOSING THE *DEBTS* SHOULD BE *SHOT!*

BJOB · BJOB

WE'LL BECOME REGINAPEG!

THE LOCAL NEWSRAG, A TV STATION-- OWNED BY ONE OF THE WHITE KNIGHTS, THE RADIO STATION WHICH BROADCASTS *DEBTS* GAMES AND OTHERS WHIPPED CROWDS OF TEENS INTO A SUNBURNED FRENZY... TO "SAVE" OUR DEBTS AND TIE UP TRAFFIC.

*N*OT *ALL* THE SHEEP WERE SUCKERED INTO THE INSANITY. A FEW SAT DOWN AND EXAMINED THE CITY'S OWN FIGURES.

SAVE OUR DEBTS!

BAA! BAA!

SAVE OUR DEBTS!

SAVE OUR DEBTS!

@#!!☆ HOCKEY FANS!

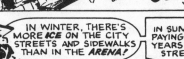

BAA BAH!

THE NUMBERS DON'T *ADD UP!*

IT'S A *BAAAAD* DEAL!

A NEW ARENA WOULD COST TOO MUCH!

IN WINTER, THERE'S MORE *ICE* ON THE CITY STREETS AND SIDEWALKS THAN IN THE *ARENA!*

GO DEBTS GO!

IN SUMMER, THE CITY HAS BEEN PAYING THE *DEBTS* LOSSES FOR YEARS AND LETTING THE STREETS GO TO POT!

GO DEBTS GO!

OUR GREAT METROPOLIS IS THE CHILD POVERTY CAPITAL OF CANADA!

THE *DEBTS* FANS RESPONSE?

mustard and they too are slated for the chopping block. Meanwhile, the CFL is constantly expanding, contracting, and moving teams around in the next desperate bid, not to please fans, but to squeeze every possible cent out of the small market franchise.

We hate to come off as waxing nostalgic (see *Zeitgeist, Nostalgia*), but what urbanite doesn't long for a time when you could love your heroes without having to think about how overpaid, overmarketed, and seemingly temporary they are? But were sports ever really different in this country?

Take the story of Saskatoon's Ethel Catherwood, who remains the only Canadian woman ever to win an individual gold medal in track and field at the Olympics. She broke the world record for the high jump in 1926, and won gold in the 1928 Amsterdam Olympics. The world fell in love with her there, with the *New York Times* reporting that she "received a tremendous ovation with the cool grace of a movie star, waving and blowing kisses to the stands." Tall, pale, and lovely, she was nicknamed the Saskatoon Lily by Saskatooners, who embraced her as one of their own. That is, until she got back home and married and divorced twice within a year. Then public opinion turned against her. Soon after, she married again, this time to a San Francisco millionaire. She left her hometown for California, and would never return to Saskatoon again.

Ethel's fame was fleeting and her adulation fickle—as soon as the public realized she was mortal, they attacked her. It would take Canada's national sporting obsession—hockey—to give us the man who remains Canada's greatest sports legend.

His name was Maurice Richard, and he lived and died in the Montreal to which he gave an incredible five Stanley Cups in a row. There were faster skaters and harder shots, but nobody could match the intensity of Richard, who made a paltry $25,000 a season at the height of his career. Perhaps his greatest goal came in the 1952 conference final, after a collision that knocked him unconscious. They carried him off the ice, and the game was winding down to a tie. Suddenly, Richard returned to the rink, blood still trickling from his six stitches. He took the puck into the corner, slipped away from a defender, and put it in the net—the Habs were going to the Stanley Cup. Richard doesn't really remember the moment: "By that time I was too dizzy to even see."

The Canadiens didn't win the Cup that year, and had to wait till 1956 for their staggering five years of greatness to begin. But Richard was already a mythical figure—his grit, determination, and temperamental outbursts represented the hopes, dreams, and frustrations of working-class French Canadians. It's hard for us to imagine now, but Richard was more than a hero; he was a living symbol. When he was suspended from action during the 1955 playoffs for striking a linesman, the infamous Richard Riot ensued, which gives us an inkling into how much the people of Montreal loved their greatest player.

SPORTS

Richard was, without a doubt, the most idolized player ever to lace up his skates. He galvanized and entranced an entire province, as Roch Carrier's famous short story "The Hockey Sweater" attests. But in urban Canada, a sports figure is as likely to be reviled as he or she is loved. Another hockey figure—on the business side of things—is legendary for being the most hated figure ever in Canadian sports.

No, we're not talking about Ottawa's profound disgust for contract hold-out and playoff pansy Alexi Yashin. We're talking about Harold Ballard, owner and president of the Maple Leafs throughout the 70s. Ballard took a once-proud franchise and sucked every cent he could out of it, counting all the while on the idiocy of the Toronto fans who, despite every setback, could not help but pack the Gardens year after losing year.

Among Ballard's many celebrated manoeuvres—and we're not going to mention his conviction for tax evasion—was his firing of popular head coach Roger Neilson and then asking him, not more than two days later, to come back and coach a game wearing a paper bag over his head. Neilson refused. Well, that was the 70s for you… In the 80s, Ballard decided to reduce the payroll by trading away Leaf all-star stalwarts Darryl Sittler and Lanny McDonald. Fans kept filling the Carlton Street Cashbox and the Leafs' situation, predictably, became ever more dire. The earth over Ballard's grave was still fresh when, in 1990, workers hurried to erase his hand- and footprints from the concrete under centre ice. A curse had been lifted, but Toronto sports fans no longer had a single glorious focal point for all their rage and disgust at the world. (And

still they wait, in vain, for the elusive Cup to finally return to town.)

Besides giving lucky cities sports figures to revere or retch over, sports in Canada has always represented the tremendous rivalry between cities that has long been part of our national character. A game between Montreal and Toronto (or Saint John and St. John's—see *Politics, Saint John vs. St. John's*) is sure to raise far more interest than when the boys fight for city pride in, say, Phoenix (which is largely populated by retired Canadians now anyway, so maybe the former Jets can make a go of it there … hmmm …).

Perhaps the most intense rivalry is between Calgary and Edmonton, two cities that have been locked in mortal combat since they were founded. In 1913 the Edmonton Eskimos were set to play the Calgary Tigers for the provincial championships. Only problem was, neither team would travel to the other city, certain that the officiating would be hopelessly skewed toward the home team. The debate threatened to derail the entire event, until finally it was agreed that the game would be played in … Red Deer! Luckily, this gave both sides ample time to practise their cheers and "fight song" on the train. Check out this glorious Edmonton version, sung at a time when our sports teams didn't threaten to disappear at the whim of

> **"Very little is known of the Canadian country since it is rarely visited by anyone but the Queen and illiterate sport fishermen."**
>
> —P.J. O'Rourke

an owner or a change in a tax variance, and our sports stars didn't make the equivalent of an average year's wages every single game of the season:

*(Sung to the tune of "Alexander's Ragtime Band")*

*Come on and cheer, come on and cheer,*
*Deacon White's great football band;*
*Come on and cheer, come on and cheer,*
*they're the gamest in the land.*
*They can play football like you've never seen before*
*plunge, run or kick up a corking big score,*
*They're just the fastest gang what am,*
*Boom bam!*
*Come on along, come on along*
*Let us give the boys a hand.*
*There's Bailey, kick it hard,*
*he's the leader of the gang.*
*So if you want to see the Eskies clean the spots off*
*Calgary*
*Come on and cheer, come on and cheer,*
*Deacon White's great football band! Hurrrrraaayyyy!!!*

And then there's the *other* kind of football, the thing the Americans persist in calling "soccer." Yes, it's harder to play than North American–style football; yes, the athletes are in better shape and have cooler haircuts (not a mullet among them, even on the Eastern European teams); yes, it's more inclusive of cultures and nations from all over the globe; and yes, dammit, with the exception of some of its brutally violent fans, it's just a better sport all round.

Over the last decade, Canadians have begun to take football, especially World Cup football, very seriously indeed. The myriad ethnic neighbourhoods in our cities (see *Zeitgeist, Community*) give us a reason to stay up all night to watch the games. When our local Koreatown celebrates (as they had occasion to do in Toronto this past World Cup) we tag along for the ride and use the victory to party on the streets. It speaks volumes to our open-mindedness that we don't particularly care if, say, Italy gets knocked out of competition, as long as we can still cheer for Brazil or Portugal. That is, unless we're actually a member of the community in question. Then losing is like a funeral and a disaster all rolled into one. But when victory does come around, it seems even sweeter for those Senegalese and Turk Canadians who don't often find their countrymen appearing on an international stage. True, the endless streams of honking, flag-bearing cars are a little annoying (see *Transportation, Traffic*), but having too much fun once every four years is still well within the tolerance range of most of us. Watching a soccer game with a gaggle of fervent expatriate fans has become as vital an urban Canadian sports tradition as the Ottawa Senators tanking in the playoffs.

## Olympics

On a snowy winter evening in Toronto last year, a press conference was held trumpeting the "arts and culture" angle of the Toronto 2008 Olympic bid. Held in the bowels of a Yonge Street theatre, the gathering consisted of bland speeches from bronze medallists and vaguely recognizable retiree artists, the presentation of an oversized game-show–style cheque (from the usually tight-fisted government of Ontario), and an ethnically correct array of children displayed like flowers in a vase. There was something about the commissioning of an official Toronto

SPORTS

Ted Grant, National Archives of Canada

Brian Orser carrying the Canadian flag at the opening ceremony of the Calgary Olympic Games in 1988. A fave to win gold, he typified Canada's Olympic experience by coming in second.

Olympics song, something about a teen camp featuring kids from all over the world, and very little about the living, breathing arts that make Toronto one of the most vital cities in North America. The press conference, as insipid as a "We Are the World"–style charity pop song, told us nothing about how the bid organizers would be presenting Toronto culture to the global masses and a lot about the organizers' worldwide publicity scheme.

The Toronto Olympic bid was essentially put together behind closed doors by a wealthy elite (is there any other kind?). Concerned that their train not be derailed by such piddling issues as poverty and cost overruns, never mind real artists, they got the jump on detractors with a multi-year campaign designed to show us how the Olympics will revitalize the city and make everyone oodles of cash. During the year or so that the bid was an ongoing concern, not a day went by without us hearing some tidbit conducted by the Summer Games 2008 Marching Band Glee Club. A seemingly endless stream

of favourable polls were obligingly regurgitated by the daily press with the urgency usually reserved for shoot-ups and pop stars. Apparently, 70 or 64 or 99% of Torontonians, or Haligonians, or work-to-rule teachers or disaffected nurses, or guys sleeping on grates on Bay Street, support, crave, and are desperate to have the Olympics. (This telephone survey of 2.3 Canadians aged 2.3 and over is considered accurate within 2.3 percentage points two times out of three…) Meanwhile, the good people of Toronto were subjected to a fusillade of ads, trinkets, and, of course, requisite Internet bumpf.

Two hundred Toronto bid representatives were in Moscow for a final $2 million dollar party—uh, that is, *push*. The entourage included Jean, Mike, and Mel as well as the standard indigenous peoples representation. (Who can blame the Mississaugas of the New Credit native band for accepting a swank free trip to Russia?) And did we mention the all-night bid bash featuring free bands, laser show, and breakfast at an entertainment complex on Lake Ontario?

In the end, even though the mayor promised that the bid wouldn't cost Toronto taxpayers a cent, experts and reporters estimate that almost a million dollars came out of the pocket of the city's taxpayers. Of course, we all know how the bid ended—with Toronto finishing a predictable and distant second to Beijing and Mayor Mel embarrassing the city by making joking comments to a reporter: "What the hell would I like to go to a place like Mombasa? I just see myself in a pot of boiling water with all these natives dancing around me." (See *Politics, Mayors*.)

All this, of course, raises the question: why the hell are Canadian cities so obsessed with getting the Olympics? We've only had the Olympics twice in Canada ever, probably because Canadians are not known for their ability to offer lavish sexual favours and scholarships upon IOC officials. (By contrast, when the evaluation team came to Toronto, we got 'em stuck in an elevator for an hour.)

The first time we had the Olympics, in Montreal in 1976, it was a disaster. The city is still paying for the stadium, which ended up costing a staggering $970 million … and it's falling apart at the seams. On September 13, 1991, the stadium was closed after a 55-ton concrete beam fell off the side of the building and onto a walkway below; on January 19, 1999, a huge piece of the roof collapsed due to an accumulation of wet snow, injuring five people (about 200 were in the stadium, setting up an auto show). The city is facing a potential $3 million bill to pull down the building, but given its homicidal tendencies, it's a move that many Montrealers wholeheartedly support.

Montreal only got the games in the first place because the IOC couldn't decide between the US and the USSR. On the second round of voting, Los Angeles took an "anything but Russia" tack and threw its support to Montreal, leaving the city with a tax burden legacy still ongoing… And by the way, Canada won no gold medals in that Summer Olympics.

The second Olympics we hosted were the 1988 Winter Games in Calgary. Tacky and not all that memorable, they featured the kinda-ridiculous "bridge of fire." Usually welcome warm-weather chinooks swooped in and delayed alpine events. Canada distinguished itself with a measly five medals, none of them gold. And a stadium was built on the edge of one of Calgary's poorest neighbourhoods, Victoria Park—against most of the community's wishes. Many people feel that the stadium was the thin edge of a drive to expand the Calgary

Stampede grounds into the same area … there's nothing quite like a constant stream of drunken idiots trickling through one's neighbourhood. About 750 people were displaced out of two apartment buildings, and nearly 1,500 students had to move out of their residences as well, but clearly, poor people and students don't count for much in Alberta either.

Nonetheless, Calgary left a sports facility legacy that was part of the reason for Canada's burgeoning Winter Olympics success in Nagano and Salt Lake (which hired 10-plus Calgarians to help plan their $3 billion party).

The fact that Canadian cities have been largely unsuccessful in securing the Olympics and staging them with memorable style doesn't discourage our cities from coveting this international money-loser. Following the footsteps of TO's lame summer bid is Vancouver–Whistler's unlikely bid for the 2010 Winter Games. The bid got off to a rocky start when Olympic rules required them to remove Whistler's name as officially part of the bid. Promo material had to be redone, no doubt adding to the tally of yet another "no cost to the taxpayer" bid.

We hate to say it, but the Canadian city would be better off without the Olympic pipe dream constantly emerging as a panacea for struggling public transit, snarled roads, and blighted waterfronts. Let's fix our problems first, and *then* invite the world to come and see how kickass we are.

## Volleyball, Indoor Beach

"People can play volleyball anywhere," says Max Slivka, one of four owners of Toronto's Beach Blast, an indoor volleyball sports complex, "but do they have sand?" He

SPORTS

gestures rhetorically at the 1,241 tonnes that carpet the six busy full-size volleyball courts of Beach Blast. Seems the former steel bridge factory near Lawrence and Caledonia has been reinvented as one more good reason to spend February in Toronto.

"You don't have to worry about anything," explains Ken Nichol, a 31-year-old who plays in the house league with co-workers from a funeral home (today they're pitted against the Bank of Montreal). "You never have to miss a game. This is a controlled environment; you always know the weather is going to be consistent." Fifty dollars an hour per court gets you and your friends the chance to chase after a ball and luxuriate under the radiant heat lamps that keep the cavernous building permanently at 65 degrees. "It's like the sun," extols Slivka, pointing at the 35-foot ceiling. With its faux boardwalk and resort-style bar, Beach Blast goes out of its way to look like summer. "People are moving toward indoor leisure activities," Slivka says. "You don't need any equipment. Just a T-shirt and a pair of shorts." That, and the kind of fervent escapism that lets indoor beach v-ball enthusiasts stuck in the frigid city imagine that they're soaking up the rays somewhere slightly more tropical than five minutes south of the 401 ...

# FOOD

**F**OOD IS A DIRECT LINK TO A COUNTRY'S CULTURE. What a country eats tells us how a people think, what they value, and what they can afford. Experiencing a country's food in that country is a distinct, exciting, yet accessible way to come to terms with another culture. Right across the world, countries, regions, even cities serve up meals particular to a single place that celebrate human ingenuity and make life worth living.

At least, that's the case almost all across the world. Things are different in Canada. The cities of the world's second-largest country by land mass have nothing resembling a distinct food tradition. And yet, paradoxically,

Goat roti

Paul Fairweather

we're here to tell you that Canadian cities can provide some of the most various, vibrant, and piquant eating experiences in North America. But first, you have to forget about eating "Canadian" food.

When picturing the frosty Canadian urban environment, people don't immediately imagine spicy ethnic cuisine with origins from all regions of the world. And yet, in the nooks and crannies of every Canadian city, weird and delightful snacks can be found—many of them hot enough to get us through even the coldest winter.

To help you expand your culinary repertoire, we're providing you with a list of some of the wondrous world foods you can discover in the Canadian city. This list comes with some advice: be adventurous. That rundown hole of a restaurant may be serving the best oxtail stew with rice and peas this side of Jamaica. A menu item you can't pronounce is nothing more than a culinary experience you haven't yet had the pleasure of encountering.

# Urban Multicultural Menu

A *Hal Anecdote:* In my first year of studies at the University of Toronto I had a roommate from Hong Kong. One night I came in late and mentioned that I was hungry. Before I knew it, we were wandering the streets of Toronto's largest Chinatown (one of many official and unofficial Chinatowns in Toronto and its suburbs), a sprawling downtown area minutes from U of T. We ended up at the now sadly defunct Sam Woo, a basement Chinese barbecue house open into the wee hours of the night on weekends. While I gaped at the whole roasted pigs and ducks dangling from the large front window, Simon said a few words in a language I didn't speak. Within moments, I was experiencing authentic Chinese glazed barbecued pork. Its rich, tangy-sweet flavour would bring me back for more until that fine restaurant inexplicably closed many years later. On one memorable return visit, I was eating my simple meal of a bowl of rice topped with slices of lean, sweet pork and drizzled with hot chili oil ($4.25 in 1989) when a food critic from one of Toronto's daily newspapers turned to me and said, "Best Chinese barbecued pork in North America."

**Kimchee** Korean appetizer staple that comes in a variety of flavours and types, though the most common is a fiery chili- and garlic-infused pickled cabbage. You'll get several types of kimchee free of charge before the start of any meal in a Korean restaurant. Try them all.

**Bibimbap** Delicious Korean one-dish wonder in which rice, bits of meat, egg, and vegetables come to your table in a sizzling hot pot. Subtle tastes of sesame and soy elevate this dish, as does a dash of the Korean hot sauce kochujang.

**Goat Roti** Roti is a wonderful flatbread wrap used in West Indies and Caribbean cuisine. Goat, in this case, is stewed with a thick brown curried gravy and nuggets of soft melt-in-your-mouth potatoes. This is the ultimate

Empanada

Paul Fairweather

urban snack (bone-in is tastier but more fiddly). You can also get roti filled with chicken, conch, spinach, shrimp, channa (chick peas), squash, and in Edmonton, bison.

**Doubles** Another West Indian snack consisting of a deep-fried pastry around a spicy corn and chickpea filling. Comes sweet or hot.

**Empanada** "Empanada" is a Spanish word meaning turnover. But the South American snack food is no old-world delicacy—it's a takeout tidbit you're meant to eat on the street. Empanadas come either in their traditional form—stuffed with savoury shredded beef, hardboiled egg, and raisins—or in a lighter vegetarian version with spinach, peppers, onions, and other goodies.

**Pupusa** Another amazing Latin American snack food. A handmade corn tortilla pancake stuffed with cheese, pork, beans, or a combination thereof, then fried on a griddle until crispy and served with a kind of spicy coleslaw. These kick the ass of the taco!

## *The Spotter's Guide to International Sandwich Silhouettes**

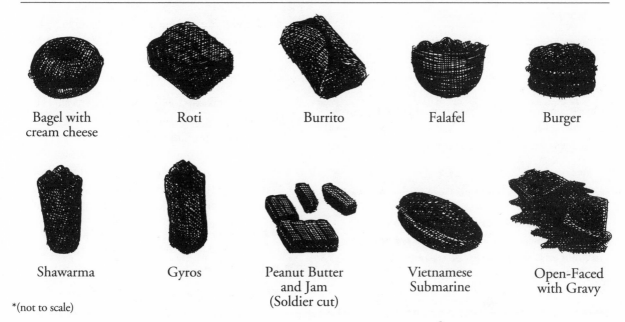

Bagel with cream cheese

Roti

Burrito

Falafel

Burger

Shawarma

Gyros

Peanut Butter and Jam (Soldier cut)

Vietnamese Submarine

Open-Faced with Gravy

*(not to scale)

URBAN MULTICULTURAL MENU

Paul Fairweather

Beef patty. Yum …

**Smoked Meat** The Jewish G-d's gift to the meat lover, smoked meat is its own entity, not to be confused with pastrami or corned beef, which try their best but don't come close. Smoked meat has more fat and juice, is cut thicker, and is spicier. It's served in a giant mound between two pieces of rye bread and is adorned with nothing more than mustard. (Nothing else is necessary.) Smoked meat can really only be had in Montreal and, even in Montreal, there are only two or three places that get the job done right—most notably Schwartz's and its neighbour across the street, The Main. (Bizarrely enough, there's a German-released techno compilation of Montreal artists called *Montreal Smoked Meat*.)

**Montreal Bagel** You really haven't lived until you've consumed a Montreal bagel fresh out of the woodburning oven, an experience you can have at places like the St. Viateur bagel factory in the old Jewish district of the city. Open 24 hours, drop by any time and you'll find workers making bagels the way they were meant to be—boiled, coated with either sesame or poppy seeds, then shovelled

into the oven until just brown. The Montreal bagel is not like any other bagel—it isn't over-sized, stuffed with raisins and chocolate chips, or doughy to the point of bland. It's flatter, crisper, and denser—and delicious. St. Viateur celebrated its 40th anniversary in 2000, and is the oldest bagel shop in Montreal. The business was launched by the late Myer Lewkowicz, a concentration camp survivor who didn't mind working 24/7 because, as he used to say: "I have bagel so I'm never short of bread, and in winter I'm always near the warm fire." (Incidentally, a search on Google for "Montreal bagel" yielded an astonishing 3,000-plus sites.)

**Kishke** The Jewish sausage. This texture-challenged mush originated in the *shtetls* of Eastern Europe and was basically just another way to get rid of stale bread and root vegetables starting to go off. Today its incarnations can involve everything from turkey necks and chicken fat (*schmaltz*) to totally vegetarian. It's often served in another *shtetl* classic—the *cholent*, a long-cooked stew of beans, potatoes, kishke, and whatever meat you can afford.

**Beef Patty** Fab takeout food from the Caribbean. Flaky golden-yellow pastry crust stuffed with savoury ground beef, ideally spiced up with the killer Scotch bonnet pepper. Sometimes eaten as the stuffing in a sandwich between two slabs of that West Indies baked treat, coco bread, by those who can't get enough carbos. Goes nice with ginger beer or golden kola.

**Kottu Roti** A Sri Lankan platter featuring fried strips of flatbread mixed with your choice of curried vegetables and meats. Also try the mutton roll!

**Hot Veal on a Bun** Italian classic in which breaded veal cutlet is deep-fried and topped with a chunky tomato

*In Canada, the time has come to address a centrally important question. If what we have in common is our diversity, do we really have anything in common at all?*

*—Reginald Bibby*

Chinese BBQ

Paul Fairweather

sauce and sautéed peppers (where the hot comes from—though you can usually also request sweet). The squeamish can usually substitute breaded eggplant for the veal.

**Cabana Sandwich** A marinated roasted pork tenderloin served hot on a crusty bun, ideally with avocado, some kind of fancy mayonnaise, and greens.

**Piri Piri Chicken** Portuguese favourite found at your local churrasqueria. The chicken is marinated, grilled until crispy, then liberally doused in piri piri, a vinegary red sauce more tangy than spicy. Also try the deep-fried cod patties sold at most Portuguese bakeries.

**BBQ Pork** You know when you're walking through Chinatown past all those glistening, dripping carcasses hanging in the windows of the restaurants? Well, one of those items is barbequed pork. It'll come to your table in strips with a reddish, crisp exterior and a dry but soft white inside. Try it with rice and an order of stir-fried Chinese greens.

**Pho** Vietnamese beef soup comes in a bowl big enough to put your head inside. Will feature savoury beef broth, your choice of beef bits, including thin strips of raw meat that cook in front of you in the still-hot broth, beef balls, and/or completely soft, near-dissolved chunks of tripe or tendon. Served with lime, crunchy bean sprouts, Vietnamese mint, Oriental basil, and tiny, excruciatingly hot peppers. Squeeze the lime and add the leaves and sprouts to the soup as you please. A little hoisin sauce and chili oil on top and you're ready to rock.

**Tandoori** An Indian method of cooking that involves coating meat, shrimp, cauliflower, or chunks of homemade cheese with a spice mixture and lowering the items into a cauldron-like clay oven. Comes out bright orange and unspeakably delicious.

**Poutine** If there's a national Québécois urban fast food treat, this is it. Fries, gravy, and cheese curds. Low-end outlets will use canned gravy and plasticky processed shredded cheese. Keep an eye out for the real thing. Newfoundland poutine: add Stove Top Stuffing under the gravy (no fooling).

**Salmon Jerky** Found in Vancouver and Victoria tourist areas, this is chewy dried and spiced salmon. It rules as a between-meals gnaw, though the locals look down upon it as strictly for the Germans and Americans.

Paul Fairweather

Pho

URBAN MULTICULTURAL MENU

# Cross-Canada Chinese Food Roundup on the Net

In the interests of arbitrarily entertaining our readers we spent several hours on Internet search engines typing in the words "Chinese food" followed by the names of various Canadian cities. Note that nothing we discovered was even remotely corroborated. Personally, we would call first. Here's what we found out:

**Montreal:** Some guy named D Stephen recommends Restaurant Kam Shing (4771 Van Horne). He says: "The meat content you get in the fried noodles at Kam Shing is two to three times what you get at Just for Noodles downtown, or Mon Shing in Chinatown."
<www.openface.ca/~dstephen/fun&food.htm>

**Winnipeg:** The website for organic veggie café and radical bookstore Mondragon suggests—surprise, surprise—a place called Delicious Vegetarian Restaurant (1467 Pembina Highway). "Completely vegan Chinese food restaurant, smoke free." <www.a-zone.org/mondragon>

**Vancouver:** Schlocky site that goes by the name BCPassport suggests two destinations: Pink Pearl (1132 E. Hastings Street), "A Vancouver institution in the middle of nowhere, but it has the best dim sum in town and is well worth the trip" and Pak Tak Chiu Chow Restaurant (in Yaohan Centre), "Succulent duckling poached in five-spice and soya brine accompanied by a garlic-and-rice-vinegar dip and boiled Dungeness crab with ginger and black vinegar." <www.bcpassport.com/food/chinese.html>

**Saskatoon:** China Inn (403 33rd Street West Avenue D) offers "Dinner for 4: 4 egg rolls Sweet & Sour Chicken Balls Deep Fried Shrimp Special Mixed Vegetable BBQ Pork Fried Rice $25.95." If that's not enough for you, Chinese Foodies Buffet House (1-833 51st East, Saskatoon) promises an evening buffet for $7.50, all you can eat: "Chinese Food (Twelve Kinds Per Day): Fried Rice, Chow Mein, Lo Mein, Shanghai Noodles, BBQ Ribs, Stir Fried Vegetables, S&S Ribs, S&S Pork, Ginger Pork, Spring Rolls, Deep Fried Shrimps, Deep Fried Wonton, Dried Ribs, Chicken Balls, Egg Rolls, Egg Foo Yung, Ginger Meat Balls, Honey Garlic Ribs, Chicken with Black Bean Sauce, Beef Stew, Rice Noodles, and many other selections. Western Food (Twelve Kinds Per Day): Pizza, Lasagna, Spaghetti, Fettuccine Alfredo, Cutlets, Pork Chops, Greek Ribs, Garlic Toast, Mash Potatoes, Homemade Fries, Grilled Cheese Sandwich, Souvlaki, Hamburger, Baked Chicken, Liver & Onion, Sausages and many other selections." <www.stn-biz.com/chinainn>

**Calgary:** Our socially conscious friends at Ecomall.com seem to think we should all head out to Buddha's Veggie Restaurant (250 Southland Crossing Shopping Centre,

9737 Macleod Trail South) for "all vegetarian, no meat, no fish. Specialties Veggie Ginger Beef, Veggie Sweet & Sour Pork, Veggie Crispy Eel." <www.ecomall.com>

**Ottawa:** We uncovered this reader's restaurant recommendation on something called chinesefood.about.com. So Good Restaurant (717 Somerset West) is a fave of this anonymous foodie: "I recently discovered this Chinese/Thai/Vietnamese restaurant. Not only was the food good on the four different times I have been there, but they also had a large selection of vegetarian (mostly vegan) dishes. It is a small place and not very pretty but the food is exceptional." <http://chinesefood.about.com/library/blrestcanont.htm>

**Windsor:** Dining alone? The New Kirin Eatery (2466 Dougall Avenue) offers a sizzling round-up of combos for one. "COMBINATION DINNER FOR ONE Served with: Wonton Soup or Hot & Sour Soup, Egg Roll, Chicken Fried Rice & Cookie No. 1 $8.95, Sweet & Sour Chicken Ball, Chicken with Mixed Vegetables No. 2 $8.95, Sweet & Sour Chicken Ball Beef with Black Bean Sauce No. 3 $8.95, Sweet & Sour Chicken Ball Beef with Mixed Vegetables No. 4 $8.95, Chicken Soo Gai Hunan Chicken No. 5 $8.95, Chicken Soo Gai Chicken with Black Bean Sauce No. 6 $8.95, Chicken Shop Suey Mongolian Beef No. 7 $8.95, Chicken Shop Suey Mongolian Beef No. 8 $8.95, Chicken Lo Mein Diced Chicken with Cashew No. 9 $8.95, Beef Chow Mein Shrimp with Lobster Sauce No. 10 $8.95, Lemon Chicken Beef with Chinese Green No. 11 $8.95, Lemon Chicken Hunan Beef No. 12 $8.95, Lemon Chicken Shrimp with Garlic Sauce." •

**Shawarma** Falafel's meaty cousin. Traditionally a giant lamb kabob that looks sort of like a skinned dachshund with its legs and head removed, it spends its day swivelling under a heat lamp on a big metal stick. Slices are cut off as needed, and the spicy meat is used as a base for a pita sandwich with familiar Middle East sandwich accompaniments: tahini, pickled turnip, tomato, onion, etc.

**Vietnamese Submarines** These palm-sized mixed deli subs (which can contain coriander, ham, pork, chili, sprouts, shredded carrot, and daikon, among other things, on a tiny baguette) are ubiquitous in Vietnamese neighbourhoods, probably because they're incredibly tasty and incredibly cheap—usually under $2.

# Beverages

**Mango Lassi** Cardamom, rosewater, mango, and yogurt give this thick Indian drink its totally unique and refreshing flavour.

**Ginger Beer** The real thing is made with real ginger. It's like super-powered ginger ale and should instantly cure what ails ya, but not leave you gasping for breath.

**Vietnamese Coffee** A metal filter on top of a tall glass will drip dark coffee into the sweetened condensed milk already pooled at the bottom of the drink. After the coffee has dripped through, stir then sip this sickly sweet but somehow comforting elixir. If you're going ice, they'll bring you another glass full of cubes that you can add to your mixture before drinking.

**Bubble Tea** The latest and greatest urban craze. A *Globe and Mail* food critic describes it as "slurping slimy tapioca balls through a large coloured straw." Apparently, this beverage came about when a Hong Kong mom was attempting to concoct a healthy after-school snack for her little ones. Vancouver is Bubble Tea headquarters in North America. Writes a *New York Times* food critic: "What makes it so appealing are the gelatinous pearls made of potato flour placed in the bottom of the glass that are sipped through an extra- wide straw. The pearls sort of ramble as you slurp them up. Vancouver has no less than 30 establishments that specialize in these drinks."

Paul Fairweather

Bubble tea

# Jason Dunda's
# Top 10 Fizzy Drinks

1. *Ting* … the divine grapefruit soda from the West Indies is, hands-down, Fizzy Drink #1. Not as sweet as most fruity sodas, Ting's tart aftertaste is the only way to cool down the palate after a volcanic roti. Available at roti shops everywhere and Kensington Market.

2. *San Pellegrino Aranciata* is truly the new shit. It kicks Orangina's sorry French ass. Available in Little Italy and at frou-frou restaurants.

3. *Ramune* is a clear fizz beverage from Japan that makes the list not only for its piquant and subtle flavour but also for its gorgeous packaging. It's sealed with a marble held in place by the pressure of the carbonation. You break the seal by pushing on the marble with a little plastic accoutrement (included). Like all high-tech devices, instructions are in Japanese, so when I first tried Ramune in San Fran, I spilled most of it. I've never seen Ramune in Canada, but if you ask me nice I might be able to hook you up.

4. *President's Choice Pink Grapefruit Soda* At 77¢ for 2 litres, this unbelievably cheap, super-sweet, super-pink drink is perfect with a BBQ. Points lost because hot pink interferes with my macho image. Loblaws or No Frills.

5. *Stewart's Orange Cream Soda Creamsicle* Mmmm. Try their Classic Key Lime too.

6. *Orbitz* is now defunct but it makes the list for good design. Orbitz has flavoured blobs of gelatin floating peacefully in clear soda water. Reminiscent of a lava lamp, this stuff came out with the lounge revival and quickly disappeared after the company realized people don't like eating their drinks. The fact that the tactile sensation was pretty close to barf didn't help matters.

7. *Coca-Cola* The sweet, black juice of heaven. Not so much a beverage as a way of life, Coke wakes you up in the morning and tucks you in at night. Coke knows you better than your mother does. Coke still respects you in the morning. Coke doesn't want to hurt you, it just wants to be your friend.

8. *Tonic Water* Try it with gin.

9. *Dr. Pepper* Next time you go to 7-Eleven, buy a Dr. Pepper Big Gulp and a pile of comic books. It's pure comfort.

10. *Chubby* makes the list because of its truth in advertising—it comes in a short, fat, plastic bottle. Unfortunately, it tastes like soap so just keep it next to your vintage Orbitz and pass it down to your children's children before you die. Available at finer dollar-stores everywhere. ●

# Restaurants

If you haven't figured it out by now, there's more to
dining out in Canada than the Olive Garden. We have
an amazing variety of places to eat, as the bewildering
number of Canadian cities claiming to have more restaurants per person than anywhere else will attest. Montreal
claims to have more restaurants per capita than any city
in North America except Manhattan, Kingston claims
to have "more restaurants per capita—at least 200—than
any other place in North America," Quebec City also
apparently offers the "greatest number of restaurants per
capita," as does Saskatoon, Winnipeg, and Victoria.
Whether or not some wonk in the marketing department is lying through his teeth is beside the point—
that's what marketing wonks do. The point is that we

care enough about eating out to be boastful about it
beyond any reasonable measure.

With all those dining establishment options, we often
turn to a different kind of wonk—the restaurant reviewer
wonk—for guidance. But what do these urban gourmet
gurus really know? We tracked one down to find out.

## Don't Shoot the Restaurant Reviewer!

Edmonton-based Gilbert Bouchard is a freelance cultural commentator, journalist, poet, and a generally smart
guy. He spent four-and-a-half years as the restaurant
reviewer for alternative weekly *See Magazine*. We got in
touch with him to decode the strange world of the restaurant reviewer. Here's what he had to say:

*What are a restaurant reviewer's credentials? Why should
we trust them?*
Like in most review efforts, "credentials" are more slip-
pery and far less useful than most people would guess.

*They only give you the cork at a restaurant to show you that it hasn't dried out. You don't need to smell or chew on the damn thing.*

—Gilbert Bouchard

Obviously the reviewer needs to have enough knowledge on the subject to say something of substance about the restaurant/movie/book without making too many errors ("I couldn't have been more outraged: the soup came to the table ice-cold—I tell you, I'll never order gazpacho at that joint again"). But at the same time the review needs to be closer to the reader of the column than the world they write about. Let's face it, a heated debate in your column about the true nature of French onion soup or the morality of flavoured crème caramel might go over well in food science classes, but not so with the average reader.

The biggest single tension point between the reviewer and the reader is the grand divide that comes with a reviewer being a big fat gourmand and being in the habit of going to way more restaurants than the average person would ever want to visit. Of course, a total passion for food and a broad context of the food world is needed for the reviews to have balance and depth, but you do have to realize that this is a factor that sets you apart from the average reader. The best thing you can do about this particular trait is to make sure your writing stays fresh and to try and not get too jaded in expectations and in attitudes toward the establishments.

As for trust, like in all endeavours, it's an earned trait. For example, you read one of my reviews and you decide you like what I've described and you go to the joint. If you like the visit and find you agreed with the assessments more than not, then you're likely to visit more joints I recommend and start to build a rapport with me as a writer.

*Why do so many reviewers seem to ignore ethnic and family places for the haute cuisine $300 meals? Is it because they're eating for free so what the hell?*

I suspect it has more to do with the fact that it's easier to write about the haute cuisine places because they're working with a very canonic cuisine, are following all the rules, and are cooking in a style that allows for a lot of subtlety—all factors that allow for loads of pontification (the same way an indie/intellectual film is way more fun to write about than a lowest-common-denominator flick, regardless of the fact that far more filmgoers will want to see *Queen of the Damned* than *My Dinner with André*). With family places (and a good number of Canadian ethnic restaurants are family-run and more peasant-style than not) you're getting dishes that are usually deep in the comfort-food zone (hence more of an emotional experience than intellectual) or part of a cuisine that's alien to the reviewer and harder to write about. As for the eating-for-free angle, I'm not sure that plays as big a role as you'd guess. I was only ever partially reimbursed for tabs I acquired doing reviews for the alternative weekly I write for (heck, for a year I paid for my own meals and only got a $20 writing fee), but I'd still eat out at high-end places because I really, really like the occasional high-end meal regardless of who's picking up the tab.

*How can the average urban dweller sense whether or not a restaurant they haven't tried before will be a good one? Any tips you've picked up on the job?*

I wish I could pass on a tip or some arcane secret to suss out hidden gems, but in reality the restaurant experience is both relationship-based and holistic. Case in point: when I really want to impress casual friends I take

RESTAURANTS

*On the first day, I asked the different people to come and I didn't really expect they all were coming. A man came in and said, "Ain't you got them chickens ready?" I said, "Yes, I've got them and I'm just ready to open up. Come back in half an hour—you'll get your chicken." I couldn't afford to buy but two chickens at a time—I'd run my husband over there to buy the chicken and he'd just cut them up right quick and I'd wash them and I'd put them on frying. Oh, he liked the chicken. I gave him a good dinner ... I kept saying to my husband, "Now you stay right here in the hall so you can run quick over to the Chinaman's and buy another chicken." And then I'd commence talking, "Oh yes, yes, so and so and so," and I'd talk to take up some time until I'd see him come in, then I'd say, "Well I must get those chickens on." Then I'd get him to pay and I'd say to my husband, "Now you get two more." So I got by that way.*

—Rosa Pryor, "Opening Doors: Vancouver's East End," Blueprint: Black British Columbian Literature and Orature

them to a handful of old standard restaurants that I've gone to forever. These are the kinds of places that I've come to trust over years of visits and also establishments that know who I am (the manager greets you by name at the door, all the servers know who you are, the bartender has named a drink after you, etc.) and that I can trust to deliver a total "dining package" (from room decor to quality of food to seamless service and also that special vibe that makes you feel totally at home). The only real advice I have to give someone who's popping into a brand-new joint and wants to maximize the experience is to treat it like a first date: be on your best behaviour and offer up the best possible attitude you can (remember, if you like the outing, this first visit is the start of a relationship, so keep your options open). I've gone to a lot of joints in the past five years and can tell you that sugar certainly attracts far better restaurant karma than

vinegar. Secondly, ask loads of questions (politely of course), which restaurant workers always love (it shows you care), and don't make them change every item on the menu to match your dietary restrictions or taste quirks.

# Open All Night

Ah, the all-night convenience store ... refuge from the elements, fount of preservative-laden sustenance, and cheap source of entertainment for the inebriated, the stoned, and the otherwise mentally incapacitated.

During the daylight hours, there's precious little reason to venture inside convenience stores, except during summer months to obtain Slurpees (which make an adequate mix for vodka). But after everything has closed—even the late-night drive-throughs—they're the last resort, and their dubious wares become proportionally more attractive.

Take the 7-Eleven "Torpedo" as an example: a stale pita rolled around a slab of rubbery mozzarella, some baloney pepperoni, and a glob of tomato sauce. Hard to imagine a less appealing snack (see *Urban Multicultural Menu* for better options). But to a drunk at 3 a.m., it's ambrosial.

Sadly (for them, anyway), the boom in home videogame consoles has tarnished some of the late-night allure of the all-night convenience store. It is no longer strictly necessary, for example, to load the entire defensive backfield of your football team into one car and then drive halfway across the city at 2:15 a.m. to find the only convenience store that has a *Discs of Tron* cabinet. However, the garish

First Loblaw, Toronto store, 1919

packaging, unearthly lighting, and aforementioned bad snacks are a consistent draw to people on drugs. One old friend suggested that late-night convenience stores could tap into an entirely new revenue stream by charging a small admission fee for the privilege of allowing such persons to roam the aisles, race grapes in the microwave, ogle porn mags, crinkle cellophane packages to experience the "texture," and mutter incoherently to other lost souls.

Of course, it doesn't have to end at the convenience store. What separates the men from the boys or the cities from the suburbs and towns is 24-hour activity. Thus, one can dine—on, say, steak and eggs literally swimming in a puddle of grease at Toronto's counter-only Vesta Lunch—at 3 a.m. These days, it's not even just diners and convenience stores that are doing the 24 thing. Try buying your groceries in the wee hours—no lines and no

fighting it out for bargains. And from Saskatoon to Fredericton, urban Canadians have the great tradition of the open-all-night Shoppers Drug Mart. Sound dull? Try spending the Saturday night hours of 2 to 4 a.m. hanging out next to the condom/and or pregnancy test racks.

# Recipes

## Darren and Hal's Urban Macaroni and Cheese (a Canadian favourite!)

*Difficulty:* Not Very (requires hot plate and pot)

Get yourself some generic mac and cheese on sale. (Don't go Kraft; why pay premium?) Get yourself a package of Schneider's hot dogs. (Don't go all-beef or anything silly

RECIPES

like that … again, why pay premium? Chicken lips and cow's ears! Yum yum!) Make the mac according to the directions. But when you're boiling the noodles, slice a couple of dogs into the mix. (Split them at the bottom for that fake calamari look!) Finish up with the fake cheese powder and the milk. Stir.

## Hal and Darren Star in … Toronto Taco Delight!

*Difficulty:* Somewhat (requires several bowls, shopping for more than two items, chopping, frying, and simmering)

You'll need taco shells, salsa, two cans of black beans, a tomato, lettuce, an onion, a garlic bulb, various spices, and a chunk of Canadian cheddar (gotta be Canadian cheddar or we're in violation of Can-Con laws). Chop and fry the onion and garlic till softish. Throw in the black beans. Add a bit of water. Add spices like salt, pepper, chili powder, hot sauce, and cumin. (You can also get those taco spice mixture pouches, which are mostly salt anyway, but they might contain bonus extras like MSG!) Simmer beans till not so wet. In the meantime, chop tomato, dice lettuce, and grate the cheddar. When the beans are ready, fill up your taco shell with, in this specific order, black beans, cheddar cheese, tomato, lettuce, and salsa on top. Take a huge bite. Great to serve to friends—watch those shells crumble all over their laps!

*Note:* "Toronto" and "Taco" sound good together (it's called alliteration) and the name of this recipe in no way suggests that the authors have a Toronto bias (which they do, since they both live there after fleeing what, no doubt, continue to be wonderfully pleasant spots to raise children and walk dogs, such as Winnipeg and Ottawa).

## Hal and Darren's Ultra-Spicy Veggie Canadian Curry

*Difficulty:* Advanced (requires specialty shopping, dicing, frying, simmering, working with hot peppers, and an understanding of the effects of several exotic spices)

Get yourself some ghee. That's clarified butter, and you can buy it in specialty shops. It isn't in the refrigeration section, 'cause it never goes bad. Melt several tablespoons in a pot. Throw in your ginger, onions, and garlic and several of those long thin green hot peppers (we're assuming you're aware that dicing hot peppers can be dangerous). Fry till softish. Add various veggies. Eggplant, cauliflower, bell peppers, frozen peas, chunks of potato—they all work. Fry till softish. Throw in a can of chopped tomatoes with all their juices. Add various spices in various quantities of abundance, including but not necessarily limited to: garam masala (tasty spice mix whose authentic use continues to elude us), cumin, coriander, hot curry powder, chili powder, cinnamon. Follow this up with no less than two heaping tablespoons of Patak's extra-hot curry paste. Stir. Simmer for around 20 minutes. Remove from heat. Add two tablespoons of plain yogurt. Stir gently. Serve with naan (tasty Indian flat bread) over a mixture of basmati and Canadian wild rice (again, the latter solves the Can-Con issue…)

**S**HOPPING IS A GIVEN IN OUR WORLD. In fact, it's almost mandatory.

Marketers focus on maintaining and extending what we can call the, uh, "positive marketing environment." Now, if what you want to do is sell frozen chocolate cake, a newspaper full of items on the homeless, wars, disease, and drug epidemics does not constitute a positive marketing environment. But in the twisted logic of advertising, the answer isn't to work toward ameliorating the homeless situation, but to eradicate reports on the bad stuff. Then sell cake.

Since 1989 the number of billboard spots in Canada has soared by 42%. Business is booming for public relations, advertising, and marketing firms hard at work smoothing over the bumps in the road to lifestyle culture. Ditto for special-interest groups (the *real* ones, not the ones conservative politicians complain about): The Canadian Association of Ice Industries, The Canadian Association of Financial Planners, The Canadian Association of Gift Planners, The Canadian Association of Japanese Automobile Dealers, The Canadian Association of Specialty Foods—all exist to foster the correct marketing environment for product. Someone says cars are polluting the air? Call up the Canadian Association of Environmentally Friendly, Totally Safe and Enjoyable Personal Transport Systems and they will tell you that it's just not so.

Another example of the way the patina of marketing whitewashes common sense: network television's consistent refusal to run anti-commercials assembled by the Vancouver-based Adbusters Media Foundation. The CBC, for instance, has been approached several times and has never allowed the AMF to purchase ad space exhorting people to turn off their TVs or to buy less stuff. Why does the CBC refuse to run the ads? After all, the Media Foundation is a paying customer. The answer is, of course, to protect the other advertisers whose message would be clouded by the bad-news rhetoric of the anti-consumer ads. (CNN finally broke their long-standing ban on Adbusters ads, using the broadcasts as a publicity ploy. But the CBC stays the course.)

The goal is not to prevent the expression of differing opinions and possibilities, *but to prevent the expression of the possibility that there are differing opinions*. Within the lifestyle culture machine we respond to the clarion call,

we do exactly what we're told, we obey. Why? Because outside the marketing-driven world of mass culture, our lives, based as they frequently are on the accumulation of meaningless crap, seem silly and trivial. But from the inside it all makes sense. To recognize the lies for what they are, though, would be to leave us bereft of meaning and purpose … which is why almost everybody admits to buying stuff they don't need and to watching too much TV, but rarely actually changes their behaviour.

As a result, our priorities are fucked. Mass culture allows us to exist in a world of fuzzy relativism, without values, judges, juries, or executioners. Once upon a time, a man discovered that his collection of 5,000 Barbie dolls had been stolen. "They meant everything to me," he told a reporter. "I could do without eating. I don't know if I can live without them." And, dear reader, who are you to judge him?

# Box Stores versus the Strange Joys of Indie Commerce

We of the rapidly aging X Generation grew up in malls (see *Malls*). They were everywhere, and they were frequently located close enough to our junior high schools that we spent as much time in the food courts as we did in class.

During the 60s, 70s, and 80s, we could pretend that malls, architectural atrocities that they were (and are), were invisible. Douglas Coupland has a term for this peculiar form of mass denial—The Emperor's New Mall:

Paul Fairweather

"The suspension of visual disbelief engendered by [the notion that shopping malls exist on the inside only and have no exterior] allows shoppers to pretend that the large, cement blocks thrust into their environment do not, in fact, exist." But box stores have rendered that pleasant little coping strategy as much a part of the past as the healthy dollar. They intrude on the real world with all the blank, menacing indifference of the Monolith in *2001: A Space Odyssey*.

Unlike a mall, no one can grow up in a box store, or even a complex of box stores, scattered like giant Monopoly houses across a quadruple-football-field-sized stretch of asphalt. The illusion of a common space connecting the stores has vanished. No room for socializing. All that remains is raw mercantile lust. *Buy this. You need it, and you need it in quantity*. Want to go to another store on the same lot? No more pleasant strolls past anemic potted rubber trees, lame fashion shows, and pleasant wrinkly old people on the benches in the centre court for you. Baudelaire called this sort of casual strolling *flânerie* (see *Transportation*) and Walter Benjamin noted that idly passing through consumer culture while remaining above it was a major coping mechanism for alienated contemporary intellectuals. Fuck you and your fancy French words, say the box stores. Go out in the cold and the rain, or better yet, drive from one side of the parking lot to the other.

What box stores sell is the illusion of plenitude, offering choice or quantity where none is necessary (How many sizes of plastic and rubber containers *do* you need around the house? Who needs an entire skid of frozen quiche, or a can of tuna as large as their head?) while

> *Canada is not really a place where you are encouraged to have large spiritual adventures.*
>
> —Robertson Davies

BOX STORES

paradoxically limiting the range of goods that would actually be available in a number of smaller stores. Box stores work according to an economic principle known as "fungibility," which basically means the degree to which one object can be substituted for another. Box stores are crammed full of highly fungible goods in large quantities, but a given item is rarely around for long. One month the store is full of wrought-iron candlesticks,

### WHAT TO DO WHEN THE FRANCHISES THREATEN YOUR 'HOOD

*Attention, budding culture jammers: you don't have to take the invasion of your neighbourhood by the megafranchises lying down (though lying down is always an option for those in favour of passive resistance). As part of the general shit-disturbing at the G8 summit in Kananaskis, Alberta, in June 2002, a loose coalition of activists, police, business people, capitalists, journalists, slackers, and union members got butt-naked under a giant banner reading "I'd rather be naked than wear GAP." It's fun, it's political, and it's a good way to even out your tan, too.*

*You can use these kinds of creative protests to prevent big box stores from ruining your neighbourhood commercial strip. It's called embarrassment. The key is to go big and go public. In Toronto, a neighbourhood successfully prevented the opening of a Starbucks mostly by getting national coverage of the plight of their local café (see Tools, Coffee for the full story). So what are you going to do the next time a box chain threatens? Get naked and get out a press release!*

the next it's translucent plastic office supplies in lollipop colours. Doesn't matter what the merchandise is, as long as it has a barcode and as long as it moves. If you gather enough useless shit in one place and convince people that they're getting it at a bargain, they'll be all over it like sharks on chum.

But as the joke goes, IKEA is Swedish for "Sorry, that's out of stock." The price we pay for box stores is the death of local variety and the disappearance of stores that stock low-fungibility, slow-moving goods—like bookstores. Despite what Heather Reisman might want to believe, books do not sell like candles. Unless they're books by Martha Stewart.

Until recently, the only good thing about box stores was that you rarely found them in the urban core. This allowed lame suburbanites to furnish their houses with the exact same set of attachable adjustable Billy bookcases and Ivar TV units while downtown folks in the know could visit an incredible array of diverse local business. (Hal once spent two entire days visiting obscure stores devoted exclusively to illumination before finally settling on an Italian floor lamp with an almost undetectable crack in it being practically given away at an incredibly pretentious style outpost called EuroLite.)

Lately, however, box stores and their strip-mall chain equivalents have been encroaching more and more on the downtown. The landscape is changing for the worse. Where once we could count on shopping as being a kind of entertainment, chains and box stores are turning everything mundane. Would you rather shop at Toys-R-The-Same or the late great Fun-O-Rama? For years, Morris Greenbaum ran the used and obscure toy store Fun-O-Rama on Toronto's Queen Street. A trip to Fun-O-Rama was like an occasion: you went to shop, but also just to see and reminisce. Big sellers included the potato gun and toy birds that drink (as seen in *Darkman* and *The Simpsons*). Fun-O-Rama made that block worth journeying to. It anchored an array of lesser thrift stores, crummy "antique" joints, and even local too-cool-for-you record joint Rotate This (which, thankfully, remains). There are many who think of Fun-O-Rama every time they meander that particular corner. But it's not enough to just fondly remember. When you find the kind of stores that are one of a kind, that make a neighbourhood, there's only one thing to do: patronize them. Don't root around and then head to the HMV to see if you can buy it for $1.50 less. (Remember, the box stores loom. One day, like the evil alien ships in *Independence Day*, they'll be there, hanging overhead, swollen with someone else's idea of a fulfilling life.)

So we'll end this mini-rant with some words of wisdom from Fun-O-Rama proprietor Morris, who, in a 1995 interview with the zine *Cussword*, spent a bit of time talking about the difference between the toys of today and the great traditions of yesteryear. A look back in time, but, also a prophetic warning for the Canadian city. Take it away, Morris:

> *The stuff today is really mass-produced. Mass production in the 50s and 60s was a couple hundred thousand, but mass production today … they have these factories in China and Taiwan that produce a couple hundred thousand per day. And they make it for months and months until there's billions of them, which sort of spoils the collectibility of it. Plus, there's not much human element to the manufacturing of the toys. With old stuff, there's things that are hand-painted—like Barbie dolls, when they first came out*

> *the eyes were hand-painted so no two Barbie dolls' eyes were exactly alike. The same thing with jigsaw puzzles—years ago they'd cut them by hand with a jigsaw, so no two had the same pieces.*

# Bookstores

We have two kinds of bookstores: those owned by Heather Reisman, and everything else.

Since those owned by Ms. Reisman are relatively easy to locate due to their grotesque profiles on the skyline (see *Box Stores*); here are a few of the others.

**Audrey's Books**  10702 Jasper Avenue, Edmonton, AB T5J 3J5, (780) 423 3487. One of the few things left in the downtown Edmonton core that's worth visiting.

**Bollum Books**  710 Granville Street, Vancouver, BC V6Z 1E5, (604) 689 3629

**Book City**  501 Bloor Street West, Toronto, ON M5S 1Y2, (416) 961 4496. Many of Canada's current crop of young writers (including André Alexis, Alana Wilcox, Chris Chambers, and Derek McCormack) have served as staffers here; these people know what they're talking about. Great remainder tables.

**Bookmark II**  5686 Spring Garden Road, Halifax, NS B3J 1H5, (902) 423 0419

**The Bookshelf Cafe**  41 Quebec Street, Guelph, ON N1H 2T1, (519) 821 3311. Great store, wine bar, rep cinema, and an amazing restaurant. Go straight to the shelf marked "Weird."

BOOKSTORES

Woman displaying *The Globe* newspaper at North Toronto Book-store, 1922

**Buzzword** 2926 13th Avenue, Regina, SK S4T IN8, (306) 522 6562

**Glad Day Books** 598A Yonge Street, Toronto, ON M4Y IZ3, (416) 961 4161. Along with Little Sister in Vancouver, a consistent foe of censorship and homophobia. Unfortunately, this role has been thrust upon them by boneheaded Customs officials who routinely snoop through and seize shipments of their stock.

**Granville Book Company** 850 Granville Street, Vancouver, BC V6Z IK3, (604) 687 2213

**Greenwoods** 10355 Whyte Avenue, Edmonton, AB T6E IZ9, (780) 439 2005, <www.greenwoods.com>. Another great Edmonton store. Good selections of SF and literature.

**L'androgyne** 3636 boul. St. Laurent, Montreal, QC H2X 2V4, (514) 842 4765

**Librairie Paragraphe** 2065 rue Mansfield, Montreal, QC H3A IY7, (514) 845 5811

**Little Sister's Books & Art** 1238 Davie St., Vancouver, BC V6E IN4, (604) 669 1753. Like Glad Day in Toronto, they spend too much of their time fighting with bluenosed Customs types, so help them out by buying local.

**McNally Robinson** Unit 4000-1120 Grant Avenue, Winnipeg, MB R3M 2A6, (204) 475 0483; 208-393 Portage Avenue, Winnipeg, MB R3B 3H6, (204) 943 8376; 3130 8th Street East, 8th Street at Circle Drive, Saskatoon, SK S7H 0W2, (306) 955 3599; <www.mcnallyrobinson.com>. Won the Canadian Chain Bookseller of the Year Libris Award for two years running; Canada's only indie megabookstore. A class act; great kids' bookstores as well. Excellent website.

**Mondragon Books** IA-91 Albert Street, Winnipeg, MB R3B IG5, (204) 946 5241. Its decor looks like the Hall of the Dwarf King, but it's really an anarchist collective. Good fair-trade coffee too.

**Munro's** 1108 Government Street, Victoria, BC V8W 1Y2, (604) 382 2464

**Octopus Books** 798 Bank Street, Ottawa, ON K1S 3V4, (613) 235 2589. A comfy little anarcho-leftist bookstore in Ottawa with some surprising, quirky selections in the poetry section.

**Orlando Books** 10123 Whyte Avenue, Edmonton, AB T6E 1Z5, (780) 432 7633

**Pages** 256 Queen Street West, Toronto, ON M5V 1Z8, (416) 598 1447. Great cultural theory, art, film, small press, poetry, and photography sections. All bookstores should strive to understand and serve their clientele this well.

**Pages On Kensington** 1135 Kensington Road NW, Calgary, AB T2N 3P4, (403) 283 6655. Excellent literary bookstore; habitually hosts readings by Canadian small-press authors.

**Prospero** 128 Bank Street, Ottawa, ON K1P 5N6, (613) 238 7683. In the 80s downtown Ottawa was choked with great bookstores, but this is one of the few that are left. Good inventory, wide selection.

**Spartacus Books** 311 West Hastings Street, Vancouver, BC V6B 1H6, (604) 688 6138

**This Ain't the Rosedale Library** 483 Church Street, Toronto, ON M4Y 2C6, (416) 929 9912. Great literature and magazine sections; a strong selection of queer writing as well. Committed to supporting the local arts and culture scene.

# Indie Record Stores

There will always be indie record stores, if only to ensure that the otherwise overeducated and socially unskilled will have a place to work. Seriously, they may not have huge inventories, but they're the best place to locate truly bleeding-edge tunes, because their buying is done locally by people who are passionate about their musical choices rather than by wage slaves trapped deep in a corporate cubicle hive. Here are a few faves:

**Black Swan Records** 3209 West Broadway, Vancouver, BC V5M 1Y1, (604) 294 5737. Imports, vinyl, and other stuff for music junkies.

**Ditch Records & CDs** 635 Johnson Street, Victoria, BC V8W 1M7, (250) 386 5874. Crazy-ass vinyl and CD store—the ceiling is papered with old album covers. Full of college and indie-rock stuff.

**Megatunes: Your Music Destination** 932 17 Avenue SW, Calgary, AB T2T 0A2. A little bit of everything you fancy, from dance imports to country to reggae.

**Metropolis Records** 162A Spadina Avenue, Toronto, ON M5T 2C2, (416) 364 0230. Mostly techno, trip-hop, ambient, and the dance stuff. Also sells some gear for DJs.

**Rotate This** 620 Queen Street West, Toronto, ON M6J 1E4, (416) 504 8447. Punk, reggae, electronica, and all else that's cool on CD and vinyl.

**Sound Connection** 10838 124th Street, Edmonton, AB T5M 0H3, (780) 425 8721. Mostly used, but lost of rarities, imports, T-shirts, posters, and other cool shit.

INDIE RECORD STORES

**Soundscapes** 572 College Street, Toronto, ON M6G 1B3, (416) 537 1620. Our fave Toronto record shop is more like a very large, very cool record collection owned by a friend. Great books and mags, too.

**Scrape Records** 17 West Broadway, Vancouver, BC V5Y 1P1, (1 800) 540 2157, <www.scraperecords.com>. Vancouver shop devoted to all things metal. Rock on, dudes.

**Tidemark Music and Distribution Ltd.** 3 Church Hill, Suite 300, St. John's, NF A1C 3Z7, (709) 754 8630; Suite 1400, 1791 Barrington Street, Halifax, NS B3J 3L1, (902) 492 2400. Sells and distributes a huge chunk of East Coast music—The Barra MacNeils, Great Big Sea, the Irish Descendants, and so on.

**Zulu Records** 1972 West 4th Avenue, Vancouver, BC V5M 1J9, (604) 738 3232. Alt, indie-rock, jazz, and second-hand stuff by the handful make this the music destination of choice in Kitsilano.

# Malls

In Northrop Frye's opinion, Canadians have a "garrison mentality" inherited from their legacy as fort, shack, and trading post dwellers—New World capitalists who relied not on the safety of making peace with their neighbours and trading partners, but on the facade of security provided by fortress-like structures.

Thus is the mall imposed on us—*forced* on us—as one of the founding principles of Canadian society. (See *Zeitgeist, Beginnings*.) If it weren't for commercial opportunities, no one would ever have bothered sending Europeans over here in the first place. That's a pretty pathetic impetus for a country. Our first Euro-style writers—chronicled in Germaine Warkentin's wonderful anthology *Canadian Exploration Literature*—set out on terrific adventures with the glamorous goal of assisting their employers in the establishment of trading posts (Canada's first strip malls).

Keeping that in mind, it shouldn't surprise us that today all Canadian cities are inundated with malls both at their centres and suburban fringes.

One Canadian city, in fact, lays claim to having "the world's largest shopping and entertainment centre." This is, of course, the West Edmonton Mall. It features submarine rides "in the world's largest indoor lake," a skating rink "ice palace," the "Galaxy Land" amusement park complete with indoor rollercoaster, the themed bars of "Bourbon Street," 58 entrances (or exits), and over 20,000 parking spots (it's the largest parking lot ever built; make *sure* you remember where you left your car). And, by the way, it also has stores. Lots and lots of stores, though

Paul Fairweather

# Dumpster Diving:
# Shopping on a Budget of Zero

**by Dottie and Rosie, from the regular "Trash Finds" column in _Tart_, the essential Winnipeg zine of arts and culture**

#1: I'm really broke. Can you give me any suggestions for furnishing an apartment?

#2: I think people are going through my garbage and it makes me feel weird. What should I do?

The relationship between these two problems seemed clear to us immediately (or at least it did last night after the cocktail party).

No, it's not that we think Strapped for Stuff is going through Tense Tosser's garbage. But it did occur to us that these two could be mutually enlightened about the universal principles of karmic redistribution.

Before we explore the Tao of trash, however, might we remind you, Tosser, that people who pick through garbage don't generally do so because they are curious about its previous owner. In fact, it is quite likely that they don't give two hoots about your version of the universe—you know, the one with you smack dab in the centre of it. Still, if it makes you feel better, take the precaution of shredding your super-private stuff, like old incriminating government documents, nudie pics, outdated sex journals and such. Unless of course you want to be famous.

The basic principle of karmic redistribution is that "one woman's trash is another one's treasure." More to the point, Tosser, just because you refused your stuff doesn't mean that it doesn't deserve a good home with someone else.

According to Marla Stewart of _Shabby Chic_, "with a bit of craftiness, trash can be transformed! Old ketchup bottles and wire coils (from notebooks) make great candle holders. To create nifty room dividers, fasten glued-together

Paul Fairweather

What are you waiting for? Dive in!

rows of empty pop or beer cans, or tomato soup tins à la Warhol, to a solid wooden base. Check with electronics distributors for discarded bubble wrap; if you can resist the obvious temptation to pop non-stop, these make unique window and/or shower curtains. And now that fall has arrived, everyone is leaving leaf-filled, industrial strength garbage bags on their lawns, completely oblivious to the fact that they can double as fantastic retro-style beanbag chairs! People are throwing out great stuff every day! The possibilities are limited only by your own imagination—and the degree to which you're willing to wade through the rubbish to recover the riches." (Look for more Shabby Chic in our next issue.)

We hope the lights are dawning here, Tosser and Strapped. The world is a beautiful place and trash is free for the taking. Finally, to those of you rich enough to be throwing stuff away, the principles of karmic redistribution do have the minor complication of requiring a little human cooperation and understanding. A bit of benevolence goes a long way, as does the occasional plate of chocolate chip cookies.

## GEORGE SIMPSON

*When you read what our early thinkers had to say about their new country, you don't get much in the way of probing analysis of the Canadian shopping experience. That is, unless you read the private notes of Canada's first bloated CEO: George Simpson, head of the Bay's North American operations from 1822 to 1860.*

*Simpson—whom Dan Francis describes in* The National Dream *as the man "who turned the canoe into a weapon of bureaucratic tyranny"—was one of Canada's earliest mall writers, combining surface observations with a surreal agenda in which real people are mere characters in the corporate narrative, characters to be condemned or saved by their capacity to consume or be consumed. Simpson's attitude is evidence; it shows how the notion of the mall, the idea of the mall, was ingrained in the Canadian consciousness since the beginning. For Simpson, each of his workers was like your typical mall food court wage slave. ("You want beaver pelt with that?") In classic corporatese, he describes his employees solely in terms of their usefulness—these are not people, but mall employees. If you knew how to drive a good bargain for the company, you'd get the nod. If you didn't, Simpson would note in his journal, as he did of one poor sap: "A large, heavy, inactive, indolent, man … perfectly useless …" Gee, we hope he wasn't planning on asking for a raise …*

National Archives of Canada

George Simpson

many of them appear at least twice, because people get too tired to walk back to a store once they've seen it (except for the old people who can rent those zippy little scooters). Interestingly enough, when it opened in 1981, only 10% of its terrain was devoted to entertainment. That number has since risen to 35%, reflecting the Canadian fascination with the mall as a place not just to shop, but to visit and enjoy.

Why would you go to a mall and experience the "street life" of a faux New Orleans when you have real city streets and locales to hang out in? The secret to the mall's attraction is that *it is not and never will be the city*. In the mall, everything is carefully planned, from the fake smiles of the underpaid salespeople to the glittering displays of items not nearly as useful and affordable as they seem to be. In the mall, there is a surface veneer: Muzak over the *bring-bring* of cash registers, designer jeans over self-starving thighs, fake waterfalls over pennies that never rust. The city can be dirty, scary, exclusive. The mall is always clean, always inviting. There are no homeless (at least, if the security guards aren't napping), no random encounters, and a limited range of predetermined options. Best of all, there is no weather in the mall.

# Fashion

We are the wrong guys to be asking about fashion. But we're big enough to acknowledge this fact and turn to people who might actually know something about the subject. Rory Lindo and Kelly Freeman are the Toronto-based dynamic duo behind the fashion label and retail mini-chain Damzels In This Dress. They've designed

**Rory and Kelly of Damsels In This Dress**

"beer" T-shirts for the Donnas; they've dressed the likes of Sarah Harmer, Neve Campbell, Kirsten Dunst, and Sarah Polley; and they've got stores across the country selling dresses on the "sweet side of tarty and the tarty side of sweet." Since they turn out fun urban clothing that normal people might actually wear and be able to afford, and since they're an answer to the cliché that the big-city Can-hipster wears nothing but black, we turned to them for some insights into Canadian urban fashion.

*A lot of urban Canadians think fashion is something for pretentious rich types. What's wrong with going around the city wearing stained boxers and whatever T-shirt you find crumpled up behind the sofa? Why should anyone care about fashion?*

Fashion is definitely not only for pretentious rich types; it's also for pretentious poor types and all those in between. Fashion is an expression of who you are. Dressing stylishly is subjective, and often requires only confidence and a little creativity. You don't have to be rich to be fashionable; all you have to do is buy our clothes. Then we can be rich and you can be fashionable! Fashion, by its own nature, is pervasive. Fashion is inevitable. It's not so much caring about fashion, but having fun with it.

*Damsels In This Dress has stores in every major city in Canada. Is there such a thing as urban Canadian style?*

According to beer commercials, Canadian style is recognized by a toque, a plaid shirt, and a beer cozy. But Canadian urbanites can be very fashion forward. They have great individual style. Whether vintage or high-priced designer labels, Canadians' wardrobes are as diverse as the country itself. And their style is on par with such fashionable cities as New York or LA.

*What Canadian city contains the most fashionable people? Why?*

Any city where lots of girls are wearing Damzels!

*The Canadian city is renowned for its terrible weather. Freezing in winter, sweltering in summer. How does the fashion designer deal with this?*

Four seasons, more fashion opportunities. Of course, we have to design seasonally, but Damzels makes dresses, not coats, so we have a little more freedom. But we do consciously try to stay away from obvious trends, so our styles can be worn from one summer to the next without looking dated. Gals appreciate being able to spend money on something they love, and that's not going to go out of style overnight.

*What's the worst Can-urban outfit? What's your ideal look for the Can-urban dweller (one gratuitious product reference only please…)?*

Problem dressing isn't uniquely Canadian; it's a problem everywhere. Specifically, men who wear dress shoes with shorts or the infamous pairing of black dress socks

FASHION

# Jason Dunda's Top 10 Sneakers

1. *Nike Spirit II* The latest in Nike's cheerleading line, available in inoffensive white and "zen grey," which begs the question: If a cheerleader falls in the forest, will anybody hear? Unsarcastically cool are the 10 interchangeable colour inserts to customize your kicks. Go team! $55US (Stateside only)

2. *Aqua Sock* Yes, it's a sneaker, and an amphibious one to boot. Extra-tight elastic laces will keep these nylon sneaks on in the roughest of Ontario Place pool waves. Deep blue with silver/yellow accents, and a super-cool transparent blue sole. Sporty! $14.99 at all Payless Shoes stores

3. *Nike Zealot* Simple and classic, this is the closest one gets to the platonic ideal of sneakers. Beige or black with a retro zig-zag (Nike calls it "herringbone") sole. $39.95

4. *Nike Air Flightposite* More H-bomb than footwear, this is an ergonomic, hypersonic, chronic, bionic, gin-and-tonic mamma jamma. Made of some kind of futuristic moulded polysynthetic alloy, it's the least shoe-like sneaker I've ever seen. Available in silver-black and chrome green, and fully Y2K compliant. $249.95 Whoosh

5. *Powerpuff Girls Sneakers* If only I could fit into these. Transparent lavender soles with little nubblies, hologram accents, even a handy velcro quick-on/quick-off tab for kids on the go. Beats the shit out of anything Mariko Mori ever made. $24.99 at Payless Shoes everywhere

6. *Blue's Clues Sneakers* Kids' sneakers kick ass. The Blue's Clues shoes feature a paw-print sole so you can pretend you're Blue himself, as well as "left" and "right" indicators printed on the insole. Hey, I could use that! $26.99 at Payless Shoes

7. *Nike Air Kukini* Tired of pesky laces? Velcro got you down? Well, with its powerful elastic foot web (read: stretchy thing) the Kukini is for you. On top of that, the green ones have elastic that looks just like alien snot. $139.95

8. *Nike Air Metal Max IV* Just like the Air Metal Max III but one better. Shiny cool metal logos are all over this shoe, proving once again that wearing a lot of metal on your feet makes you run faster. $199.99

9. *Lower Eastside* I took these handsome black suede-y numbers home with me and two days later they started falling apart. I ultimately blame myself since I live on the south side of Chicago, not the east. From now on I promise to keep it real. $31.99 (Payless)

10. *Cross Trekkers* Genuine vinyl sneaks with a non-skid, non-marking sole, perfect for gym class. Special features include boring all-white design and a clear plastic blob on the side you can pretend is full of air. $39.99 (Payless)

Suggested accessories: Power Rangers Galaxy Knapsack, $11.99; Orange Nike trainer T-shirt, $67.50; Payless Sneaker Laces, $2.99; Nike Golf Clubs, $1600.

and sandals. Also, just about anything that comes free with a two-four. On the flipside, the ideal Can-urban outfit would be a saucy Damzels dress worn on a babe with attitude, really bitchin' shoes, breezin' down the street on a bright summer day.

## THE MISSISSAUGA ANIME SHOPPING GUIDE

*Surfing the web one late night for, uh, a present for someone else, we came across this fabulous list dedicated to shopping for Asian cartoon kitsch in the sprawling city of Mississauga. Check out the site <www.interlog.com/~riwasa/shopping/canada/ontario/mississauga.htm> for the full effect. And, naturally, that wasn't us you saw prowling the aisles of the Dixie Park Trading Centre…*

***The Comic Den!*** *3032 Kirwin Avenue, Mississauga, ON L5A 2K6 The Comic Den has an excellent selection of anime-related goods. The store has English, and some Japanese, manga and comics, and carries anime-related magazines such as Animerica, Newtype, and Animage. There's also some anime merchandise available, such as trading cards, posters, etc.*

***E.K. Trading: Cards and Comics*** *Unit 210 Dixie Park Trading Centre Has a fairly good selection of anime DVDs (including box sets), plus some anime comics, graphic novels, magazines, wall scrolls, figures, cards, and soundtracks.*

***Pringo Trading (formerly Manly Trading Corp)*** *Unit 123 Dixie Park Trading Centre Carries a lot of anime-related merchandise, video tapes (mainly Dragonball and some Neon Genesis Evangelion), posters, stickers, cards, and calendars. Slightly cheaper prices than UC Stationery and Gifts.*

***UC Stationery and Gifts*** *There's a large selection of cards here, from Yu Yu to Dragonball to Sailor Moon. Despite this, they haven't ordered any new, updated stuff recently (such as Neon Genesis Evangelion), but this may change. They also have a small selection of older Macross and Dragonball soundtracks, posters, and a few computer games.*

***North Star Hobbies and Collectables*** *1185 Dundas Street East, Mississauga, ON L5A 3M4 North Star sells anime-related models at different scales, including ones from Gundam, Tekkaman, Macross, and Patlabor.*

***Sekyo*** *Kanip Trading Corporation, 30 Eglinton Avenue West, #12, Mississauga, ON L5R 3E7 Sekyo is a Japanese place that sells everything: anime books, anime games (for Playstation, PC, Super Famicon, etc.), soundtracks, videos, you name it! Right now, they're selling a lot of their books for $1.50 a piece (titles such as Ranma 1/2 and Dragonquest), with some of their other books going for $3.00+. Anime tapes (which are recorded from television in Japan) are $10 each. Each tape comes with four different cartoons. The more popular ones (such as Gundam X and Dragonball GT) come in special tapes (up to four episodes of the series per tape).*

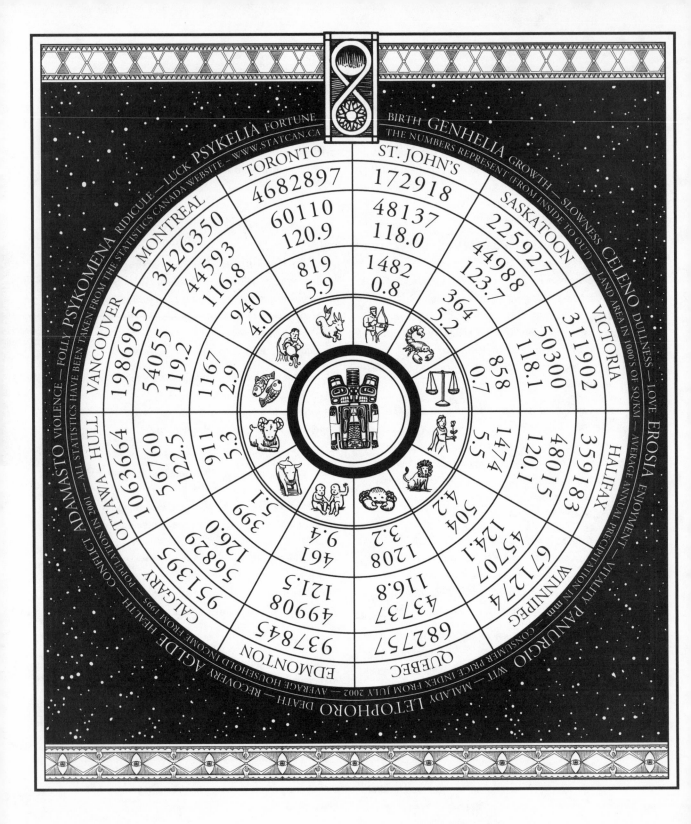

# Calendar

AN ALMANAC WITHOUT A CALENDAR is about as complete as a trip to Alberta without loading up on tax-free liquor.

In that dubious spirit, we offer you this calendar, devoid of almost all functional value (no weather forecasts, no holidays, no phases of the moon), with a smattering of titillating, context-free miscellaneous historical information and the birthdates of the celebrities that we cling to as an affirmation of Canada's worth in the eyes of sneering Yankees.

Knowledge is a beautiful thing.

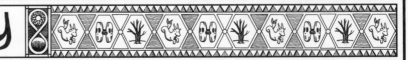
| Day | Birthdays | Events | |
|---|---|---|---|
| 1 Jan |  | *1991* | GST goes into effect; |
| | | *1994* | NAFTA goes into effect … January 1 should be called "Screw the Canadian Consumer Day" |
| 2 Jan | Frederick Varley | *1918* | Montreal Wanderers hockey arena burns down |
| 3 Jan | Bobby Hull | *1863* | First Canadian covered skating rink opens in Halifax; "hockey moms" invented; |
| | | *1992* | Miss Canada Pageant scrapped (in 1991, Nicole Dundson was the last Miss Canada) |
| 4 Jan | Matt Frewer, Dave Foley (Kids in the Hall), Vanity | *1995* | Denis Lortie paroled (shot 10 people in the Quebec legislature in 1984) |
| 5 Jan | | *1874* | First election in Winnipeg: 304 registered voters and 331 cast ballots; |
| | | *1986* | Gretzky becomes the first NHL player to score 100 or more points in seven consecutive seasons |
| 6 Jan | | *1845* | Eighty people riot in the streets of Stratford, Ontario, after a city council election |
| 7 Jan | | *1955* | TV cameras in Parliament for the first time … "Question Period" becomes number one with a bullet in the Nielsen Ratings |
| 8 Jan | Mike Reno (Loverboy), Sarah Polley, Alex Colville, David Milne | *1954* | First crude oil shipped by pipeline from Edmonton to Sarnia … Alberta effectively doomed to become the westernmost suburb of Toronto |
| 9 Jan | | *1899* | Record low Manitoba temperature of -52.8°C |
| 10 Jan | Craig Russell, Frank Mahovlich | *1815* | British government bans Americans from settling in Canada … the long trend of Canadians moving to California and Florida begins |
| 11 Jan | Sir John A. Macdonald, Jean Chrétien | *1922* | Leonard Thompson becomes the first person whose diabetes is successfully treated with insulin |
| 12 Jan | | *1995* | Neil Young (the Leader of Our People) is inducted into Rock and Roll Hall of Fame |
| 13 Jan | Emily Carr | *1881* | Edmonton's population increases to 263; |
| | | *1982* | Anne Cools becomes the first black Canadian to serve in the Senate |

| Day | Birthdays | Events | |
|---|---|---|---|
| 14 Jan | Ronnie Hawkins | 1976 | The Eaton's catalogue nixed; |
| | | 1982 | Clifford Olson gets life for murdering 11 kids; |
| | | 1990 | Laurence J. Peter dies … author of *The Peter Principle*, which states that employees rise to the level of their incompetence |
| 15 Jan | | 1892 | James Naismith, from Almonte, Ontario, first publishes his "Rules of Basketball" in the YMCA's *Triangle* magazine |
| 16 Jan | | 1905 | Frank McGee scores 14 goals as the Ottawa Silver Seven beat Dawson City (Yukon) 23-2 for the Stanley Cup … it's the most lopsided playoff game in Stanley Cup history; |
| 17 Jan | Jim Carrey, Jacques Plante | 1861 | Mass Montreal protest against forced return of escaped slaves to US; |
| | | 1888 | Big Bear dies |
| 18 Jan | Gilles Villeneuve, Mark Messier | 1977 | McClelland & Stewart and Bantam Books launch Seal Books in order to publish paperbacks by Canadian authors |
| 19 Jan | | 1649 | First executioner in Canada, a pardoned criminal, performs his inaugural assignment at Quebec City on a 16-year-old girl found guilty of theft; |
| | | 1996 | Winnipeg Jets sold to Phoenix, Arizona (where they play exclusively for an audience of retired Canadians) |
| 20 Jan | | 1892 | Almonte, Ontario–native James Naismith hosts world's first organized basketball game; |
| | | 1994 | Telesat Canada's Anik E-1 communications satellite spins out of control; newspapers, radio, and TV broadcasters scramble to get news feed |
| 21 Jan | | 1983 | JoAnn Wilson—the ex-wife of Saskatchewan politician Colin Thatcher, son of ex-Premier Ross Thatcher, who will be found guilty of first-degree murder—found murdered in her garage |
| 22 Jan | | 1991 | Northrop Frye dies; |
| | | 1992 | Roberta Bondar goes into space on the Discovery |
| 23 Jan | | 1954 | Leafs undefeated for 18 games straight; |
| | | 1995 | Canadian Airborne disbanded in disgrace after murdering a Somali boy |
| 24 Jan | Michael Ontkean | 1885 | CPR telegraph lines reach from Vancouver to Halifax … teenage girls overjoyed |
| 25 Jan | | 1932 | First trans-Canada phone call made by the governor general, the Earl of Bessborough, who speaks to the lieutenant governor of each province |

| Day | | Birthdays | Events | |
|---|---|---|---|---|
| 26 | Jan | Wayne Gretzky | 1990 | Donald Marshall Jr. is acquitted 19 years after being falsely convicted of stabbing Sandy Seale … Marshall, a Mi'kmaq, served 11 years as a result of racism and bureaucratic stupidity |
| 27 | Jan | Mordecai Richler, Don Shebib | 1859 | Ottawa becomes Canada's capital |
| 28 | Jan | Sarah McLachlan | 1916 | Manitoba's Temperance Act allows use of liquor at home but prohibits public bars |
| 29 | Jan | | 1796 | Yonge Street opened … Sam's and first hookers appear shortly thereafter |
| 30 | Jan | | 1985 | New Brunswick premier Richard Hatfield found not guilty of possession … marijuana was found in his bag during a Royal Visit security search ("I'm just holding for the Queen, man") |
| 31 | Jan | Timothy Eaton | 1991 | HBC gets out of the fur business it entered in 1670 |

# FEBRUARY

| Day | | Birthdays | Events | |
|---|---|---|---|---|
| 1 | Feb | Conn Smythe | 1893 | Coldest day on record in Saskatchewan (-56.7°C) |
| 2 | Feb | | 1955 | Coldest day in New Brunswick (-47.2°C) |
| 3 | Feb | Stompin' Tom Connors | 1916 | Parliamentary Reading Room in Ottawa catches fire, guts most of Parliament Buildings; |
| | | | 1947 | Thermometers in Snag, Yukon, at -64°C (-83°F), the lowest temperature recorded in Canada and likely the lowest temperature on record in North America … all brass monkeys are moved inside |
| 4 | Feb | Conrad Bain, E.J. Pratt | 1924 | First Winter Olympic Games in Chamonix, France … Canadians win the hockey gold, our first Winter Olympic medal |
| 5 | Feb | | 1973 | Construction of CN Tower begins |
| 6 | Feb | | 1977 | Premier René Lévesque drives over a man lying in a Montreal street … coroner rules no criminal responsibility … Lévesque fined $25 for not wearing his glasses at the time of the accident |

| Day | Birthdays | Events | |
|-----|-----------|--------|---|
| 7 Feb | | 1922 | Lila Acheson Wallace of Virden, Manitoba, sells the first 5,000 copies of *Reader's Digest*, the most-read periodical in history |
| 8 Feb | Billy Bishop | 1879 | In a lecture at the Canadian Institute in Toronto, Sandford Fleming first proposes the adoption of Universal Standard Time, whereby the world is divided into 24 equal time zones, each with a standard time |
| 9 Feb | | 1974 | Gordon Sinclair's recording of his radio commentary, "The Americans (A Canadian's Opinion)," peaks at #24 on the pop singles chart; |
| | | 1996 | Donovan Bailey sets world record for the 50-metre dash with a time of 5.56 seconds |
| 10 Feb | Adrienne Clarkson | 1763 | France signs the Peace of Paris, ending the Seven Years War … France gives up Canada, keeping only St. Pierre and Miquelon and part of Louisiana; |
| | | 1983 | Canada signs agreement allowing US testing of military equipment in Canada, including cruise missiles |
| 11 Feb | Leslie Nielsen | 1869 | Second-last public execution in Canada … Patrick James Whelan hanged in a snowstorm before a crowd of 5,000 people for the murder of Thomas D'Arcy McGee … denies he did it; |
| | | 1922 | Banting and Best discover insulin |
| 12 Feb | Lorne Greene | 1990 | Tire-dump fire in Hagersville, Ontario, set by teenage boys, forces hundreds of families from their homes, causes massive air pollution |
| 13 Feb |  | 1833 | Hamilton, the oldest city in Ontario, is incorporated; |
| | | 1937 | Halifax native Harold Foster (1892–1982) publishes his first Prince Valiant comic strip, which will run for 42 years; |
| | | 1969 | Terrorist bomb explodes at Montreal and Canadian Stock Exchanges, injuring 27 |
| 14 Feb | Boom Boom Geoffrion, Meg Tilly | 1927 | Toronto Maple Leafs Conn Smythe takes over the Toronto St. Patricks team and renames them the Maple Leafs; |
| | | 1979 | North York becomes a city and the suburbs begin to take over … |
| 15 Feb | | 1965 | Maple Leaf flag replaces the Red Ensign; |
| | | 1996 | Prime Minister Jean Chrétien lays the smackdown on a protestor during Flag Day ceremonies |
| 16 Feb | Lanny McDonald | 1971 | Prime Minister Pierre Trudeau tells an opposition member exactly what to do; later spins it as "fuddle-duddle" |

FEBRUARY

| Day | Birthdays | Events | |
|---|---|---|---|
| 17 Feb | Loreena McKennitt | 1973 | Newfoundland record low of -51°C; |
| | | 1989 | Ottawa temporarily blocks import of Salman Rushdie's novel *The Satanic Verses* |
| 18 Feb | Robbie Bachman | 1972 | 44.2 inches of snow fall in Kitimat, BC |
| 19 Feb | | 1996 | The toonie design is unveiled … vending machine manufacturers rejoice |
| 20 Feb | Phil Esposito, Buffy Sainte-Marie | 1985 | First successful US cruise missile test in Canadian airspace |
| 21 Feb | | 1961 | Ontario Royal Commission endorses water fluoridation … our precious bodily fluids are corrupted; |
| | | 1824 | 18-year-old Saint John boy hanged for stealing 25 cents |
| 22 Feb |  | 1813 | Canada invades the US across the St. Lawrence in retaliation for the War of 1812; |
| | | 1995 | Lucien Bouchard returns to House of Commons after recovering from flesh-eating disease, receives standing ovation; |
| | | 1994 | Health Canada project finds traces of cigarette smoke compounds in fetal hair … the first biochemical proof that even offspring of nonsmoking mothers are affected by passive smoke |
| 23 Feb | Marc Garneau | 1906 | Tommy Burns of Hanover, Ontario, defeats Marvin Hart in 20 rounds to take the World Heavyweight Boxing Championship |
| 24 Feb | Manon Rhéaume | 1887 | Vancouver loses city charter after failing to control rioting against Chinese immigrants; |
| | | 1905 | Members of the Ottawa Silver Seven, winners of the Stanley Cup, celebrate their victory by booting the Cup onto the frozen Rideau Canal … Captain Harry Smith retrieves it unharmed the following day |
| 25 Feb | | 1940 | World's first televised hockey game … Montreal Canadiens lose 6–2 to the New York Rangers in Madison Square Gardens |
| 26 Feb | Hagood Hardy | 1851 | George Brown founds Toronto Anti-Slavery Society |
| 27 Feb | Charles Best | 1977 | Keith Richards of the Rolling Stones is arrested in Toronto by the RCMP and charged with possession of heroin with intent to traffic and possession of cocaine … police seize 22 grams of heroin, 5 grams of cocaine, and narcotics paraphernalia |
| 28 Feb | Dorothy Stratten, Rae Dawn Chong, Guy Maddin | 1877 | University of Manitoba founded; |
| | | 1985 | Ernst Zundel convicted for distributing hate literature … no one seems to notice that he also believes the Earth is hollow |
| 29 Feb | Henri Richard | 1980 | Gordie Howe becomes the first NHL player to score 800 career goals |

# MARCH

| Day | Birthdays | Events |
|-----|-----------|--------|
| **1 Mar** | *Monique Bégin* | |
| **2 Mar** | *Al Waxman* | **1983** Federal government drops rule requiring licences for private ownership of satellite TV dishes; <br> **1989** Track coach Charlie Francis tells Dubin Inquiry that his pupil Ben Johnson and other athletes knowingly took banned steroids |
| **3 Mar** | *Norman Bethune, Alexander Graham Bell, James Doohan, William Kurelek* | **1994** Alan "The Eagle" Eagleson indicted on 32 counts of embezzlement, fraud, and racketeering |
| **4 Mar** | *Catherine O'Hara* | **1969** RCMP replaces dog teams with snowmobiles; <br> **1977** Rolling Stones record *Love You Live* in Toronto; <br> **1982** Bertha Wilson appointed first woman to sit on Supreme Court of Canada |
| **5 Mar** | | **1872** Toronto Typographical Union goes on 17-week strike against the *Globe* newspaper for nine-hour workday ... they're all arrested anyway |
| **6 Mar** | *Ken Danby* | **1834** Toronto incorporated as city; <br> **1962** Sons of Freedom Doukhobors bomb electric power pylon near Riondel, BC; <br> **1889** Émile Zola's novels seized and destroyed by Canadian Customs officers after they're ruled obscene |
| **7 Mar** | *Douglas Cardinal (architect, Museum of Civilization)* | **1965** Roman Catholic churches in Canada celebrate Mass in English or French for the first time |
| **8 Mar** | *Thomas Fuller (architect, Parliament Buildings)* | **1965** Government grants free tuition to all Newfoundland first-year students at Memorial University in St. John's |
| **9 Mar** | | **1977** Terry Fox loses right leg above the knee to cancer ... fitted with artificial leg |
| **10 Mar** | *Shannon Tweed, Tommy Hunter, Kim Campbell* | **1876** Alexander Graham Bell makes the first successful test of his new invention, the telephone ... transmits the first intelligible speech to the next room, telling his assistant, "Come here, Watson. I need you" ... they subsequently order out for pizza |
| **11 Mar** | *Elias Koteas* | **1992** Environment Canada begins issuing weekly ozone warnings |

MARCH

| Day | | Birthdays | Events | |
|---|---|---|---|---|
| 12 | Mar | Irving Layton | 1921 | Stephen Leacock becomes founding president of the Canadian Authors Association |
| 13 | Mar | Robin Duke (comedian), W.O. Mitchell | 1971 | FLQ terrorist Paul Rose gets life for the murder of Quebec labour minister Pierre Laporte in Montreal; Jacques Rose, Francis Simard, Bernard Lortie also sentenced |
| 14 | Mar | Megan Follows | 1923 | World's first hockey broadcast by radio, Edmonton beats Regina 1–0; |
| | | | 1978 | Statistics Canada reports that unemployment passed the 1,000,000 mark for the first time |
| 15 | Mar | David Cronenberg, Mary Pratt | 1894 | Nova Scotia prohibits alcohol; |
| | | | 1906 | Alberta legislature opens first session in temporary quarters at the Thistle skating rink in Edmonton; |
| | | | 1990 | Sikhs in the RCMP can finally wear turbans and other religious garb while in uniform |
| 16 | Mar | | 1946 | John Dick's headless, armless, and legless torso found on Hamilton Mountain, leading to the sensational trial of his wife; |
| | | | 1955 | Maurice "Rocket" Richard of the Montreal Canadiens is suspended from the NHL; triggers riot next day at Montreal Forum |
| 17 | Mar | | 1985 | Shamrock Summit: Mulroney kisses Reagan's Blarney Stone |
| 18 | Mar | | 1892 | Former governor general Lord Stanley donates a silver cup as an award for the best hockey team in Canada |
| 19 | Mar | Kristjana Gunnars | 1885 | North West Rebellion: Louis Riel takes hostages and sets up Provisional Government of Saskatchewan |
| 20 | Mar | Bobby Orr, Brian Mulroney (Canada's most hated prime minister) | 1986 | Sondra Gotlieb, wife of Canada's then-ambassador to the US Alan Gotlieb, slaps an aide in public during a reception for Prime Minister Brian Mulroney |
| 21 | Mar | Ed Broadbent, Jehane Benoît | 1970 | The Guess Who release their hit single "American Woman"; |
| | | | 1991 | Supreme Court rules 9–0 that a fetus is not a legal person |
| 22 | Mar | William Shatner, Elvis Stojko | 1929 | Off the Gulf of Mexico, US Coast Guard ship sinks Canadian schooner I'm Alone, which had 2,800 cases of liquor on board |
| 23 | Mar | | 1752 | Canada's first regular newspaper, the Halifax Gazette, begins publication |
| 24 | Mar | David Suzuki, John Robert Colombo | 1936 | Stanley Cup game is longest in NHL history, at 176 minutes and 30 seconds … Detroit Red Wings beat Montreal Maroons 1–0 after 16 minutes and 30 seconds of the ninth period (sixth overtime) |

| Day | Birthdays | Events | |
|---|---|---|---|
| 2 Apr | | 1968 | First Canadian lottery (aka "poverty tax") launched in Montreal to help pay for Expo 67; |
| | | 1991 | Victoria: Canada's first woman premier, Rita Johnston, replaces Vander Zalm |
| 3 Apr | Richard Manuel (The Band) | 1992 | Congregation of Christian Brothers formally apologizes to victims of physical and sexual abuse at the 94-year-old Mount Cashel orphanage in St. John's |
| 4 Apr | Evelyn Hart | 1893 | New Ontario Legislature at Queen's Park is built on the former site of a lunatic asylum |
| 5 Apr | | 1971 | Frances Phipps becomes the first woman to reach the North Pole |
| 6 Apr | Walter Huston | 1909 | Commander Robert Peary claims to have reached the North Pole with a party of six, including his servant Matthew Henson and four Inuit … he began his journey (his sixth attempt) at Ellesmere Island … his claim has since been thoroughly debunked |
| 7 Apr | | 1868 | After delivering an anti-Fenian speech in Parliament, Thomas D'Arcy McGee is shot and killed by a Fenian assassin; |
| | | 1869 | last public hanging in PEI |
| 8 Apr | Mary Pickford | 1751 | William Pigott opens the first inn in English Canada in Halifax |
| 9 Apr | | 1917 | Canadians take Vimy Ridge, turning the tide of World War I |
| 10 Apr | | 1990 | GST passes in the House of Commons |
| 11 Apr | | 1940 | Quebec City: Women are allowed into the chamber of the Quebec Legislature for the first time, to hear Premier Godbout's speech asking for the vote for Quebec women |
| 12 Apr | | 1980 | Terry Fox begins his Marathon of Hope in St. John's; runs until he reaches Thunder Bay on September 1, when cancer spreads to his lungs |
| 13 Apr | | 1993 | BC government allows logging of half of Clayoquot Sound, the last old-growth rainforest on Vancouver Island |
| 14 Apr | | 1869 | Noon cannon on Parliament Hill fired for the first time |
| 15 Apr | | 1912 | Cape Race, Newfoundland: Robert Hunston and James Goodwin hear the first distress call from the RMS *Titanic*, en route to New York |
| 16 Apr | Joseph-Armand Bombardier | 1874 | Louis Riel (1844–1885) is expelled from the House of Commons as a fugitive |

| Day | Birthdays | Events | |
|-----|-----------|--------|---|
| 25 Mar | Jean de Brébeuf, Jeff Healey | 1903 | Anglo-American Convention defines the Alaska–Canada bo[...] US president Theodore Roosevelt had threatened to send i[...] if the boundary was not fixed the way the US wanted … Ca[...] gets screwed, with no seaports in northern BC or the Yukor[...] |
| 26 Mar | Martin Short | 1908 | Prince Edward Island bans cars |
| 27 Mar | Jack Warner, Karen Kain, Jann Arden | 1935 | John Buchan, Lord Tweedsmuir (author of *The Thirty Nine [...]* the first modern thriller) appointed governor general of Ca[...] establishes the Governor General's literary awards in 1937[...] |
| | | 1982 | "Take Off to the Great White North," by Bob and Doug McK[...] (Rick Moranis and Dave Thomas from SCTV) with Geddy L[...] Rush on vocals, peaks at #16 on the pop singles chart |
| 28 Mar | | 1928 | Ottawa gets its first automatic streetlight system |
| 29 Mar | | 1991 | BC premier Bill Vander Zalm, under investigation for dodg[...] estate dealings in the sale of his Christian theme park Fant[...] Gardens to a Taiwanese billionaire, says he will step down [...] his Social Credit party chooses a new leader |
| 30 Mar | Céline Dion | 1885 | Cree chief Poundmaker (Pitikwahanapiwiyin) attacks and s[...] rounds Battleford, Saskatchewan … local settlers forced to [...] shelter in NWMP barracks for a month; |
| | | 1954 | Toronto Transit Commission opens first subway in Canada [...] Yonge Street |
| 31 Mar | Gordie Howe | 1975 | CN Tower (555.35 metres) becomes world's tallest free-sta[...] structure … Rick/Simon and the other Toronto Islanders are[...] impressed; |
| | | 1984 | Steve Fonyo begins cross-Canada run |

| Day | Birthdays | Events | |
|-----|-----------|--------|---|
| 1 Apr | | 1975 | Radio and TV stations begin giving the temperature in Cels[...] |
| | | 1992 | NHL Players Association launches first players' strike in its 7[...] history |

APRI[...]

| Day | Birthdays | Events | |
|-----|-----------|--------|--|
| 17 Apr | | 1918 | First secret session of Parliament (during wartime); |
| | | 1982 | Queen Elizabeth II signs the Royal Proclamation of Canada's Constitution, ending British authority in Canada ... the Constitution incorporates the Charter of Rights and Freedoms; |
| | | 1991 | Ottawa bans Meme breast implant |
| 18 Apr | Rick Moranis, Eric McCormack | 1763 | Marie-Josephe Corriveau is hanged in Quebec City for murdering her abusive husband Louis Dodier ... her corpse hangs for a month in an iron cage at Lauzon |
| 19 Apr | Sharon Pollock | 1904 | Great Toronto Fire burns for two days, causes $12 million in damages and destroys 104 buildings covering 14 acres; |
| | | 1912 | Mystery man "Jerome" dies at about age 58; found on a Nova Scotian beach with both legs amputated ... he refused to talk or write, and died unidentified |
| 20 Apr | Toller Cranston | 1769 | Pontiac dies; |
| | | 1963 | Wilfred O'Neill, a 65-year-old night watchman, is killed by a terrorist bomb placed in a garbage container at the Montreal army recruiting centre ... he is the first victim of the FLQ; |
| | | 1968 | Ralph Plaistead and Jean-Luc Bombardier lead the Canadian-US expedition to the North Pole on four snowmobiles; the trip takes 42 days and is the first indisputable arrival at the Pole ... Bombardier, the nephew of snowmobile inventor Joseph Armand Bombardier, is the first Canadian to reach the Pole; |
| | | 1982 | Peter Pocklington is held hostage in his Edmonton home for almost 12 hours by a gunman demanding $1 million |
| 21 Apr | | 1918 | Bertangles, France: "Red Baron" Manfred von Richthofen shot down and killed over the Western Front during a dogfight with Captain Roy Brown of Carleton Place, Ontario |
| 22 Apr | Sandra Birdsell | 1979 | Rolling Stones benefit concert for the blind in Toronto is part of the conditions for Keith Richard's release from drug charges |
| 23 Apr | Tony Esposito, Margaret Avison | 1981 | Paramount Canada's Wonderland amusement park opens north of Toronto; one Canadian writer notes that "the big purple mountain looks a lot better when you're on mushrooms" |
| 24 Apr | Alan Eagleson | 1985 | Supreme Court of Canada allows Sunday shopping in most provinces |
| 25 Apr | | 1890 | Crowfoot dies; |
| | | 1940 | Quebec women allowed to vote and run for office in provincial elections, 22 years after women were granted the federal vote; |

| Day | Birthdays | Events | |
|-----|-----------|--------|---|
| | | 1972 | Paula the cat, a 10-month-old tabby, survives a fall from the 26th floor of an apartment building in Toronto |
| 26 Apr | | 1900 | Fire in Hull spreads across the river to Ottawa, kills seven and does $10 million in damage |
| 27 Apr | | 1644 | Wheat planted in Canada for the first time |
| 28 Apr | | 1996 | Winnipeg Jets lose for the last time before being sold to Phoenix |
| 29 Apr | Peter Jennings | 1995 | Kitchener butchers make the world's longest sausage (28.77 miles) |
| 30 Apr | | 1789 | Parrtown and Carleton merge to become Saint John, the first incorporated city in Canada |

# MOY

| Day | Birthdays | Events | |
|-----|-----------|--------|---|
| 1 May | Glenn Ford | 1921 | Quebec provincial government takes control of liquor sales … Quebec is the only "wet" area on the continent |
| 2 May | Abraham Gesner | 1670 | Charles II grants a Royal charter (The Hudson's Bay Company) to his cousin Prince Rupert and his pals … the charter gives them an exclusive monopoly over commerce in lands flowing into Hudson Bay, which is most of the northern part of the continent |
| 3 May | | 1915 | Lt.-Col. John McCrae composes his poem "In Flanders Fields" while overlooking the grave of another officer at Ypres; |
| | | 1969 | Jimi Hendrix is arrested for heroin possession at Toronto International Airport |
| 4 May | | 1958 | Johnny Wayne and Frank Shuster make the first of a record 67 appearances on *The Ed Sullivan Show*; |
| | | 1992 | The Yonge Street riot in Toronto |
| 5 May | | 1950 | The Winnipeg flood causes $100 million in damages |
| 6 May | | 1990 | Prime Minister Mulroney says tough economic measures by his government will continue to make him unpopular with the public … he's right, and will go on to become the most unpopular Canadian politician, ever, whose legacy is the near-destruction of the Tory party |

| Day | Birthdays | Events | |
|---|---|---|---|
| 7 May | | 1945 | VE Day (World War II ends) ... happy Haligonians and 10,000 soldiers riot for two days; |
| | | 1988 | Mila Mulroney struck in the stomach by a placard during a labour rally outside a Tory gathering in Moncton; a man is arrested but no charges are laid |
| 8 May | George Woodcock | 1906 | Canada's first train robbery ... Bill Miner holds up a CPR train, gets only $15 and is captured a couple of days later; |
| | | 1982 | Gilles Villeneuve dies at 225 kph in Belgium; |
| | | 1984 | Quebec City: Canadian Army Corporal Denis Lortie sprays the Quebec National Assembly with sub-machine gun fire, killing three and wounding 13; |
| | | 1987 | The loonie (aka "the northern peso") replaces the dollar bill |
| 9 May | Don Messer, Hank Snow | 1977 | Downtown Toronto fire does not destroy Eaton Centre ... oh well ... |
| 10 May | Gaëtan Boucher | 1924 | Edmonton: end of prohibition in Alberta; |
| | | 1995 | Ontario Court gives lesbian couples the right to legally adopt children |
| 11 May | Mort Sahl  | 1870 | Sir John Rose delivers a bank draft for £300,000 (the equivalent of $11 million) to the Hudson's Bay Company in full payment for the title to Rupert's Land. The land includes all territories drained by rivers flowing into Hudson Bay (most of today's Prairie provinces, northern Ontario, northwestern Quebec, and portions of the Northwest Territories). The HBC keeps blocks of land around its trading posts and 1/20 of the fertile belt (2.8 million hectares); |
| | | 1984 | creation of CSIS |
| 12 May | Farley Mowat, James Houston, Bruce McCulloch | 1989 | Ben Johnson admits to Dubin Inquiry that he used anabolic steroids |
| 13 May | Roch Carrier, Mary Walsh | 1991 | Baltej Dhillon of Regina becomes the first RCMP officer to wear a turban |
| 14 May | Gump Worsley, Tom Cochrane | 1946 | House of Commons passes the Canadian Citizenship Act, the first nationality statute in Canada to define its people as Canadians ... Canadian citizenship to be distinct and primary over being a British subject ... to take effect January 1, 1947; |
| | | 1984 | Jeanne Sauvé sworn in as Canada's first female governor general |
| 15 May | James Wiseman, Turk Broda | 1919 | Winnipeg General Strike begins ... 30,000 workers from 52 unions walk off the job, paralyzing the city for 41 days; |
| | | 1965 | Igor Vodic beats Quebec's Mad Dog Vachon to become the National Wrestling Association champion; |
| | | 1981 | SCTV debuts on NBC |

MAY

| Day | Birthdays | Events |
|---|---|---|
| 16 May | Kevin McDonald | **1990** Fire breaks out at St. Amable near Montreal, Quebec's largest tire dump (3 million tires) … burns for four days |
| 17 May | | **1993** Stompin' Tom Connors is awarded an honorary Doctor of Laws degree from Fredericton's St. Thomas University;<br>**1996** David Cronenberg's *Crash* premieres at the Cannes Film Festival … audiences are scandalized by characters sexually aroused by traffic accidents … wins the Special Jury Prize several days later |
| 18 May |  | **1966** Paul-Joseph Chartier killed in Parliament Buildings washroom by a bomb he intended to throw into the House of Commons;<br>**1989** Stratford Festival cuts two anti-Semitic references in its production of Shakespeare's *The Merchant of Venice* after meeting with officials of the Canadian Jewish Congress |
| 19 May | | **1780** Complete darkness falls on eastern Canada and the New England states at 2 p.m. … cause never explained |
| 20 May | Dave Thomas, Stan Makita, Otto Jelinek | **1980** Quebec votes No by 59.56% in René Lévesque's referendum on a mandate to negotiate Quebec's sovereignty-association with the rest of Canada |
| 21 May | Raymond Burr | **1920** Montreal radio station XWA broadcasts the first regularly scheduled radio programming in North America;<br>**1986** Keith Alexander becomes the first corporate executive sent to jail for pollution (dumping toxic contaminants into Toronto sewers) |
| 22 May | | **1965** Mad Dog Vachon beats Igor Vodic to become the National Wrestling Association champion;<br>**1984** Rick Hansen ends his heroic Man in Motion tour in Vancouver (26 months, 40,000 km, 34 countries) … raises $15 million for spinal cord research |
| 23 May | | **1886** Canadian Pacific Railway Engine 374, the first transcontinental passenger train, arrives in Vancouver |
| 24 May | Robert Bateman, Tommy Chong, Marian Engel | **1918** Women over 21 get the federal vote;<br>**1936** Bank robber Norman "Red" Ryan shot and killed by police while trying to rob Sarnia liquor store |
| 25 May | Mike Myers, W.P. Kinsella | **1905** Peterborough, Ontario, is incorporated as a city |
| 26 May | Jay Silverheels, Levon Helm, Aritha van Herk | **1969** John Lennon and Yoko Ono begin their second Bed-In for Peace in the Queen Elizabeth Hotel in Montreal … record "Give Peace a Chance" |

| Day | Birthdays | Events | |
|---|---|---|---|
| 27 May | Bruce Cockburn | 1900 | Berliner Gramophone Co. of Montreal registers the famous dog and gramophone symbol (His Master's Voice) as the company's Canadian trademark |
| 28 May | Johnny Wayne, Bruce McDonald, Dionne Quints, Lynn Johnston | 1845 | Fire in Quebec City destroys two-thirds of the city as well as nearby towns St-Roch and St-Jean |
| 29 May | | 1985 | Steve Fonyo completes cross-Canada marathon begun 14 months earlier in Newfoundland … raises $9 million for cancer research |
| 30 May | | 1848 | Fredericton gets city charter |
| 31 May | Monika Schnarre | 1954 | CBWT-TV Winnipeg goes on the air … the first prairie television station |

| Day | Birthdays | Events | |
|---|---|---|---|
| 1 Jun | Alanis Morrisette | 1938 | Toronto-born cartoonist Joe Shuster teams up with Jerry Siegel to create Superman, who makes his first appearance in DC Comics' Action Comics Series issue #1; |
| | | 1966 | CFTO in Toronto transmits the first Canadian colour TV signal; |
| | | 1973 | Marshall McLuhan appointed to Papal Commission for Social Communication to examine the Vatican's relations with the media |
| 2 Jun | | 1965 | Government sets retirement age for senators at 75 |
| 3 Jun | Colleen Dewhurst | 1972 | Mob of 2,000 fans fail to crash a Rolling Stones rock concert in Vancouver … 31 policemen injured; |
| | | 1989 | Official opening of SkyDome, Toronto's $500 million domed stadium … 50,000 baseball fans soaked by rain when retractable roof opens |
| 4 Jun | Tom Longboat | 1990 | Daniel Maston charged with spiking a Moncton lunch-room cooler with radioactive heavy water, exposing eight co-workers to high radiation |
| 5 Jun | Joe Clark | 1967 | Royal Canadian Mint ordered to begin converting dimes and quarters to pure nickel to head off silver speculators |

JUNE

| Day | Birthdays | Events | |
|-----|-----------|--------|---|
| **6 Jun** | | *1861* | Niagara Falls: Maid of the Mist becomes the first boat to navigate the Niagara River's rapids; |
| | | *1944* | D-Day: 14,000 Canadians and some other guys storm Normandy … 715 Canadians are wounded, 359 dead |
| **7 Jun** | Jacques Cartier (born sometime between June 7 and December 23), Jenny Jones, John Turner | *1956* | At Niagara Falls, most of an Ontario Hydro power generating station collapses into the Niagara River gorge |
| **8 Jun** | | *1900* | PEI passes the first Canadian prohibition law |
| **9 Jun** | Michael J Fox | *1846* | Hamilton, Ontario, gets city charter |
| **10 Jun** | Preston Manning, Linda Evangelista, Saul Bellow | *1947* | Harry S. Truman becomes the first US president to pay a state visit to Canada |
| **11 Jun** | | *1992* | Martensville, Saskatchewan: Police charge Ron and Linda Sterling, their son Travis, and six others with 170 counts of sexual assault and forcibly confining children … most charges are dropped |
| **12 Jun** | Scott Thompson | *1947* | First broadcast of radio show *Sergeant Preston of The Yukon* |
| **13 Jun** |  | *1833* | John Wilson kills Robert Lyon in the last fatal duel in Ontario … the two law students and former friends quarrelled over remarks made by Lyon about a local teacher, Elizabeth Hughes … Wilson will be acquitted of murder … later marries Hughes and becomes an MP and judge; |
| | | *1985* | Supreme Court of Canada rules that almost all laws in Manitoba are constitutionally invalid because they were written in English only |
| **14 Jun** | Arthur Erickson | *1887* | Canadian Pacific steamer *Abyssinia* is the first passenger ship from the Orient to dock at Vancouver |
| **15 Jun** | Josiah Henson | *1789* | Josiah Henson (born a slave in Charles County, Maryland, in 1789 … died in Dresden, Ontario … escaped to Canada in 1830 and founded a settlement and labourer's school for fugitive American slaves … he was the model for the eponymous Uncle Tom) |
| | | *1859* | Hudson Bay Company pig breaks into potato patch of American squatter and nearly triggers British-American war over ownership of one of the San Juan Islands |
| **16 Jun** | Gino Vannelli | *1967* | Monterey Pop Festival … Buffalo Springfield (including Neil Young) plays |

| Day | | Birthdays | Events | |
|---|---|---|---|---|
| 17 | Jun | Tommy Burns (world heavyweight champ 1906; the only Canadian ever to hold the title) | 1871 | Anna Swan of Nova Scotia, at 2.27 metres (7'5"), marries Martin Buren of Kentucky, at 2.19 metres (7'2") … the world's tallest married couple work for Barnum Circus; |
| | | | 1962 | Rioting prisoners cause $3 million in damages at St. Vincent de Paul Penitentiary in Montreal |
| 18 | Jun | Kurt Browning | 1980 | *The Blues Brothers* movie opens in NYC |
| 19 | Jun | Guy Lombardo | 1938 | Bloody Sunday … RCMP and Vancouver police use tear gas and clubs to remove strikers from the art gallery and post office; |
| | | | 1983 | BC Place opens in Vancouver … the 60,000-seat domed stadium costs $126 million |
| 20 | Jun | Anne Murray | 1877 | Hamilton: Alexander Graham Bell installs the world's first commercial telephone service; |
| | | | 1942 | Japanese submarine shells isolated Estevan Point on Vancouver Island, with little damage … the only time Canadian land territory comes under fire in World War II |
| 21 | Jun | Joe Flaherty | 1734 | Marie-Joseph Angélique, a black female slave, is hanged in Montreal for setting fire to her master's house in protest for her treatment; |
| | | | 1749 | Founding of Halifax |
| 22 | Jun | George Vancouver, Graham Greene | 1983 | The Canadarm is used by the NASA shuttle to release and retrieve the SPAS-01 satellite |
| 23 | Jun | | 1974 | PC prime minister John Diefenbaker is sworn in as an MP for the 12th consecutive time, a record in Canadian politics; |
| | | | 1975 | Alice Cooper falls off stage in Vancouver, breaking six ribs; |
| | | | 1985 | Bomb planted on Air India Boeing 747 jet out of Montreal explodes over the ocean south of the coast of Ireland … 329 dead … planted by Sikh terrorist, who is later captured in London … it's the greatest loss of Canadian lives in commercial flying history |
| 24 | Jun | Jean Charest | 1968 | Pierre Elliott Trudeau is showered with rocks and bottles on the reviewing stand during St-Jean Baptiste Day riot; on so-called "Lundi de la matraque" (Nightstick Monday) 290 are arrested, 130 injured; |
| | | | 1989 | The Who begin their North American tour at same Toronto venue where they played their farewell performance in 1982 … |
| 25 | Jun | Denys Arcand, Mark McKinney | 1968 | Lincoln Alexander is the first black Canadian elected to the House of Commons |
| 26 | Jun | | 1976 | Opening of the CN Tower … at 1,821 feet, it's the world's tallest self-supporting structure |

JUNE

| Day | Birthdays | Events | |
|---|---|---|---|
| 27 Jun | Charles Bronfman | 1989 | Food poisoning from tapioca pudding strikes 130 nuns in a Sherbrooke, Quebec, convent; |
| | | 1995 | The RCMP grants an exclusive marketing licence for its likeness and image to the Walt Disney Company, who will pay the force royalties and control copyright infringement |
| 28 Jun | | | |
| 29 Jun | | 1985 | Vancouver businessman Jimmy Pattison pays $2.229,000 for a yellow Rolls-Royce formerly owned by the Beatles |
| 30 Jun | Joyce Wieland, Murray McLauchlan | | |

# JULY

| Day | Birthdays | Events | |
|---|---|---|---|
| 1 Jul | Dan Aykroyd, Pamela Anderson, Geneviève Bujold, Michelle Wright | 1923 | Parliament passes legislation that virtually suspends all Chinese immigration to Canada … known to Chinese community as Humiliation Day … in 1885, Chinese immigrants were required to pay an entry fee, or head tax, of $50 for entry into Canada … by 1900, as immigration continued, the amount was raised to $100; |
| | | 1970 | Winnipeg: Pierre Trudeau tells Canada Day heckler concerned about unsold grain, "Relax mister. You can't carry the weight of the world on your shoulders every day. This is a fun day" |
| 2 Jul | Robert Ito, Evelyn Lau | 1941 | RCAF authorized to enlist women |
| 3 Jul | | 1901 | Billy Cochrane drives the first automobile in Calgary, a steam-powered "Locomobile" steered by a tiller rather than a wheel |
| 4 Jul | Hiram Walker (distiller of Canadian Club rye) | 1893 | Tug of war team from Zorra Township, Ontario, wins world championship at the Chicago World Fair |
| 5 Jul | Robbie Robertson | 1937 | Yellow Grass, Saskatchewan: Temperature reaches 45°C, the highest ever recorded in Canada |
| 6 Jul | | 1924 | Winnipeg-born inventor and radio pioneer William Stevenson sends the first photo across the Atlantic to England by radio; |
| | | 1993 | Justice Francis Kovacs sentences Karla Homolka to two concurrent 12-year prison terms for manslaughter in the sex slayings of Ontario girls Kristen French and Leslie Mahaffy |

| Day | Birthdays | Events | |
|---|---|---|---|
| 7 Jul | | 1969 | House of Commons passes the Official Languages Act, making French and English the official languages of Canada |
| 8 Jul | Raffi | 1943 | Canadian gold millionaire Harry Oakes found burned and beaten to death in his villa … murder remains unsolved; |
| | | 1995 | First CFL game between two US teams … Las Vegas Posse vs. Sacramento Gold |
| 9 Jul | | 1960 | Seven-year-old Roger Woodward survives a 162-foot plunge over the Horseshoe Falls because he's wearing a lifejacket … the first person to go over by accident and live … his first word when rescued is "gosh" |
| 10 Jul | Joe Shuster (Superman creator), Alice Munro, Saul Bellow, Elwy Yost, Kim Mitchell, Rik Emmett | 1972 | Leonid Brezhnev, leader of the USSR, when asked by *Time* magazine how many ballistic missiles were aimed at Toronto, replies: "None; I have nothing against the Indians"; |
| | | 1985 | French secret agents sink the *Rainbow Warrior* with an underwater bomb, killing one crew member |
| 11 Jul | Liona Boyd | 1750 | Fire almost completely destroys the recently settled Halifax |
| 12 Jul | Gordon Pinsent, Barbara Astman | 1812 | Windsor: US brigadier general William Hull crosses the Detroit River with 2,500 troops and occupies the town of Sandwich … first American invasion in the War of 1812; |
| | | 1963 | Terrorists destroy the Queen Victoria monument in Montreal's Dominion Square |
| 13 Jul | Deborah Cox, Peter Gzowski | 1995 | Geddy Lee of Rush sings "O Canada" at an all-star game in Baltimore |
| 14 Jul | Northrop Frye, Moshe Safdie | 1976 | House of Commons abolishes the death penalty by a free vote of 132–124 |
| 15 Jul | | 1909 | George-Étienne Cartier's Manitoba Act comes into effect … creates a new bilingual province in the West, recognizes Métis land claims by setting aside 566,000 hectares, gives English and French languages equal status, guarantees Protestant and Roman Catholic educational rights … Manitoba enters the Dominion as our fifth province |
| 16 Jul | | 1945 | US scientists explode the first atomic bomb using Canadian U-235 refined in Port Hope, Ontario; |
| | | 1988 | Wayne Gretzky marries Hollywood starlet Janet Jones |
| 17 Jul | Art Linkletter, Donald Sutherland | 1972 | Bomb placed under a ramp at the Montreal Forum explodes, blowing up an equipment truck and destroying 30 speakers belonging to the Rolling Stones |

| Day | Birthdays | Events | |
|---|---|---|---|
| **18 Jul** | *Margaret Laurence, R. Murray Schafer, John Diefenbaker* | **1973** | Christine Demeter found bludgeoned to death in her Mississauga home … husband of the former fashion model is later convicted of hiring an assailant to kill her in order to collect $1 million insurance policy |
| **19 Jul** | *Atom Egoyan* | **1981** | Hailstones the size of tennis balls fall on Toronto, destroying millions of dollars' worth of property … Canadians living elsewhere rejoice |
| **20 Jul** | *Tantoo Cardinal* | **1871** | BC enters Confederation; |
| | | **1977** | CRTC declares that Radio-Canada French-language service has no separatist bias |
| **21 Jul** | *Marshall McLuhan, Norman Jewison* | **1896** | Canada's first motion picture showing via Thomas Edison's Vitascope at the Ottawa Electric Railway Company's West End Park |
| **22 Jul** | *Alex Trebek, Albert Warner* | **1981** | Quebec's licensed taverns are required to post a notice saying that women are allowed to enter … taverns licensed before 1979 can still bar women |
| **23 Jul** |  | **1900** | Government bans immigration of criminals and "paupers" to Canada; |
| | | **1983** | Air Canada 767 runs out of fuel in midair due to confusion with metric system and makes emergency landing in Gimli, Manitoba |
| **24 Jul** | *Ed Mirvish, Jackson Beardy, Anna Paquin, Chief Dan George* | **1988** | Edmontonians make the world's largest milkshake weighing 54,914 pounds, 13 ounces, with 44,689 lbs 8 oz of ice cream, 9,688 lbs 2 oz of syrup, and 537 lbs 3 oz toppings; |
| | | **1991** | Quebec police find over 270 barrels of hashish floating in the St. Lawrence, after smugglers try to transfer the drugs from a tug onto life rafts; |
| | | **1995** | Regina filling station attendant Dick Assman appears on *Late Show with David Letterman* |
| **25 Jul** | *Steve Podborski* | **1911** | Bobby Leach survives drop over Niagara Falls in a steel barrel … spends 23 weeks in hospital; |
| | | **1990** | Lucien Bouchard announces formation of the Bloc Québécois |
| **26 Jul** | *Austin Clarke* | **1967** | French president Charles de Gaulle ends controversial Canadian tour after rebuke for declaring "Vive le Québec libre"; |
| | | **1983** | Cookie Gilchrist is the first player to refuse induction into the Canadian Football League Hall of Fame |
| **27 Jul** | *Maury Chaykin* | **1991** | 2,000 people riot after MC Hammer concert … 90 jailed, 60 treated for injuries; |
| | | **1996** | Donovan Bailey wins gold in Atlanta Olympics, running the 100-metre sprint in 9.84 seconds, a new world record |

| Day | Birthdays | Events | |
|---|---|---|---|
| 28 Jul | Malcolm Lowry, Terry Fox | 1979 | Grade A egg dropped from the CN Tower observation deck lands unbroken in a net |
| 29 Jul | Geddy Lee, Peter Jennings, J.S. Woodsworth, Pat Lowther | 1977 | 12-year-old Emanuel Jacques' torture and murder in an apartment above a Toronto massage parlour leads to police crackdown on Yonge Street |
| 30 Jul | Paul Anka, Jack McClelland, Tom Green | 1900 1996 | At Canada's request, Japan bans emigration of citizens to Canada; Consumers Distributing goes bankrupt … suburbanites now have to buy their vibrators elsewhere |
| 31 Jul | Saul Rubinek | 1972 1987 | Ottawa announces that first-time offenders for cannabis possession will not be jailed; Tornadoes in Edmonton cause $150 million in damages … 36 killed and 250 injured, mostly in an Edmonton East trailer park |

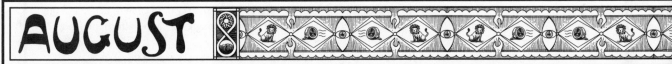

# AUGUST

| Day | Birthdays | Events | |
|---|---|---|---|
| 1 Aug | Anne Hébert | 1992 1995 | Troy Hurtubise plunges to his death while demonstrating bungee jumping … Canada's first bungee-related death; Ottawa: Former NHL player and sportscaster Brian Smith shot in the head by a mental patient as he's leaving work at CJOH-TV … dies the next day |
| 2 Aug | Jack Warner, Bob Rae | 1862 1970 | Victoria is incorporated as a city; Disastrous Manseau Pop Festival is held 80 kilometres southwest of Quebec City in the pouring rain … only 10,000 people show up … Jimi Hendrix, Allman Brothers, and Little Richard are no-shows |
| 3 Aug | Marcel Dionne | 1876 1914 | Alexander Graham Bell makes the first intelligible telephone call from building to building in Brantford, Ontario … hears his uncle recite Hamlet's "to be or not to be" soliloquy; Government suspends coined money payments to conserve gold supply |
| 4 Aug | Maurice Richard | 1637 | Huron council figures out that the smallpox epidemic comes from the Jesuits, with predictable results |

| Day | Birthdays | Events |
|---|---|---|
| 5 Aug | Tom Thomson | **1940** Fascist Montreal mayor Camilien Houde is arrested by the RCMP for sedition and interned for the remainder of World War II |
| 6 Aug | | **1991** Bob Rae recognizes Ontario First Nations' right to self-government |
| 7 Aug | James Randi, Anna Swan (7'6" giantess, with P.T. Barnum's circus) | **1858** Ottawa officially becomes capital of the Province of Canada |
| 8 Aug | Ken Dryden | **1907** Bill Miner, the Gentleman Bandit, escapes from a New Westminster penitentiary and flees to the US, where he continues his bank-robbing career until his death in a Georgia prison … <br> **1991** Ron Joyce sells Tim Hortons, Canada's top doughnut chain, to Wendy's for $300 million |
| 9 Aug | David Steinberg, Graeme Gibson | **1988** Wayne Gretzky is traded by Edmonton Oiler owner Peter Pocklington to Los Angeles Kings with two other players |
| 10 Aug | Peter Martin/Oronhyatekha (doctor—first native Canadian to get a degree from a Canadian university) | **1966** Daylight meteor streaks across the sky from Utah to Canada … the only known meteor to skip through the Earth's atmosphere and leave it again; <br> **1993** Man immolates himself on Montreal's Mount Royal |
| 11 Aug | Izzy Asper | **1931** Tim Buck, a machinist trained in politics at the Lenin School in Moscow, is arrested for belonging to an "unlawful association" |
| 12 Aug | Jane Siberry | **1992** Canadian Trade Minister Michael Wilson signs NAFTA |
| 13 Aug | Bobby Clarke | **1993** Valery Fabrikant sentenced to life in prison for the murder of four Concordia University professors |
| 14 Aug | Ernest Thompson Seton <br>  | **1934** Millionaire brewer John Labatt is abducted at gunpoint by three men, who ask for a ransom of $150,000, which the kidnappers never received … first recorded kidnapping for ransom in Canada; <br> **1980** Dorothy Stratten is murdered by her husband Paul Snider; <br> **2000** goodmagazine.com declares "Mark Kingwell Week" … from the editor: "In the end, it didn't even matter that, in my opinion, the stories written for Kingwell Week were shallow, hastily crafted garbage. The time that was spent sending press releases to persuade the media—and hence the public—that we were somehow, on some level, related to cultural critic and intelligentsia-member Mark Kingwell was far more effective than any piece of writing on the site ever could be." |
| 15 Aug | Oscar Peterson, Natasha Henstridge | **1972** Harold Ballard, president of Maple Leaf Gardens, is convicted of 47 charges of fraud, tax evasion, and theft |

| Day | | Birthdays | Events | |
|---|---|---|---|---|
| 16 | Aug | James Cameron, Harold Foster (originator of the adventure comic books Prince Valiant, Tarzan) | 1947 | Catholic Church abolishes meatless Tuesdays and Fridays |
| 17 | Aug | | 1996 | Ottawa actor Matthew Perry appears on the cover of *TV Guide* |
| 18 | Aug | Simon Fraser | 1968 | Canadian National Exhibition opens on a Sunday for the first time |
| 19 | Aug | Matthew Perry, Morley Thomas | 1942 | Canadians storm Dieppe … 3,500 wounded, 900 killed, and 1,874 taken prisoner; |
| | | | 1981 | Alice Cooper cancels a concert at Toronto's CNE at the last minute; fans riot, police arrest 31 … $25,000 in damages |
| 20 | Aug |  | 1969 | Frank Zappa temporarily disbands the Mothers of Invention after an eight-day tour in Canada … says he's tired of people who clap for all the wrong reasons; |
| | | | 1987 | Federal government bans smoking in public service offices; |
| | | | 1990 | Kahnawake: Army moves to dismantle barricades on the Mercier Bridge south of Montreal put up by Mohawks |
| 21 | Aug | Josée Chouinard, Kim Cattrall | 1965 | Quebec's Mad Dog Vachon defeated by The Crusher … loses National Wrestling Association championship; |
| | | | 1993 | Claude McKenzie of the Innu pop group Kashtin hits and injures a 10-year-old girl with his car … pleads guilty to drunk driving causing bodily harm … sentenced to nine months in jail and ordered to undergo treatment for alcoholism |
| 22 | Aug | Frank Marino | 1964 | The Beatles give their first Canadian concert in Empire Stadium for 20,000 fans; |
| | | | 1992 | Charlottetown Accord signed; |
| | | | 1952 | CBC tele-cine projectionist inserts a slide upside down … Canada's first known TV gaffe |
| 23 | Aug | William Southam | 1820 | Lost pig enters the Bank of Montreal on St. James Street in Montreal; |
| | | | 1890 | Moncton becomes a city |
| 24 | Aug | René Lévesque, Alex Colville, Linda Hutcheon | 1988 | Toronto: Minnesota North Stars hockey player Dino Ciccarelli sentenced to 24 hours in jail and a $1,000 fine for assault; released after two hours … first NHL player to be jailed for a penalty on ice; |
| | | | 1992 | Valery Fabrikant shoots to death four fellow professors at Concordia University |

AUGUST

| Day | | Birthdays | Events | |
|---|---|---|---|---|
| 25 | Aug | Monty Hall, Conrad Black | 1917 | Calgary court gives the death sentence to Sinnisiak and Uluksuk, two Inuit found guilty of the 1913 murder of an Oblate missionary … first trial of Inuit in a Canadian court |
| 26 | Aug | Rick Hansen | 1970 | Canadian folk singer Joni Mitchell performs at Isle of Wight Pop Festival … bursts into tears when a spectator jumps on the stage, grabs her |
| 27 | Aug | Alex Lifeson | 1966 | FLQ terrorists bungle holdup at Montreal's Jean-Talon cinema … six arrested, aged 19 to 22 |
| 28 | Aug | Robertson Davies, Jason Priestly, Shania Twain | 1872 | James Butler "Wild Bill" Hickok stars in the Grand Buffalo Hunt at Niagara Falls … first Wild West Show in Canada |
| 29 | Aug | Peter Jennings | 1883 | Thomas Ahearn, head of the Ottawa Street Railway Company, demonstrates the electric stove at Ottawa's Windsor Hotel … it's the world's first dinner cooked on an all-electric stove |
| 30 | Aug | Raymond Massey, Don Getty | 1959 | End of Montreal streetcar service |
| 31 | Aug | Alan Fotheringham | 1527 | The first letter from Canada … John Rut of St. John's writes to King Henry VIII |

# SEPTEMBER

| Day | | Birthdays | Events | |
|---|---|---|---|---|
| 1 | Sep | Henri Bourassa, Mitsou | 1971 | BC is the first province to ban tobacco advertising; |
| | | | 1992 | Statistics Canada says lung cancer soon to pass breast cancer as leading killer of women … more men than women quitting smoking; |
| | | | 1995 | Toronto: Paul Bernardo is found guilty of first-degree murder in the sex-slayings of Ontario schoolgirls Leslie Mahaffy and Kristen French … he's sentenced to life in prison with no parole for 25 years |
| 2 | Sep | Keanu Reeves | 1912 | First Calgary Stampede; |
| | | | 1986 | Cathy Evelyn Smith is sentenced to three years in jail for involuntary manslaughter in the drug overdose that killed comedian John Belushi in March 1982 |

| Day | Birthdays | Events | |
|-----|-----------|--------|--|
| 3 Sep | | **1979** | Toronto's CFMT-TV, the world's first full-time private multilingual TV station, goes on the air, broadcasting in 26 languages to an audience of 4.5 million |
| 4 Sep |  | **1972** | Art thieves rob the Montreal Museum of Fine Arts of paintings and art objects worth $3 million |
| 5 Sep | Frank Schuster | **1945** | Cipher clerk Igor Gouzenko defects from the USSR Embassy with more than 100 secret documents under his coat, detailing the workings of a major Soviet spy ring in Canada … results in 20 espionage trials and nine convictions |
| 6 Sep | George-Étienne Cartier, W.A.C. Bennett | **1977** | Whitby, Ontario: Leslie MacFarlane dies at age 74 … she wrote the first 20 books of the Hardy Boys series, and made almost nothing on them |
| 7 Sep | | **1985** **2001** | William Shatner's *TJ Hooker* moves from ABC to CBS; Pride TV launched in Toronto |
| 8 Sep | Barbara Frum, Rogie Vachon | **1966** **1976** | Montreal-born actor William Shatner as Captain Kirk and the crew of the Enterprise begin their mission in Gene Roddenberry's sci-fi space epic *Star Trek* on NBC TV; Vancouver band Heart's debut album *Dreamboat Annie* goes gold |
| 9 Sep | Brett Hull | **1979** **1996** | Lynn Johnston premieres her *For Better or For Worse* cartoon strip in selected newspapers … two years later, she has 50 million readers worldwide; Mario Lemieux signs a 12-month contract with the Penguins worth $10 million |
| 10 Sep | Margaret Trudeau | **1988** | CTV Network switches from ground microwave to satellite transmission |
| 11 Sep | Daphne Odjig | **1888** | Toronto: Governor-General Lord Stanley records an address to the US president onto an Edison phonograph cylinder, creating the world's oldest known sound preserved on a record |
| 12 Sep | George Chuvalo, Michael Ondaatje, Niel Peart | **1959** | Toronto actor Lorne Greene stars as Pa Cartwright in the new NBC-TV western drama *Bonanza*, with Michael Landon, Dan Blocker, and Pernell Roberts … it's the first Western broadcast in colour |
| 13 Sep | Laura Secord, Dany Laferrière | **1981** **1991** | Soviet Union wins its first Canada Cup hockey tournament, defeating Team Canada 8–1 … later caught trying to smuggle the Cup out of the country; 35-tonne beam falls from Montreal's Olympic Stadium when 16 reinforcing rods break … a chunk falls on the sidewalk but no one is hurt |

SEPTEMBER

| Day | Birthdays | Events |
|---|---|---|
| 14 Sep | | **1936** Vanier, Ontario nurse Dorothea Palmer arrested for distributing birth control information … acquitted at subsequent trial, which made distribution legal |
| 15 Sep | *Fay Wray* | **1885** St. Thomas, Ontario: P.T. Barnum's famous circus elephant Jumbo charges and is killed by a Grand Trunk train in the railway yard; <br> **1949** Canadian Mohawk actor Jay Silverheels stars as Tonto in first episode of *The Lone Ranger* |
| 16 Sep | *Jennifer Tilly* | **1991** Jenny Jones debuts *The Jenny Jones Show* … born in London, Ontario, Jones started her career as a rock drummer … she worked as a backup singer/arranger with Wayne Newton, formed her own band, worked on the game show and standup comedy circuit, and developed a popular comedy show, which led to a contract with Warner Brothers |
| 17 Sep | | **1952** Edwin Alonzo Boyd captured in a barn near Toronto after the biggest manhunt in Canadian history; <br> **1978** Lorne Greene stars in the debut of the ultra-cheesy space opera *Battlestar Galactica* series |
| 18 Sep | *John Diefenbaker, Daryl Sittler, Archie Belaney (Grey Owl)* | **1942** CBC authorized to begin a national radio service; <br> **1989** NDP leader Bob Rae is arrested with 15 others near a stand of old-growth white pines in Temagami, Ontario |
| 19 Sep | *Daniel Lanois, Sylvia Tyson, Don Harron* | **1985** Tunagate: Fisheries Minister John Fraser orders recall of 1,000,000 cans of rancid tuna … resigns September 23 … later elected Speaker of the House of Commons |
| 20 Sep | *Guy Lafleur* | **1816** Opening of the first stagecoach line from York to Niagara |
| 21 Sep | *Leonard Cohen* | **1854** London, Ontario, gets city charter; <br> **1957** Raymond Burr stars as Perry Mason in the television debut of the series |
| 22 Sep | | **1966** Cuban nationalists attack Cuban Embassy in Ottawa with a bazooka; <br> **1982** Michael J. Fox appears in the debut of *Family Ties*; <br> **1988** Brian Mulroney apologizes in the name of the Government of Canada for the World War II internment of Japanese Canadians; <br> **1994** Matthew Perry appears in the premiere of *Friends* |
| 23 Sep | *Walter Pidgeon* | **1992** Manon Rhéaume becomes the first woman to play in a NHL exhibition game for the Tampa Bay Lightnings |

| Day | Birthdays | Events | |
|---|---|---|---|
| 24 Sep | Phil Hartman | 1927 | Conn Smythe changes the name of the NHL's Toronto St. Patricks hockey team to the Maple Leafs; |
| | | 1952 | Thieves make off with six boxes of gold bullion worth $300,000 from an unguarded building at Malton Airport ... gold is never found; |
| | | 1844 | Canada defeats US in the first international cricket match |
| 25 Sep | Glenn Gould, Ian Tyson | 1942 | Squadron leader K.A. Boomer downs a Japanese fighter off the Alaska coast ... the RCAF's only air combat in North America |
| 26 Sep | | 1988 | Ben Johnson is stripped of his Olympic gold medal for steroid use |
| 27 Sep | Randy Bachman | 1972 | Ottawa bans the sale of firecrackers; |
| | | 1989 | Elton John apologizes to 35,000 people for poor sound quality at a concert in SkyDome |
| 28 Sep | Jean Vanier | 1885 | Rioting in Montreal over mandatory smallpox vaccination; |
| | | 1962 | Canada launches its first orbiting satellite, *Alouette 1*; |
| | | 1972 | Paul Henderson scores on Vladislav Tretiak ... Team Canada beats USSR 6–5 |
| 29 Sep | | 1994 | Supreme Court of Canada rules that a man accused of sexual assault can use the defence that he was too drunk to know what he was doing |
| 30 Sep | | | |

# October

| Day | Birthdays | Events | |
|---|---|---|---|
| 1 Oct | Ben Wicks | 1951 | Charlotte Whitton becomes Canada's first woman mayor |
| 2 Oct | | 1995 | Alanis Morissette's *Jagged Little Pill* hits #1 on the Billboard chart |
| 3 Oct | Neve Campbell, A.Y. Jackson | 1992 | The bodies of two cult members of the Order of the Solar Temple are found in a burned-out condominium in Ste. Agathe, north of Montreal ... the next day 48 more members will be found dead in Switzerland ... three more bodies are found at Ste. Agathe on October 5 |
| 4 Oct | | 1998 | Nine Canadians victimized by CIA brainwashing experiments at McGill University in the 1950s reach an out-of-court settlement for $750,000 |

OCTOBER

| Day | Birthdays | Events | |
|---|---|---|---|
| 5 Oct | Mario Lemieux | 1786 | Womanizing Prince William (aka "Coconut Head" to Navy friends) becomes the first member of the Royal Family to visit Halifax; |
| | | 1984 | Marc Garneau is the first Canadian in space |
| 6 Oct |  | 1973 | UFO sighted by two people in St-Mathias-de-Chambly; |
| | | 1927 | Warner Brothers premieres the world's first talking film (*The Jazz Singer*) |
| 7 Oct | | 1913 | William Stewart Herron discovers oil near Calgary, launching Alberta's first oil boom; |
| | | 1969 | Montreal's 3,700 police and firefighters stage a 16-hour wildcat strike, resulting in violence, looting, and arson plus one policeman and one civilian dead |
| 8 Oct | | 1904 | Edmonton and Prince Albert are incorporated as cities |
| 9 Oct | Aimee Semple McPherson | 1984 | Peter Greyson is sentenced to 89 days in jail for pouring red ink on an original copy of the 1982 Constitution Act in protest against cruise missile testing in Canada |
| 10 Oct | Pete Mahovlich | 1970 | Quebec labour minister Pierre Laporte is kidnapped by the FLQ while playing football with his son outside his suburban Montreal home; |
| | | 1978 | Female pages in House of Commons for the first time |
| 11 Oct | | 1869 | The Red River Rebellion begins in Winnipeg; |
| | | 1934 | Pro-fascist demonstration at Montreal's Monument National |
| 12 Oct | Dorothy Livesay | 1856 | The first street lighting by coal gas goes on in Quebec City |
| 13 Oct | Evelyn Dick | 1992 | Michael Ondaatje is the first Canadian to win the Booker Prize |
| 14 Oct | Dave Schultz (the Hammer) | 1979 | Wayne Gretzky scores his first NHL goal in Edmonton |
| 15 Oct | John Kenneth Galbraith | 1981 | In the largest drug seizure in Canadian history, the RCMP seize a $200 million shipment of methaqualone at Collingwood airport; |
| | | 1986 | University of Toronto professor John Polanyi is joint winner of the Nobel Prize for Chemistry |
| 16 Oct | Fred Turner (BTO), Paul Kariya | 1970 | Trudeau invokes the War Measures Act in response to the FLQ Crisis |
| 17 Oct | Norm Macdonald, Margot Kidder, Rick Mercer | 1967 | Montreal composer Galt MacDermot opens his rock musical *Hair* on Broadway; |
| | | 1986 | Winnipeg's CKND-TV is the first television station in Manitoba to broadcast in stereo |

| Day | Birthdays | Events | |
|---|---|---|---|
| **18 Oct** | Pierre Trudeau | **1929** | The Supreme Court of Canada rules that the word "person" in Section 24 of the British North America Act refers to both male and female persons and that Canadian women are eligible to be summoned to and serve as members of the Senate of Canada; |
| | | **1980** | Toronto: First elephant born in Canada |
| **19 Oct** | | **1987** | Black Monday stock market crash |
| **20 Oct** | Nellie McClung, Tommy Douglas | **1964** | Mad Dog Vachon beats Verne Gagné to become National Wrestling Association champion |
| **21 Oct** | | **1926** | McGill student kills Harry Houdini by punching him in the stomach before Houdini has a chance to brace himself … 10 days later Houdini dies from internal injuries; |
| | | **1976** | Saul Bellow wins the Nobel Prize for Literature |
| **22 Oct** | Louis Riel | **1976** | Toronto: The last Who show in North America with Keith Moon alive |
| **23 Oct** | Lawren Harris | **1978** | Neil Young's beach house in Zuma, California, burns down in a forest fire |
| **24 Oct** | Eustache Martin (in 1621, the first French child born in North America) | **1901** | Anna Edson Taylor, a 50-year-old Michigan teacher and non-swimmer, is the first person known to go over Niagara Falls in a barrel and survive; |
| | | **1903** | Carlisle, Saskatchewan: The coach of the Carlisle Industrial School for Indians football team has football-shaped patches sewn to the front of his players' sweaters to fool an opposing team |
| **25 Oct** | Wendel Clark | **1951** | Montreal is the first Canadian city to reach a population of over 1 million; |
| | | **1923** | Frederick Banting and J.J.R. Macleod win the Nobel Prize for Medicine for their discovery of insulin; |
| | | **1993** | Progressive Conservatives lose 152 of 154 seats in the Commons, dropping to two seats and losing official party status |
| **26 Oct** | | **1986** | New Brunswick premier Richard Hatfield is charged in Saint John with possession of 26.5 grams of marijuana |
| **27 Oct** | | **1871** | Montreal: David MacDonald wins a competition by lifting 725 kilos, but the exertion kills him; |
| | | **1951** | London, Ontario: Radiation treatment for cancer used in Canada for the first time |
| **28 Oct** | | **1741** | Fish glue first made in Quebec |
| **29 Oct** | Denis Potvin | **1923** | Halifax: The *Bluenose* defeats the American schooner *Columbia* in an international boat race |

| Day | Birthdays | Events | |
|---|---|---|---|
| 30 Oct | | 1968 | Frank Sinatra records "My Way," lyrics by Ottawa native Paul Anka; |
| | | 1995 | Premier Jacques Parizeau loses the Quebec referendum on sovereignty (50.6% Non, 49.4% Oui), blaming "money and the ethnic vote" for defeat |
| 31 Oct | John Candy | 1962 | FLQ founded |

# NOVEMBER

| Day | Birthdays | Events | |
|---|---|---|---|
| 1 Nov | Tie Domi | 1952 | Montreal: Canada's first English-language hockey telecast |
| 2 Nov | k.d. lang | 1959 | Montreal Canadiens goalie Jacques Plante is the first NHL goalie to wear a mask on a permanent basis |
| 3 Nov | William Kurelek | 1930 | Windsor: Opening of auto tunnel to Detroit … the world's first vehicular tunnel from one country to another |
| 4 Nov | Howie Meeker | 1920 | Radio station CFCF Montreal, the oldest commercial radio station in the world, broadcasts the first commercial radio show; |
| | | 1992 | Montreal: Manon Rhéaume is the first woman to sign a professional hockey contract |
| 5 Nov | Bryan Adams, Harold Innis | 1995 | Jean Chrétien's wife Aline stops an intruder carrying a knife outside their bedroom at 24 Sussex Drive; |
| | | 1995 | Montrealer David Boys becomes World Scrabble Champion |
| 6 Nov | Fred Penner | 1984 | Regina: Former Saskatchewan cabinet minister Colin Thatcher is found guilty of murdering his ex-wife JoAnn and is sentenced to life in prison; |
| | | 1991 | Canadians put out the last of 751 oil well fires started by Saddam Hussein's troops during the Gulf War |
| 7 Nov | Joni Mitchell, Audrey McLaughlin | 1810 | Antoine Romaine is pilloried in Quebec City for running a whorehouse |
| 8 Nov | Morley Safer, Luba Goy | 1976 | Oakville, Ontario: US–Canadian syndicate pays $235,000 for "Hanover Hill Barb" … the highest price ever paid for a cow; |
| | | 1995 | Whistler: Country Dick Montana, lead singer of the Beat Farmers, collapses and dies on stage |

| Day | Birthdays | Events | |
|---|---|---|---|
| 9 Nov | Marie Dressler | 1965 | Niagara Falls: The largest power failure in North American history … over 30 million people in Ontario, New York, Connecticut, Rhode Island, Massachusetts, Vermont, and New Hampshire lose power for most of the night |
| 10 Nov | | 1975 | The *Edmund Fitzgerald* sinks near Sault Ste. Marie on Lake Superior |
| 11 Nov | | 1967 | St. John's: Clinton Shaw sets the world's distance record for roller skating 7,885 kilometres from Victoria |
| 12 Nov | Neil Young | 1965 | Quebec's Mad Dog Vachon beats The Crusher in Denver to become NWA champ; |
| | | 1966 | Dick The Bruiser defeats Mad Dog Vachon in Omaha to become NWA champ; |
| | | 1984 | In history's first space salvage, shuttle astronauts use the Canadarm to retrieve a satellite |
| 13 Nov | George Grant | 1985 | The National Research Council develops the world's first microwave oven for thawing plasma |
| 14 Nov | Frederick Banting | 1835 | The opening of Canada's first insane asylum in St. John; |
| | | 1992 | London: Artist Greg Curnoe dies after a cycling collision with pickup truck |
| 15 Nov | | 1960 | A Toronto panel declares that D.H. Lawrence's *Lady Chatterley's Lover* is not obscene according to the Criminal Code |
| 16 Nov | Barry Morse | 1885 | Louis Riel hanged in Regina; |
| | | 1983 | Margaret Trudeau files for divorce |
| 17 Nov | Gordon Lightfoot | 1623 | Canada's first highway connects the Lower and Upper Towns of Quebec |
| 18 Nov | Margaret Atwood | 1980 | Conn Smythe, builder of Maple Leaf Gardens and founder of the Toronto Maple Leafs, dies |
| 19 Nov | | 1804 | A Scottish actor named Ormsby opens Canada's first English-language theatre in Montreal with two plays |
| 20 Nov | Wilfrid Laurier | 1995 | Montreal: Brian Mulroney files a $50-million lawsuit against the federal Department of Justice and the RCMP, alleging damage to his reputation by police investigations alleging kickbacks in the sale of Airbus jets to Air Canada in 1988 |
| 21 Nov | Foster Hewitt, Samuel Cunard | 1899 | The first automobile appears on Montreal streets |

NOVEMBER

| Day | | Birthdays | Events | |
|---|---|---|---|---|
| 22 | Nov | Yvan Cournoyer, Floyd Sneed | 1963 | The Toronto Stock Exchange closes in mid-session for the first time due to John F. Kennedy's assassination |
| 23 | Nov | P.K. Page, bill bissett | 1809 | After Canada's first piracy trial, Edward Jordan is hanged … his tarred corpse hangs on a gibbet at the entrance to Halifax Harbour |
| 24 | Nov | | 1922 | After complaints from golfers on public courses, Edmonton's city council approves a bylaw outlawing swearing in public |
| 25 | Nov | Tom Thompson, Holly Cole | 1968 | Police charge 104 students with trespassing after a three-day occupation of Simon Fraser University's administration building |
| 26 | Nov | Rich Little, Robert Goulet | 1917 | NHL founded in Ottawa |
| 27 | Nov | Nicole Brossard | 1861 | Montreal gets its first streetcars |
| 28 | Nov | Lotta Hitschmanova, Paul Shaffer | 1907 | The first dial telephones in Canada are used in Sydney, Nova Scotia |
| 29 | Nov | George Brown, Stan Rogers, Howie Mandel | 1963 | Trans-Canada Airlines DC-8F crashes in the woods north of Montreal with 111 passengers and seven crew, four minutes after takeoff from Dorval Airport |
| 30 | Nov | Lucy Maud Montgomery, Dr. John McCrae, Colin Mochrie | 1972 | David Kootook is found dead with other plane crash victims … he had starved to death rather than eat the human flesh of dead passengers (immortalized in Stompin' Tom Connors' song "The Martin Hartwell Story") |

# DECEMBER

| Day | | Birthdays | Events | |
|---|---|---|---|---|
| 1 | Dec | George Bowering | 1919 | Ambrose Small sells his chain of theatres to Trans-Canada Theatres for $2 million and disappears the following day; |
| | | | 1994 | Lucien Bouchard loses a leg to flesh-eating bacteria |
| 2 | Dec | | 1973 | The Who are jailed overnight for $6,000 in damages to a hotel after a show at the Montreal Forum |
| 3 | Dec | Eli Mandel, Miriam Waddington | 1979 | Chang Kuo-tao, the last survivor of the 12 founding members of the Chinese Communist Party, dies in a Toronto nursing home, age 82 |

| Day | Birthdays | Events | |
|---|---|---|---|
| 4 Dec | Roberta Bondar | 1905 | Quebec City riot after Sara Bernhardt performance; |
| | | 1937 | Canadian department stores stock Dionne Quintuplet dolls but Shirley Temple dolls remain the Christmas fave |
| 5 Dec | | 1837 | William Lyon Mackenzie leads 800 rebels eight kilometres down Yonge Street from Montgomery's Tavern to Toronto; |
| | | 1983 | Hell's Angels come to Quebec, and a series of pitched battles with rival local gang Rock Machine begins |
| 6 Dec | Susanna Moodie  | 1917 | The Halifax Explosion results when the French munitions freighter *Mont Blanc* (carrying 2,300 tons of picric acid, 200 tons of TNT, 35 tons of high-octane gasoline, and 10 tons of gun cotton) hits the Belgium steamship *Imo* … downtown Halifax is levelled in the largest manmade explosion before the A-bomb … 2,000 dead, 8,000 injured, 10,000 homeless, $50 million in damages |
| 7 Dec | Max Braithwaithe | 1982 | Hugh Hambleton, a Laval University professor, is convicted of spying for the USSR in the 50s |
| 8 Dec | | 1969 | Toronto: Jimi Hendrix is released on drug possession charges, saying that he's "outgrown" drugs … Hendrix dies of an overdose about two years later |
| 9 Dec | | 1851 | The first North American branch of the YMCA opens in Montreal |
| 10 Dec | Michael Snow, John Colicos | 1987 | The first death in Montreal from tainted mussels |
| 11 Dec | | 1962 | Ronald Turpin and Arthur Lucas are hanged in Toronto's Don Jail, marking Canada's last judicial hanging |
| 12 Dec | Robert Lepage, Steve Podborski | 1970 | Roy Spencer, father of Toronto Maple Leafs player Brian "Spinner" Spencer, is killed by the RCMP outside a Prince George TV station … Spencer Sr. had forced the station off the air at gunpoint because it wasn't carrying a Leafs-Blackhawks game |
| 13 Dec | Emily Carr, Christopher Plummer | 1993 | Kim Campbell, the first woman prime minister, resigns after being left holding the Mulroney bag and having to endure endless "Tory, party of two" jokes following a devastating election |
| 14 Dec | Deanna Durbin | 1916 | Quebec City: Quebec bans women from becoming lawyers |
| 15 Dec | | 1979 | St. Catharines, Ontario: Chris Haney and Scott Abbott invent the Trivial Pursuit game |
| 16 Dec | Donovan Bailey, André-Philippe Gagnon | 1994 | The last direct VIA train runs between Montreal and Halifax |

DECEMBER

| Day | Birthdays | Events | |
|---|---|---|---|
| 17 Dec | William Lyon Mackenzie King, Eugene Levy | 1875 | Montreal riots over scarcity of bread |
| 18 Dec | Brian Orser, Wilf Carter | 1968 | British sculptor Henry Moore donates 600 works to the Art Gallery of Ontario |
| 19 Dec | | 1917 | The first two NHL games are played (Montreal Canadiens vs. Ottawa Senators, 9–4; Montreal Wanderers vs. Toronto Arenas, 10–9) |
| 20 Dec | | 1891 | Montreal strongman Louis Cyr resists the pull of four horses in London, England |
| 21 Dec | Kiefer Sutherland | 1966 | Parliament passes national Medicare Act |
| 22 Dec | Lucien Bouchard | 1973 | Pierre Berton is quoted in Canadian Magazine as saying, "A Canadian is somebody who knows how to make love in a canoe" |
| 23 Dec | Yousuf Karsh, Patrick Watson | 1977 | After protests from owners of vending machines, the Royal Canadian Mint postpones bringing in smaller pennies |
| 24 Dec | | 1781 | Baron von Riedesel puts up Canada's first Christmas tree in Sorel, Quebec; |
| | | 1879 | Temperature in Winnipeg drops to a record -44.3°C |
| 25 Dec | Alannah Myles | 1855 | Kingston: Soldiers in the Royal Canadian Rifles clear ice from Lake Ontario and use field hockey sticks and lacrosse balls to play the first game of hockey; |
| | | 1924 | The cross on Montreal's Mount Royal is lit for the first time |
| 26 Dec | Ronnie Prophet | 1908 | Jack Johnson, the first black heavyweight champion, gains his title by knocking out Canada's Tommy Burns in Australia |
| 27 Dec | Elizabeth Smart | 1942 | A troop train with 13 coaches collides into another train west of Ottawa, killing 36 people and injuring another 155 |
| 28 Dec | John Molson, Lou Jacobi, Brad Fraser | 1980 | Pierre Trudeau says on CTV that if Canada breaks up because of his constitutional proposals, it's "not worth holding together" |
| 29 Dec | | 1967 | Parliament drops the death penalty for murder |
| 30 Dec | William Aberhart, Stephen Leacock, Ben Johnson | 1989 | Canada is the first country in the world to ban smoking on domestic airlines |
| 31 Dec | Burton Cummings, Elizabeth Arden | 1929 | Guy Lombardo and his Royal Canadians play "Auld Lang Syne," the band's theme song, at midnight in their first annual New Year's Eve Party at the Hotel Roosevelt Grill ... the singing of "Auld Lang Syne" at midnight on New Year's becomes an annual tradition |

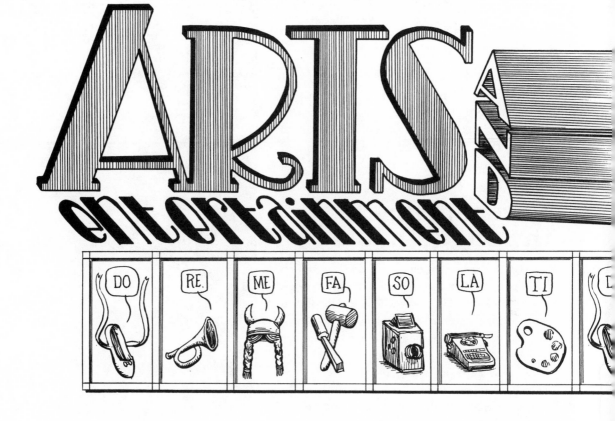

# ARTS AND entertainment

LOOK, WE CANADIANS KNOW WE'RE FUNNY. Anybody who's even remotely humorous south of the border is Canadian (Bill Hicks doesn't count because he's dead).

We also know we rock. Neil Young—the true leader of our people—and legions of others (see *Urban Tunage*) have proved *that* beyond a shadow of a doubt (we maintain that Céline Dion is really not our fault, but rather some sort of horrible mutation resulting from overexposure to toxic US broadcasts over the years).

And we know we can write, make movies, visual art, and all that other stuff. Question is, do *you* know it? What follows are a few of the startling and vibrant number of ways that urban Canada says no to global monoculture.

# Newspapers:
# The Juggernauts

Though we malign and complain and write countless letters to the editor that never get published, we can't seem to give up our daily and weekly newspapers: their health and vitality are often questioned, but their necessity never is. In an age of the generic and the global, a city counts on its newspapers to cover the minutiae of backroom development politics and the successes and failures of its civil servants (including the police and the politicians) and, basically, to give voice to all the disparate but local communities that make up a great city. If a paper is doing its job, it is read, discussed, berated, and read again. If it's disconnected from the city, relies on wire feeds and global pop stars for its content, and doesn't reflect where it comes from, it will eventually die, no matter how many cleavage-laden ladies it puts on its covers or what political slant it occupies.

The earliest papers were, of course, in the cities. John Bushell, a printer from Boston, issued the first Canadian newspaper, the *Halifax Gazette*, on March 23, 1752. The next 60 years or so would see most of Canada's Eastern provinces publish their own, including the *Quebec Gazette*, which eventually morphed into the *Quebec Telegraph-Chronicle*, a weekly in Quebec City founded in 1764 that dubbed itself "North America's oldest newspaper."

By 1871 there were a staggering 16 newspapers in Montreal. Around the same time, the West's newspapers were slowly emerging. Calgary's first paper, the *Calgary Herald, Mining and Ranch Advocate and General Advertiser*, appeared in 1883 and was an ardent supporter of the Conservative party and the cattle industry (some things never change). But Alberta's first newspaper was actually launched in Edmonton, when Frank Oliver brought back a second-hand press from Winnipeg in 1880. The press was so small that it was said to be the tiniest newspaper in the world. In stark contrast to the *Herald*, the paper hated John A. Macdonald's Conservatives and battled for the rights of Western settlers. In 1881 Oliver's paper featured the headline: "Edmonton Population Increases to 263."

Unlike today's bland acceptance of the status quo, our newspapers quickly became mouthpieces of dissent—and many of their proprietors paid the price. In 1835 Joseph Howe had to defend himself when he was brought to trial for trashing Halifax police and judges in his paper, the *Nova Scotian*. The judge wanted him found guilty, but the jury acquitted him and he was later elected to the provincial legislature.

Meanwhile, in what was then York and soon to be Toronto, rabble rouser William Lyon Mackenzie spent 12 years running the *Colonial Advocate* (1824–1834). King's paper "excelled in extremes and abuses" and made a name for itself by running personal attacks on the official upper-class families at a time when there were already something like seven newspapers publishing in York. Young men whose families were maligned actually sacked the office. King sued and was rewarded substantial damages. In a tradition common at the time but rare in our age (when we often suspect our politicians can barely spell), King went into politics and became Toronto's first mayor.

Today, we have fewer choices in daily newspapers. Many are in the hands of the same three or four big companies, resulting in blandness and boredom as papers rerun one another's content and cut back on local reporting to hype up the bottom line. To fill the gap we have a coterie of monthly and weekly "alternative" newspapers,

## CENSORSHIP CRITIC PROVES HIS POINT

*The Winnipeg-based, media-mogul Aspers control a majority of the daily newspapers in Canada—and their various acts of censorship have made them the most despised newspaper-owning family of all time.*

*In March 2002 a* Toronto Star *columnist gave a speech in Regina criticizing the Asper policies. According to the Canadian Journalists for Free Expression (CJEF), the report filed on the talk by Asper-owned* Regina Leader-Post *reporter Michelle Lang began like this: "CanWest Global performed 'chilling' acts of censorship when it refused to publish several columns containing viewpoints other than those held by the media empire, a* Toronto Star *columnist said Monday." But when the article appeared in the paper, it was uncredited and began with the sentence: "A* Toronto Star *columnist says it's okay for CanWest Global to publish its owners' views, as long as the company is prepared to give equal play to opposing opinions." Staff at the paper were not impressed.*

*Not long after the speech incident, the Aspers decided to ditch Russell Mills, 30-year veteran publisher of the* Ottawa Citizen. *His crime? Publishing opinions about the prime minister not approved by head office.* Ottawa Citizen *staff engaged in a byline boycott to protest his dismissal.*

many of which started in the 60s as rallying cries against the Establishment but, having enriched their owners, now seem to care more about target markets than breaking difficult stories. A good example of the alt-weekly philosophy in Canada is Vancouver's *Georgia Straight*, which regularly grosses around 10 million dollars a year. Its publisher, Dan McLeod, attributes its success to having made the move from "being a protest voice in our day, to being a service."

NEWSPAPERS

Canadian cities are replete with chain newspapers controlled from afar and stuffed with articles encouraging conspicuous consumption. They made their reputation crusading for the little guy, but make most of their money as a cog in the machine of a monopoly addicted to corporate ads. Is there any hope for the next Mackenzie King, muckraking journalist turned mayor? Well, one of the greatest newspaper editions in recent years was actually a spoof of the *National Post* slipped into *Post* boxes and handed out all over Vancouver. The work of Guerilla Media, the cleverly executed sendup of the right-wing rag everybody loves to hate featured such headlines as "New Poll Shows 100% Support for United Alternative" and a full-page ad for "The Conblob," "with special conglomeration effects created by Rogedon Lucre's ideological right-wing magic." So don't despair yet; there is a light at the end of the tunnel.

# Radio

The CBC is Canadian as a roomful of drunken Mounties staging a crokinole tournament. And, since most of us grew up listening to the Hog Report over lunch and hearing Mom talk about what that funny Peter Gzowski said this morning, there's really little need to cover those bases here.

Instead, here's a quick plug for independent radio across the nation. The Canadian Society for Independent Radio Production has a great web page <www.radiosite.ca/links.html> that lists Canadian community and non-profit radio websites and related resources, including stations that stream their broadcasts over the Internet.

Radio-Locator <www.radio-locator.com/cgi-bin/page?page=provs> provides comprehensive lists of Internet radio stations for every province (and internationally, for that matter)—use 'em before the Recording Industry Association of America shuts it all down.

# TV

Used to be that TV was the Great Satan, source of all that was evil ... at least in the eyes of our parents and religious zealots everywhere. And perhaps with good reason. As Kelly Simpson opines in "Thalidomide, the Super Soldier and Me: A Paranoid Tirade" from classic Canuck zine *Virus 23*, TV's bad influence had everything to do with the production of the much-maligned generation to which the authors of this tome proudly belong:

*We lived in a world where we were constantly exposed to the acid leftovers of everyone around us, and consequently spent about five years in a "contact high." ... Sid and Marty Krofft (Pufnstuf: "Holy Smokes Jimmy! Witchie-Poo's givin' me a heavy!") and other children's programmers allowed us to grow up in a world where acid logic and psychedelic art were the norm. Consider any one of the animated sequences on Sesame Street and you'll see what I mean (let alone the twisted relationship between Big Bird and his imaginary friend Mr. Snuffalufagus) ... We didn't have to do acid; everyone did it for us.*

... But that was a much less sophisticated world; times have changed, and we all care about the idiot box a little bit less than we used to, given that the range and

## CANADIAN SEINFELD

New York my ass: there are Canadian references aplenty on Seinfeld, especially where Kramer is concerned:

- "The Blood": Kramer asks to use Jerry's TV because he's taping Canadian Parliament on C-Span.

- "The Label Maker": Jerry has Superbowl tickets but can't give them to Kramer because Kramer only likes Canadian football.

- "The Maid": Kramer is on Jerry's couch, under a Hudson's Bay Company blanket.

- "The Couch": Poppy tells Kramer he gets his ducks from Newfoundland.

And then there's always product placement:

- "The Calzone": The show where Kramer cooks his clothes, and claims he's going to Montreal and can pick up some Cuban cigars for Jerry.

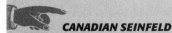

## CANADIANS IN SPACE

Here are a few of the Canadians who populate the Star Trek universe:

- Geneviève Bujold—original choice for Captain Janeway on Voyager

- Kim Cattrall—Lieutenant Valeris, Star Trek VI: The Undiscovered Country

- Gordon Clapp—Hadran, Star Trek: The Next Generation

- John Colicos—Kor (the first Klingon), Star Trek (also Baltar on Battlestar: Galactica)

- Nicole DeBoer—Lieutenant Ezri Dax, Star Trek: Deep Space 9

- Angela Dohrmann—Ricky, Voyager

- James Doohan—Scotty, Star Trek

- Matt Frewer—Rasmussen, Star Trek: The Next Generation (also Max Headroom!)

- Tom Jackson—Lakanta, Star Trek: The Next Generation

- Kerrie Keane—Police Chief Alexana Devos, Star Trek: The Next Generation

- Barbara March—Lursa

- Andrea Martin—Ishka (Moogie), Star Trek: Deep Space 9

- Derek McGrath—Blue-skinned cadet Chell, Voyager

- Christopher Plummer—General Chang, Star Trek VI: The Undiscovered Country

- Duncan Regehr—Ronin, Star Trek: The Next Generation and Shakaar, Star Trek: Deep Space 9

- Saul Rubinek—Kivas Fajoy, Star Trek

- Alan Scarfe—Romulan Admiral Mendak, Star Trek: The Next Generation; Romulan Tokath, Star Trek: The Next Generation; Augris, Voyager

- William Shatner—Captain James Tiberius Kirk, Star Trek

- Linda Thorson—Carduassian Gul Ocett, Star Trek: The Next Generation

- Gwynyth Walsh—B'Etor, Star Trek: The Next Generation

TV

number of sinful activities available to Canadian urbanites has (thankfully) broadened.

Canadians now watch at least an hour less TV per week than we did at TV-watching's peak in 1998, when we each averaged 23.5 hours glued to the screen. In particular, children and young adults watch less of it. The Internet is part of the reason, but we all rent and watch more movies now as well. It remains to be seen whether the addition of a hayrack full of digital channels of indifferent quality will lure the lost viewers back.

## A Homegrown Network: Moses & MuchMusic

Ensconced in the Wesley Building (the finest example of Industrial Gothic architecture in Toronto, constructed in 1914 by the Methodist Church) on the corner of Queen Street West and John in the heart of Toronto is the CHUMCity empire. CHUM Limited owns and operates 28 radio stations, eight local independent television stations, 17 specialty channels, and "an environmental music distribution division" (i.e., elevator music). Thanks to them, we have CityTV (Canada's largest independent televison station), MuchMusic, MuchMoreMusic, MusiquePlus, MusiMax, Bravo!, Alberta's Access, the Edmonton-based Canadian Learning Television, CablePulse24, SPACE: The Imagination Station and Star!. CHUM also runs a number of digital channels— FashionTelevisionChannel, BookTelevision: The Channel,

CourtTV Canada, Drive-In Classics, SexTV: The Channel, MuchLoud, and MuchVibe.

Moses Znaimer is, in many respects, a classic Canadian success story. He was born in Kulab, Tajikistan, and arrived in Montreal with his parents in 1948, a refugee from a "Displaced Persons" camp in Nazi Germany. According to (his own) legend, Moses purchased the family's first television set with his bar mitzvah money.

Today, of course, Znaimer is Marshall McLuhan lite, king of an empire built on late-night softcore porn (the

CityTV … everywhere?

fabled "baby blue movies") and music videos, touting quasi-revolutionary concepts such as "videography" (making reporters act as their own camera crew); "Speakers Corner" (either "the first effective electronic parallel to the 'letter to the editor'" or narcissism on the hoof, depending on whom you ask); and "ChumCity: The building that shoots itself" (which either "reinvents the television 'factory' as a perpetual performance and demystifies the television process in a way that's important for the democratization of the medium" or sets new lows for sloppy camera work). Znaimer's three-hour *TVTV* special catered to his megalomania, presenting him as, in turn, Lenin and the biblical Moses, bringing down the new laws of TV for the people. Maybe someone should have pointed out the irony of delivering the sentence "TV is the triumph of the image over the printed word" written on a stone tablet. At least he ditched the ponytail.

## Public Access Cable

Public Access Cable TV was the Internet of the 70s and 80s—just about anyone could use it, and just about anything was possible. Back in that day, people were running weird, aesthetically freaky and/or politically charged shows and even commercials of their own devising in places like Kenora, Toronto, Winnipeg, and Vancouver.

Before there was public access cable, there was community-produced video. It began in Canada in the early 1920s, when Canadian filmmaker Robert Flaherty allowed an Inuit hunter to participate in the production decisions of the first documentary, *Nanook of the North*, released in 1922.

**MOSES ZNAIMER'S LAWS OF TV**

1. TV is the triumph of the image over the printed word.
2. The true nature of television is flow, not show; process, not conclusion.
3. As global television expands, the demand for local programming increases.
4. The best TV tells me what happened to me, today.
5. TV is as much about the people bringing you the story as the story itself.
6. In the past, TV's chief operating skill was political. In the future, it will have to be mastery of the craft itself.
7. Print created illiteracy. TV is democratic. Everybody gets it.
8. TV creates immediate consensus, subject to immediate change.
9. There never was a mass audience, except by compulsion.
10. Television is not a problem to be managed, but an instrument to be played.

In the 60s, that first effort inspired the members of a project called Challenge for Change, a documentary film series associated with The National Film Board. While the Challenge for Change series got off to a rocky start—the subjects of the first films were ridiculed by their neighbours for participating—those difficulties led directly to the involvement of the films' subjects in the very making of the films themselves. In December 1966, filmmaker Fernand Dansereau permitted each of his documentary's subjects to view the uncompleted film and to contribute to the editing process. When the crew went to Fogo Island in Newfoundland, the initial plan for one long film switched to the production of many short films as a result

TV

of the islanders' preference. Dansereau and the other CFC filmmakers hadn't planned to involve their subjects so explicitly, but these initial accidents and spur-of-the moment decisions changed the course of the series, and ultimately the course of Canadian broadcasting.

In the early 70s, community-produced video fed directly into the development of public-access cable when Challenge for Change supplied video equipment and training to Town Talk, a civic organization in Thunder Bay, Ontario. Town Talk also obtained four hours a week on the local cable system for community programming and began cablecasting in November 1970. Other experiments soon followed. In the Lake St. John area of Quebec, 10% of the population became involved in cable TV, mostly through the school system. Eventually, on July 16, 1971, the Canadian Radio and Television Commission required all cable companies to provide public access channels. (See <www.geocities.com/iconostar/history-public-access-TV.html> for more history.)

One of Canadian public-access cable's oddest moments was a Winnipeg show called *Survival*. Every episode opened the same way—with an extreme close-up on a twitching, ski-masked face, that would, after a minute or so, scream in an apoplectic, high-pitched voice: "WEEEEEEE MUST SURVIVE THE INEVITABLE SOCIO-ECONOMIC COLLAPSE AND/OR NUCLEAR HOLOCAUST. THERE WILL BE MUTANTS!" (for anyone who missed the point, there were usually subtitles).

This was "Trevor Winthrop-Baines," and *Survival* was his talk show. Trevor and his regular guests, including "Concerned Citizen Stan," discussed the finer points of how to construct a bomb shelter, stock it with food and weapons, and, um, kill the mutants that would presumably attack it. (The show even inspired a local rock band to record a short-lived single called "Kill the Mutants.")

Juvenile crap? Maybe ... everyone in Darren's junior high loved it. Trevor Winthrop-Baines and Concerned Citizen Stan grew up to be Greg Klymkiw and Guy Maddin, members of the Winnipeg Film Group and two of Winnipeg's (and this country's) most interesting alternative filmmakers (see *Movies*).

## Canadian Shows That Didn't Suck (and a Few That Do)

Following are a handful of short essays on a few of the highlights from Canadian urban television programming over the last several decades. We won't even pretend to be comprehensive—why bother?—because you probably can't find this stuff on the tube now anyway. Note that we're purposely ignoring the vast majority of lame soulless copycat works featuring detectives in Vancouver and Bay Street types in Toronto. Those shows are as forgettable as the following are memorable. So just take these few scraps of cathode nostalgia (see *Nostalgia*) and try to wring what little comfort you can from their pale blue light.

***King of Kensington*** Long before you could say bad words during prime time on CBC (thank you, Ken

Courtesy CBC

What a guy. Al and Company ruled
Kensington Market and the airwaves.

Finkleman), the best that we could muster as a half-hour Canadian sitcom was *King of Kensington*. It starred Al Waxman as Larry King, an average guy who ran a variety store in Toronto's Kensington Market with his wife Kathy and his mother Gladys. *King of Kensington* began its first regular season on CBC in September 1975 and ran to the end of March 1980.

Even if it was only competently mediocre, *King of Kensington* was still better than 90% of what passes for TV comedy. Jumping the Shark <www.jumpthe shark.com>, the infamous website that details the moment at which all sitcoms invariably take a turn for the worse (named after the episode of *Happy Days* where Fonzie jumps a shark tank in Al's parking lot on his motorcycle), claims that *King of Kensington never* jumped the shark … unless it was during the episode where Al and Kathy get divorced. One reader at JTS observed, "The message to me and all my friends in our teens appeared to be that a perfectly fine marriage between decent, funny people could fall apart for *absolutely no good reason*. Thanks for the trauma, Waxman."

Al Waxman, the eponymous King, starred in over 1,000 TV shows, plays, and films and received the Order of Ontario and the Order of Canada for his contributions to Canadian cultural identity. Shortly before his death at the age of 65, it had become obvious to anyone who paused to think about it that Al was the Canadian Once and Future King, forever enshrined in the collective imagination as our sovereign. During the merciless "Talking to Americans" segment of *This Hour Has 22 Minutes*, Rick Mercer began bearing greetings to Americans from Al Waxman, the King of Canada.

***Kids in the Hall*** When asked where he got his material, Jack Benny frequently quipped, "From the kids in the hall," referring to the long line of hungry young gag writers who were perpetually queued up outside his office.

What made (and continues to make) KITH great is that they fuse intelligence with outrageousness—a combination that no troupe since Monty Python's Flying Circus has managed consistently. We could blather on all day about their characters—Buddy Cole, the Chicken Lady, Mr. Tiscic the Head-Crushing Man, Bruno Puntz Jones and Francesca Fiore, Manservant Hecubus, the Cops, the Hookers, Queen Elizabeth, Gavin the Annoying Kid, Satan, and the people in the corporate offices of AT & Love—but even a comparatively lame stable of writers will occasionally crank out an interesting character or two.

Their real genius manifested itself in the moments of absolute jaw-dropping incredulity that the show produced: Scott Thompson leaping onto the stage while the word "FAGGOT" appeared across the bottom of the screen in huge red letters; Dave Foley in a blood-drenched suit, explaining apologetically to a suburban woman that because he was an *axe* murderer, he really

*arts & entertainment* **145**

TV

couldn't accept the loan of her *hatchet* (Foley's uncanny resemblance to Paul Bernardo only making matters worse); Mark McKinney in a chicken suit masturbating to an explosive, feathery orgasm on a coin-op horsey ride at the mall; a baseball player buying a 20-dollar whore for Bruce McCulloch's "Cancer Boy"; Kevin McDonald in drag. In the context of Canadian television in the early 90s, this was highly subversive stuff; citing it out of context a full decade later fails to convey the full impact.

The Kids in the Hall (Dave Foley, Bruce McCulloch, Kevin McDonald, Mark McKinney, Scott Thompson) formed in Toronto in 1984, though the roots of the troupe go back to 1981 in Calgary. In 1986, SNL producer Lorne Michaels saw one of their Toronto shows; by 1989, they had their own show, which aired for five years on HBO, CBS Comedy Central, and the CBC. They disbanded in 1994 to work on their own projects, but have done two reunion tours to date, with fans clamouring for one last glimpse of characters from their glory days.

(NB: Many others added to the genius of KITH— including Paul Bellini, the fifth Kid and one of their best writers; Shadowy Men on a Shadowy Planet's Don Pyle, Brian Connelly, and the late, lamented Reid Diamond, who served up the instrumental surf-rock soundtrack for every episode; and the show's many regulars, from the It's A Fact Girl to the 30 Helens.)

Online episode guide and sketch transcripts: <www.kithfan.org/work/transcripts/index.html>.

***Degrassi (Original Flavour)*** When cultural anthropologists of the future unearth ancient VHS tapes of *Beverley Hills 90210* and the various *Degrassi* shows, they'll have no trouble telling which was produced in the US and which was produced in Canada. The *Degrassi* shows are almost embarrassing to watch because they're so frank, candid, and unencumbered by all the gloss and fluff of *90210*. Sure, everybody fantasized about Brenda and Brandon and Kelly and Dylan, but you could actually *be* Joey or Spike or Wheels or Caitlin. As one fan site puts it, "*Degrassi* was about real life and all the fun that goes along with it: suicide, pregnancy, cool high-school bands [the Zit Remedy, featuring Joey, Snake, and Wheels], eating disorders, bullies, pornography, getting beaten by your bearded boyfriend, getting the courage to dump that same bearded boyfriend, hitch-hiking, booze, fake IDs, and the most important of all: the art of 'buying everything in the drugstore so you can blend a package of condoms into the purchase...'"

The Degrassi empire was the brainchild of Linda Schuyler, a former junior high school teacher, and Kit Hood, a video editor and former child actor. There were three series in all: *The Kids of Degrassi Street*, *Degrassi Junior High*, and *Degrassi High*, followed by *School's Out* (a made-for-TV movie) and a documentary miniseries called *Degrassi Talks*. As we write this, the first episodes of *Degrassi: The Next Generation* are hitting the airwaves (no word yet on whether the new cast features any Klingons).

While the series were great, it was *School's Out* that was the crown jewel of the Degrassi universe's credibility. Everyone drinks beer—*a lot*. Joey shags Tessa, even though he's still dating the virginal Caitlin. Wheels works on his crappy car all summer at the same time as he's developing a serious drinking problem (an ominous pattern is developing ...). Tessa gets knocked up, is rejected by Joey and books an abortion; meanwhile, Joey and Caitlin get back together and then *they* do

## CANADA AND THE SIMPSONS

*Yes, we know we're funny, but on The Simpsons, they're laughing at us, not with us … (actually, at least two Canadians write for the show: Jeff Poliquin from Saskatchewan and Tim Long from London).*

- *"When Flanders Failed" (7F23): Homer is watching the CFL draft picks for the Roughriders and the Rough Riders.*
- *"Dog of Death" (8F17): In a financially tight moment, the Simpsons dress Maggie in a Crown Royal bag.*
- *"Homer's Triple Bypass" (9F09): Homer to Marge: "Don't worry, Marge. America's health-care system is second only to Japan, Canada, Sweden, Great Britain and well, all of Europe, but you can thank your lucky stars we don't live in Paraguay!"*
- *"Homer vs. Patty & Selma" (2F14): Marge's international coffee flavour: "Montreal Morn."*
- *"Bart on the Road" (3F17): The episode where Bart, Milhouse, Martin, and Nelson take a trip to Knoxville, telling their parents that they're staying at the Sheraton Hotel in Canada for a National Grammar Rodeo. On the way, they pass a car with a squabbling family inside; when Nelson beans the father in the back of the head, he yells, "That's it! Back to Winnipeg!" Later, Martin wakes up in the backseat, believing he's in the great cornfields of Canada. On the way, they see Cronenberg's Naked Lunch. Nelson says, "I can think of at least two things wrong with that title."*
- *"You Only Move Twice" (3F23): Bart is moved to a remedial class and meets a student who says, "I moved here from Canada, and they think I am a little slow, eh?"*
- *"The Canine Mutiny" (4F16): Bart gets a credit card and buys Vancouver smoked salmon for Marge.*
- *"Homer vs. New York State" (4F22): Bart yells from the Statue of Liberty: "Hey, immigrants! Beat It! Country's full!" The captain says "Okay, folks. You hear the lady. Back into the hold. We'll try Canada."*
- *"The Fly King" (5F11): Ralph Wiggum is the Canadian delegate at Lisa's model United Nations. When a fight breaks out, Ralph starts singing "O Canada."*
- *"The Bongo Show" (5F15): Bart's newscast: "Some say the birds flew to Canada; others say Toronto."*
- *"Homer to the Max" (AABF09): President Clinton makes a rapid departure after being told that Quebec has the bomb.*
- *"E-I-E-I-(ANNOYED GRUNT)" (AABF19): The Simpsons watch a Zorro flick partially funded by the National Film Board of Canada.*
- *"Saddlesore Galactica" (BABF09): Bachman Turner Overdrive are playing; Bart asks, "Who are those pleasant old men?"*
- *"Skinner's Sense of Snow" (CABF06): In Vegas, the Simpsons watch the French-Canadian "Cirque de Purée."*
- *"The Bart Wants What It Wants" (DABF06): The Simpsons go to Toronto—jokes aplenty. (See the epigraph to this book).*

the nasty. Allison nearly drowns; Snake saves her. Wheels gets liquored up and cracks up his car, killing a kid in the process; Lucy, in the passenger seat, leaves the scene on a spinal board. Snake goes to jail, Caitlin goes to university, Simon and Alexa get married. Not bad for CBC.

Unfortunately, some of the Degrassi actors took the gritty realism a little too much to heart. Tyson Talbot was jailed for one year for attacking two teachers and a student in 1990. Byrd Dickens, who played Scott, was arrested in August 1991 in connection with three sexual assaults and was acquitted a year later.

TV

***This Hour Has 22 Minutes*** … aka her Majesty's Loyal Opposition. For nine years now, Mary Walsh, Cathy Jones, Greg Thomey, and Rick Mercer (recently replaced by Colin Mochrie) have constituted the closest thing that Canada has to a functioning left-wing critique of Big Government.

*22 Minutes* <www.22minutes.com> bases its format and title on the controversial *This Hour Has Seven Days*, which ran from 1964 to 1966. The creation of Patrick Watson and Douglas Leiterman, *Seven Days* was a satirical public affairs show in the best CBC tradition—meaning that it was in turn based on a British program, *That Was the Week That Was*. Those who do not remember the past are condemned to view it in reruns.

In some respects, the shock value of the guerrilla media tactics practised by *Seven Days* has lost some of its oomph in our media-saturated world. Back in that day, putting KKK members on stage with black civil rights leaders and interviewing Miss Canada contestants in their nighties was pushing the envelope of the permissible. For these sorts of antics, Watson and Leiterman were fired and the show was cancelled by the CBC brass.

But Walsh and company have had a few amazing moments of their own: convincing Arkansas governor Mike Huckabee to congratulate Canada on tape for preserving the "national igloo" that houses the Parliament of Canada; presenting Prime Minister Jean Chrétien with a Genie for Best Actor in a Continuing Role; and, gloriously, after Alliance leader Stockwell Day's assertion that they would hold a referendum whenever a write-in demanded one, penning an online petition "calling for a national referendum on the very important issue that the government of Canada force Stockwell Day to change his first name to Doris." The petition received hundreds of thousands of signatures in a matter of days, and has since toured the art galleries of the nation, which is more than can be said for Mr. Day.

***The Newsroom*** Ken Finkleman, Canada's only TV auteur, plays high-strung, self-obsessed TV news director George in this sarcastic send-up. Filmed on location at CBC headquarters in Toronto, in *The Newsroom* reality often slipped into the fiction, making this short-lived but much remembered series that much more acerbic. Written by Finkleman and adroitly acted by an ensemble cast who refuse to crack up no matter how acid the antics, *The Newsroom* is a great example of what Canadian TV could and should be, despite its obvious derivation from *The Larry Saunders Show*. In the opening scene of the first episode, news producer Jeremy is talking to George about the day's headlines. Apparently, 200 people died when a train crashed and fell into the Congo river. The following conversation ensues.

> *George: Are there piranha in the Congo?*
> *Jeremy: I wouldn't swim there.*
> *George: Make it "piranha-ridden" Congo.*
> *Jeremy: How about "piranha-infested" Congo?*
> *George: Better.*

Thirteen brilliant episodes.

# Movies

When it comes to Canadian movies, the situation is truly abysmal … not because there aren't great movies to see, but because our cities fail us by never showing them. More than 90% of what gets onscreen in this country is

The Bingo Robbers hold up a drug store.

Hollywood dreck, and when a filmmaker puts a great movie together such as the ones we're gonna shortly tell you about, there's a good chance that even if it gets rave reviews and wins awards, it won't show up in your city.

It's a terrible thing and a perpetual problem. The only way we can do something about it is to go see Canadian movies when they do get that whopping one-week run at the smallest theatre in town. Instead of ignoring Canadian cinema, we should be celebrating it. The worst Can-Con dog is more interesting than the vast major- ity of Hollywood movies. To prepare you for your future as an urban Canadian film buff, here's a roundup of essentials to rent from your local video store. (And don't get us started about the lameness of video stores. Suffice it to say you ain't gonna find these at Blocksuckers.)

***Bingo Robbers*** (**Lois Brown, 2000**)  The bulk of *Bingo Robbers* takes place in the '76 Chrysler that Vallis calls home. Accompanied by Nancy—who alternates between despising and desiring her deadbeat drummer pal—the two cruise the streets of St. John's brooding over love, violence, and the best way to take down the 24-Hour Bingo Extravaganza without alerting their relatives— many of whom are sure to be in the hall when they strike. Canada's first digital video feature film.

***Parsley Days*** (**Andrea Dorfman, 2000**)  A Halifax hip- ster soap opera in which bike-repair instructor Kate finds out she's pregnant, has a mid-20s life crisis, and strug- gles to reassess her priorities and escape the influence of her various counter-culture pals, including a herbalist who advises her that if she eats enough parsley she'll spontaneously abort. Meanwhile, hypersensitive sex- counsellor boyfriend Ollie tries to figure out what's wrong, and Kate has hilarious and lustful encounters

with an unknown teen who cruises through town on a red bike, taunting her with his permed locks.

***Last Night*** (**Don McKellar, 1998**)  The world is end- ing. How are you going to spend your last night? This sad, moving comedy examines the reaction of a loosely knit group of Torontonians. McKellar's short film *Blue*, with David Cronenberg as a porn-obsessed carpet sales- man who somehow fails to notice the lustful attentions of his secretary, is also a treat.

***Rude*** (**Clement Virgo, 1995**)  Interlocking inner-city Toronto stories tied together by the pirate radio DJ Rude. Gritty, but with a fantasy element.

***Ginger Snaps*** (**John Fawcett, 2000**)  The elder of a pair of outcast suburban goth sisters succumbs to lycan- throphy (werewolfism) at the onset of menstruation and eats her first boyfriend in their ticky-tack, half-finished basement. Cool.

***Twilight of the Ice Nymphs*** (**Guy Maddin, 1997**) Psychos, horny widows, mesmers, and more populate

MOVIES

*Arthur Lipsett plundered NFB discards for material, and made intricate collages that relied on pace and soundtrack to jar watchers into the familiar strangeness of A bombs exploding, animals in cages, and the blank faces of urban life. His brilliant short films like* Very Nice, Very Nice *and* 21-87 *captured the anxiety of sweeping technological change and ensuing alterations to Canadian life by using a high-speed pastiche of cut-and-paste found footage. Lipsett's techniques would have been more at home on MuchMusic than they were among the gentle animations and earnest instructional documentaries of the Film Board's golden age. Ahead of his time, Lipsett influenced filmmakers as diverse as Stanley Kubrick and George Lucas, and was even nominated for an Academy Award.*

*But Lipsett struggled with manic depression, and his ability to fuse questions around the ideology of urbanity and technology with a distinct bleak humour went undervalued and underappreciated. He made his last hopelessly flawed work for the Film Board in 1971, and drifted away, all but forgotten. Arthur Lipsett took his own life in 1986.*

this fantastic confection from Winnipeg's weirdest and best filmmaker. A sort of prairie Brothers Grimm flick, if you know what we mean. Also watch for the documentary about the making of the film, narrated by Tom Waits, and Maddin's other twisted masterpieces, including *Careful*, *Archangel*, and *The Heart of the World*.

***Rabid* (David Cronenberg, 1976)**  Early Cronenberg is an acquired taste (marijuana helps), and this tale of a feral lady (played by porn queen Marilyn Chambers) spreading deadly rabies across Montreal via a weird retractable stinger thing under her arm, somehow

acquired after surgery following a car accident, tells you why.

***Goin' Down the Road* (Donald Shebib, 1970)**  Re-released for its 20th anniversary in 1990, this is the ultimate tale of rural/urban disillusion. Set mostly in Toronto, the film follows two uneducated blue-collar drifters as they leave Nova Scotia to find their fortune in Toronto. The harsh cityscape sucks them in and spits them out, leaving them broke, desperate, and finally turning to crime. Lots of shots of littered streets and bright flashing advertisements cutting through the night sky. Is there a moral here? The classic SCTV parody ("Lots of jobs for you and me!") is almost as good.

***Léolo* (Jean-Claude Lauzon, 1992)**  "Because I dream," says Leo, "I'm not." Trapped in a Montreal tenement slum with a dysfunctional family (including a dad memorably obsessed with everyone's bowel movements), Leo must find a way to distance himself from the horrors of his life. The result is a sumptuous, wonderful, but incredibly bleak movie that blends fantasy, possibility, and failure.

***Cube* (Vincenzo Natali, 1997)**  A group of six strangers with varying shortcomings and abilities awake to find themselves imprisoned inside a moving maze of interconnected cubes that's peppered with deathtraps (in the opening sequence, one guy gets chopped into tiny little pieces by a giant hard-boiled egg slicer). A science fiction allegory for big-city life in the new millennium. See if you can guess who survives.

***The Adjuster* (Atom Egoyan, 1991)**  Still the thinking person's fave Egoyan film, even for those who believe that his work isn't relevant to anyone who lives outside of Toronto's Annex neighbourhood. The story of a Toronto

# Rage of the Citizenry–Cruel Face of the Business–The Innocent Victims

by Malcolm Fraser, from *Moving Picture Views*, Toronto

*Moving Picture Views* is published out of the newly expanded city of Toronto, known far and wide as our nation's centre for film and television production. The lion's share of this production consists of American TV network series, miniseries and specials: hastily knocked-off product of the utmost mediocrity. The attraction of our city lies in its fortuitous combination of two factors: a lack of visual character (enabling it to substitute for a generic U.S. city) and the continually plummeting value of our currency.

Another quality of our town was mentioned in a recent issue of *Filmmaker* magazine, wherein producer Dolly Hall was quoted as enthusing: "Even a simple thing like closing off a city street is so much easier in Canada because nobody hassles your parking production assistants … in Toronto, closing down a whole street is just another film shoot, and the locals don't even blink."

Having spent three years working in precisely the area described above—clearing streets of their cars through pamphleteering and verbal harassment in preparation for the arrival of the film trucks—I can attest that the only value of Hall's statement lies in its humour. People in Toronto hate film crews; the best reaction I can hope for after telling someone they can't park, or have to move their car, is a sarcastic roll of the eyes, though more often it's a hostile and profanity-laced tongue-lashing followed by the person either dramatically driving away or parking despite my request and walking off in a self-righteous huff.

I should stress here that I not only sympathize but agree with anyone who resents or dislikes film crews. The presence of a crew in one's neighbourhood is a drag; the vast majority of workers in the film industry could charitably be described as personally and professionally unpleasant. They yell and swear a lot for no reason. They wear sunglasses when it's not sunny. They refer to lesser crew members in the third person, and in a manner more befitting objects. They call vehicles "vehicles" (e.g., "Can I get that vehicle moved, please?"). Their treatment of the people whose neighbourhoods they invade ranges from ignorance to belligerence. Their appalling lack of simple manners, work ethic, and basic human decency is matched only by their disregard for the environment that surrounds them: they throw garbage everywhere, and leave their minivans on for hours with neither activity nor occupant.

Nonetheless, the general population's reaction to film-crew invasion is a source of unending irritation to me. I do not defend film crews because of any lofty importance attached to film—as stated, most of the film shot in Toronto is worthless garbage. I do, however, think that in the greater scheme of things, the inconvenience caused by the

continued

> **People in Toronto hate film crews; the best reaction I can hope for after telling someone they can't park, or have to move their car, is a sarcastic roll of the eyes, though more often it's a hostile and profanity-laced tongue-lashing.**

MOVIES

# SNACKING WITH THE STARS: *A Guide to Sneaking Food on Film Shoots*

## Identifying the Shoot

*Look for the following items in abundance:*

Two-way radio

Pylon

Big trailer

Cop

Road block

Lighting rig

## Finding the Food

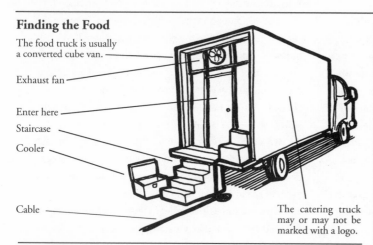

The food truck is usually a converted cube van.

Exhaust fan

Enter here

Staircase

Cooler

Cable

The catering truck may or may not be marked with a logo.

## Your Disguise

Black scruffy clothes

Utility belt w/ multi-tool pouch

Clipboard

Tape

## Helpful Words and Phrases

**"I'm a Daily"**
Translation: "I'm a temporary worker who you probably wouldn't recognize."

**"I'm a friend of the associate producer"**
The AP is a cryptic yet important position.

**Craft Services**
Refers to the company who provides the food on the film shoot.

**Call Sheet**
This extensive photocopied document provides lots of information about the shoot including the names of all the key personnel, shoot schedule and shot list. They are frequently distributed at the craft services truck.

**Subs  (short for Substantials)**
These are the hot meals that are prepared for the crew 3 hours after they start and 3 hours after every meal.

---

### ----IMPORTANT----
#### CRAFT SERVICES PROTOCOL

a) Do not go into fridges, cupboards, or shelves.
b) Serve yourself from the food on trays.

---

presence of a film crew is disproportionate to the fury that Toronto residents regularly unleash on powerless crew employees such as myself.

I recall working in an upper-middle-class residential neighbourhood (incidentally, the absolute worst kind for this sort of work; people at either end of the economic spectrum are much more friendly and helpful) and flexing my diplomatic muscles in the hope of getting a gentleman to move his car from the front of his house to a block away, a journey of some twenty seconds.

"I know it's a bit of a drag," I allowed.

"Yeah, it's a lot of a drag, actually," he snapped.

I had to bite my tongue on the words: "Well, actually, you know, not really. There are much, much worse things that

*In the greater scheme of things, the inconvenience caused by the presence of a film crew is disproportionate to the fury that Toronto residents regularly unleash on powerless crew employees.*

can happen to a person than to have the distance between your house and your car be twenty seconds instead of five seconds." It should always be remembered, though, that for a certain class of person, slight inconvenience is, in fact, the absolute worst thing that can happen.

Clearly, the conflict between the insensitive, uncouth film crews and the uptight, idle residents of Toronto cannot be resolved by mere diplomacy at this juncture. As one caught between the residents and the crews, my allegiances are torn, but my dislike of film crews wins out in the end. With that in mind, I hereby propose the following measures for residents to escalate the conflict in order to get the upper hand.

1. Don't yell at the pamphleteers or pylon-watchers. They have no power; most of the time they don't even know the people they're working for. It is also unlikely that you can say anything to them that they don't hear several times daily (note: "I pay taxes!" is second only to "Hey, can I be in the movie?" in the pantheon of idiotic passerby comment). You probably have subordinates of your own that you can take out your frustrations on.

2. If you have a parking permit for your car, you can stubbornly hold your ground. Eventually, they will try to pay you off. If money doesn't satisfy your powerlust, just stay put. You're allowed to; that's what the permit is good for. They'll have to figure out some way to work around it, and if they don't, who cares? (Note: if you don't have a permit, none of the above applies and they can tow your car if they want to.)

3. Almost all the vehicles on a film set (note the correct use of "vehicles," as it applies to all manner of automotive devices) have the keys in them at all times, either in the ignition or under the sun visor (or, if the "transport" guys are really tricky, in the gas pump pocket at the vehicle's side). You can take a minivan for a joyride, or grab the keys and drop them down the sewer.

4. A crew needs quiet when they're shooting. You can blast your radio, lawnmower or other noise polluter and ruin everything. They will eventually offer you money to stop. (Once, a crafty film crew sent a famous actor over to ask a radio-blaster to stop—but this was a notoriously nice famous actor, and most of them aren't nice at all, so don't get your hopes up.)

5. Special note for the poverty-stricken and/or freeloaders: there is a truck full of snacks on every film set. Go in and get free food. If anybody looks suspicious, or asks who you are, tell them you're a set dec daily.

If enough havoc is wrought, perhaps film crews will be taken down a peg and forced to behave more properly towards their fellow human beings. I really doubt it, though. Most residents just like to complain; they'll never do anything about it—besides, all you can really do (other than the suggestions above) is go to city hall and wade through red tape, which will probably discourage you pretty quickly. I strongly suspect that inflamed residents will simply continue to do what they always have: yell and swear at the people lowest on the ladder. In this, at least, they are united with their enemies on the crew.

MOVIES

insurance man who gets a little too involved in the lives of his clients, creating an artificial family in a bleak, half-finished housing tract. Features Maury Chaykin's best performance. Sterile, austere, and fascinating.

*Jesus of Montreal* **(Denys Arcand, 1989)**  Well, okay, the name kinda says it all. Jesus in—you guessed it—Montreal. No, seriously though, in this deep, meaningful flick, a group of actors stages a socially relevant passion play. Gradually, script and life begin to blur.

*Maelstrom* **(Denis Villeneuve, 2000)**  A talking fish being chopped into pieces narrates the story of Bibiane, a budding fashion outlet mogul in her late 20s who's so busy spiralling out of control that she barely notices ploughing over a fishmonger with her sportscar.

*Waydowntown* **(Gary Burns, 2001)**  Funny movie in which Calgary 20-somethings bet on who can survive for a month without leaving the office/mall/apartment complex their lives revolve around. Also check out *House Party* and *Suburbanators* for more Alberta angst.

## Film Shoots

Even though Toronto is unmistakably Toronto and Vancouver even more distinctively Vancouver, Canadian cities are always being used as generic stand-ins for lame American movies and TV series set in New York or San Francisco. Infamously, in Jackie Chan's chop-socky classic *Rumble in the Bronx*, the mountains around Vancouver figure prominently in the background. Who knew you could ski in Yonkers? We've also witnessed Toronto's distinctive "Red Rocket" streetcars go whizzing by wrinkly old David Carradine in *Kung Fu: The Legend Continues*

in what's supposed to be San Francisco's Chinatown district. Do filmmakers *really* think we're that stupid?

Evidently, judging by the way they occupy their locales. Film crews sweep down and clog up entire blocks with trailers, pylons, tripods, and giant lights that glare into residents' windows all night long. Rude types in security windbreakers make sure that we don't deign to walk on our city streets or sidewalks during a precious shoot. When one citizen in Toronto's Kensington Market struck back by allegedly whistling loudly on the set, she was apparently handcuffed, thrown in the back of a cruiser, strip-searched, and jailed overnight.

# Comics: Revenge of the Nerds

Being a big name in the comic world doesn't amount to much in Canada.

If you're Julie Doucet, one of the world's most respected and well-known alternative comic artists, it leads to getting your very personal and funny yet frightening work published in several European countries as well as your own, while still struggling for recognition in your home province.

"I work in English so I can sell my work in the US," says Doucet, a francophone Montrealer who's lived everywhere from Berlin to New York. "So I'm not as known in Quebec as I guess I could be. I'm well known in alternative circles in the US, but in English Canada, I don't know who reads my comics. I published a book of comics in France, but it's very difficult to find it in Quebec."

So goes the strange, fabulous world of Canadian comics. The truth is, our cities harbour some of the best graphic novelists or comic artists (whatever you want to call them) in the world. In addition to Julie, names like Seth, Joe Matt, Chester Brown, and David Collier are renowned in pockets of comic culture everywhere.

Chris Oliveros runs *Drawn & Quarterly*, North America's foremost publisher of adult alternative comics. Although he's based in Montreal and publishes the work of Canadian artists, he notes that the majority of interest in *Drawn & Quarterly* publications comes from the United States and Europe.

Indeed, when we talk about adult-themed comics or graphic novels, we aren't talking about the action adventure sagas of Superman, the X-men, or even the angst-ridden Spiderman you remember from your adolescence. These works are intensely personal, quiet, and meticulous. If they're overlooked, it's because they downplay their unique ability to convey something important about the world. These are stories about life—urban life—and none of Canada's great comic talents thinks for a second that telling their

adult stories in a form still thought of by most people as kidstuff will lead them to fame and fortune.

Which isn't to say these artists don't have their deserved admirers. Indeed, growing legions of fans are coming to appreciate their work—even in the Canadian cities where they work.

What follows are descriptions of and selections from our fave urban Canadian comic artists—both those who subsist in the underground, publishing sporadic works of zine genius, and the *Drawn & Quarterly* talents more familiar to those who regularly haunt the Beguiling and similar venues across the nation. (Note for those who have not yet known the bliss of the graphic novel: Toronto's Beguiling is the Markham Street institution unparalleled for knowledge and selection of adult Can-comics.)

## Can-Comics: The Big Names

**Chester Brown** Perhaps Canada's most formally daring cartoonist, Brown moved in *Yummy Fur* (one of the longest-running alternative comics ever) from the sardonic, scatological humour of *Ed the Happy Clown* through Biblical parables to minimalist neurotic autobiography (*The Playboy*). He's most recently blessed us with the surreal intricacy of *Underwater*, and is currently shaping an austere but compelling

COMICS

retelling of the story of Louis Riel and the Métis Rebellion.

**David Collier**  Collier takes on big subjects, but doesn't shy away from autobiography and inserting himself into the story. His *Portraits from Life* gives us illustrated accounts of the lives of figures as diverse as David Milgaard, the fake "Indian" Grey Owl, and the Saskatoon Lily, Ethel Catherwood, the darling of the 1928 Amsterdam Olympics (see *Attractions, Sports*).

**Julie Doucet**  Montreal's premier comic talent and among the top cartoonists in the world. There's something utterly compelling about Julie's autobiographical stories. Maybe it's the obsessively detailed drawing style, or the naive and innocent way her alter ego does things ranging from destroying the city during a menstrual Queen Kong–style rampage to making yet another poor career choice.

**Joe Matt**  Known for his autobiographical tales of lust, masturbation, and more masturbation in *Peep Show*. Matt shows us the horny urban antisocialite up close and personal … disturbingly so.

**Seth**  Professional anachronist Seth imbues his characters with a moody, expressionistic gravity that perfectly captures the mythical 1950s over which he obsesses (see *Zeitgeist, Nostalgia*). His 1996 book *It's a Good Life If You Don't Weaken*, set in a grey Toronto as sad as it is compelling, is

the testament of a perfectionist with a yearning for yesteryear.

**Maurice Vellekoop**  Another *Drawn & Quarterly* alumnus whose work Bruce LaBruce describes as "a light-hearted yet disturbing cross between Edward Gorey and Tom of Finland," Vellekoop's archly queer drawings have been featured in everything from homemade chapbooks to *Vogue*. Collections include *Vellevision* and *Maurice Vellekoop's ABC Book: A Homoerotic Primer* (winner of the 1999 Firecracker Alternative Book Award for best sex book).

## The Indies

**Marc Bell**  This permanent slacker delves into obsessive autobiographical weirdness wherever he resides through the vehicle of his peripatetic Mojo Action Companion Unit. Our favourite character: Black Sabbath Shrimpy.

**Fidele Castree**  This up-and-coming Montrealer perfectly captures a queasy sense of the unexpected as her child-like characters roam around under text like "Then, she takes a mink scarf and strangles it. She puts the body in a garbage bag."

**Mark Connery**  Creator of the hermaphroditic Rudy the Magic Kat and his polymorphous friends, such as Phil the Triangle (who frequently looks more like

By Julie Doucet from *My New York Diary* (Drawn & Quarterly, 1999)

# Literature (the New Urban)

If the literature of a city is the map of its collective soul, then Canadian cities are in trouble. Many of the books written in the last decade completely re-imagine the placid urbanity of Canada's cities, repopulating them with scores of angry disenfranchised quasi-citizens who see in its crowded streets, its suburbs, its offices, its stores, and its shitty overpriced apartments not the gilded benevolence of potential riches but the desperate poverty of every individual's lost desire. A new group of Canadian writers has emerged to challenge the twin myths of Canada as a pristine wilderness with clean and terribly pleasant cities. In this new urban literature, city dwellers struggle for identity and, in some cases, survival as they hunger for something bigger and better than subsistence, bureaucracy, and the daily grind.

Granted, there's resistance to this fledgling, unconscious movement. Many Canadian writers share an implicit agreement not to portray our fair land as an urban environment obsessed with the accumulation of wealth, as a country at odds with its own metaphorical love of wilderness, as a country of strip malls and highways and subdivisions and addicts in gutters. New urban writing, in contrast, turns its back on the values that Canadian literature has espoused over the last three decades. It's anti-society, amoral, and, worst of all, anti-literary.

a heart). Connery's stories come so frustratingly close to making sense that it'll make your head hurt.

**Sophie Cossette** It takes a Montrealer to give us this kind of kink—busty 1950s-style broads engage in everything from bondage to larceny. X-rated to the extreme, Cossette's work crosses every boundary of bad taste. Yum!

**Tony Walsh** Created one of the most memorable big-city comic characters ever, the violent and macabre Ratboy of the *Planet Ugly* and *He Is Just A Rat* series. Whether he's scrapping with his nemesis Rotten Chicken Lips or mucking it up in his day job at Meaty Burgers (okay, so he only lasts one day), Ratboy can be counted on to behave disgracefully.

**Brad Yung** A Vancouver satirist whose ongoing series *Stay As You Are* never fails to offer priceless send-ups of West Coast urban slackerdom. Perhaps best known for the panel where a Yung alter ego engages in "apathy practice."

**Matt B.** Autobiographical comics from Toronto that manage to combine wide-eyed innocence with the urban sleaze of everyday life.

And yet, as a movement, it continues to grow, an unsubtle reaction to the upper-class mannerism of Robertson Davies, the gentle dilemmas of Alice Munro and Carol Shields, and even the ethnic nostalgia of Mordecai Richler. This is a literature to reflect the fact that Canada has the most doughnut stores per capita in the world (even before the looming Krispy Kreme incursion). According to the catchy advertisements you used to have to read in the bar bathroom while taking a piss, Canadians also consume the largest number of Slurpees in the world. These statistics point to a country whose literature has, over the last two decades, done it a great disservice. How many people eat doughnuts and drink Slurpees in the canonized works of Canadian writing? From snacks to stupid jobs, shockingly few of our writers have had much to say about the mundane details of urban life.

This, then, is new urban writing's unifying principle. Urban writers speak less of personal travails and existential showdowns with an indifferent landscape and more of lives lived in a shared metropolis, in the shadow of a promise that cannot be kept.

New urban Canadian writing provides some insight into the way generations of perpetual undergraduates (the "avant-grad," if you will) and professional waiters envision their country and their lives. But no matter how many adjectives we hang on it, this new urban Canadian writing will remain ambiguous. After all, are our cities not disingenuous, anonymous, and yet, somehow, deeply personal places? Like the urban spaces it represents, new Canadian urban writing is an ugly glorious sprawl, as compelling as it is horrifying.

These urban fictions are the flipside of population analysis. Statistics of the soul, they tell us about our cities and our lives. They frequently feature drugs, sex, and, occasionally, murder. Do they condemn the amoral, the seedy, the violent? Not really.

Imagine Dany Laferrière wandering through the streets in search of a single soul to join him for a meal of roasted park pigeon (his loneliness not just the epitome of the loneliness that is part and parcel of recent arrival in a strange land, but of being one of millions of similarly disenfranchised strangers). Laferrière confronts the new Canada of cities, a country of multiple citizenships and unspoken municipalities, where the challenge is no longer to explore the discovered wild but to examine the fallacies and dangers of exploration turned inward to the cloistered confines of consciousness. The stories of new urban literature are brutal yet lucidly reserved; these writers eschew the grotesque violence found in the urban literature of the United States. Well, usually …

With neither US-style hostility nor the fading insistence on old-world tradition, Canada's new urban writing, still wet pavement in the perplexing, interlocking sidewalk of 21st-century society, is as distinctive and compelling a reflection of post-industrial reality as anything in the sprawl of the developed world. It's in the cities—and in the writing that they've spawned—that

---

*Coming from Canada, being a writer and Jewish as well, I have impeccable paranoia credentials.*

*—Mordecai Richler*

---

LITERATURE

we'll rediscover and reinvent Canada. New urban Canadian fiction is not a plot convention but a force that explores the very real tensions in people's lives. It's not a movement of writing, but a movement to portray the way Canadian city dwellers live. (See *Poetry; Zeitgeist, Beginnings; Denizens, Immigrants; Shopping, Malls.*)

## Your New Urban Literature Primer

You already know about Richler, Atwood, Ondaatje, and the other barons of urban CanLit. Now it's time to get to know some of the seedier parts of the CanLit city.

### The Veterans

*The Golden Galarneaus,* **Jacques Godbout** The eighth novel by the veteran Montreal writer, essayist, and filmmaker. Richly plotted, this is the tale of a bumbling, innocent security guard embroiled in his brother's affairs as he searches for meaning in the malls and galleries of the world.

*Girl on the Subway and Other Stories* and *Malignant Humors,* **Crad Kilodney** The original original, Crad spent decades selling his books (and audiotapes he surreptitiously made of people harassing him) on Toronto streets before giving it all up in 1995. He vows never to write again, which

is too bad, because stories such as "Lightning Struck My Dick" have a brutal clarity and an existential (but never self-pitying) manner of propelling themselves forward. These days, Crad makes his living as a stock market speculator.

*Neuromancer, Count Zero, Mona Lisa Overdrive,* **William Gibson** The tripartite bible of cyberpunk and far, far, beyond the need for paraphrase, these books are the bricolaged map to the aesthetics of hip urban alienation. Essential.

*The Wednesday Flower Man,* **Dianne Warren** Finely crafted stories of tiny urban dramas. In the title story, a woman working in a floral shop obsesses over a man whose mysterious regular Wednesday floral deliveries lead her to near ruin.

*Henry Kafka and Other Stories,* **Stuart Ross** The Captain Canada of chapbook surrealism, Ross's stories feature saxophone-playing birds, Jewish angst, and an urban landscape full of surprises.

### The Weird

*Despair and Other Stories of Ottawa,* **André Alexis** The banal exterior of these Ottawa denizens gives way to a sinister labyrinth of possibilities. Funny and dark, it's the capital as you've yet to imagine it.

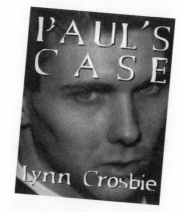

*Pontypool Changes Everything,* **Tony Burgess** A savage Swiftian allegory for our times, imagining the populace of the suburbs and small towns around Toronto as a horde of flesh-eating zombies. Soon to be a movie from Bruce McDonald.

*Paul's Case,* **Lynn Crosbie** The implications of Paul Bernardo's evil as told through diary, comics, poetry, news clippings, and more. Canada's most dangerous and subversive book?

*The Real Story,* **France Daigle** Set in a postmodern Moncton and told in an elliptical but epic style, this small book takes us in surprising directions, managing to be erotic and sterile at the same moment.

*Wish Book,* **Derek McCormack** Imagine a John Waters remake of the classic Tod Browning circus horror film *Freaks* and you're halfway there. McCormack is an amazing stylist, producing incredibly tight pages of deceptively simple-seeming James Ellroy-like sentences.

*Degrees of Nakedness,* **Lisa Moore** Travelling taxidermist sets up in the strip mall and meets a woman looking for distraction. This leads to romantic interest. Need we say more?

*The Child Garden,* **Geoff Ryman** A story of lesbian love between a purple girl and a polar bear in a future city where people eat language like candy and the walls of spaceships sprout flowers. This

kinder, gentler version of a William S. Burroughs novel from one of Canada's most brilliant expats won every award that contemporary SF has to offer.

*New Motor Queen City,* **Patricia Seaman** Eight excerpts from Mexican romance novels get the cut-up Situationist/ Roy Lichtenstein treatment from Seaman, who reorders their narratives and rewrites the dialogue to strip bare the follies of brides and bachelors everywhere. It's all here, from torrid tales of ancient Egypt told entirely in hieroglyphs to blaxploitation flicks, stolen skateboarder dialogues, and an oddly touching tribute to Kathy Acker.

*Dad Says He Saw You at the Mall,* **Ken Sparling** A compelling portrait of suburban family life. The protagonist struggles to find meaning in the quotidian antics of his children, wife, and co-workers. Told in a sparse prose full of pathos and humour, this is one of Canada's few legitimate cult classics.

*If you look at a book about Casa Loma, you will see that it originally had three bowling alleys. This was in 1914, the year construction in the castle ended.*

*When Tutti first learned she was pregnant, we went looking for a house to buy. I'm not as naive as I once was. I understand now why a guy might want to build a castle in the middle of a big city. And why he might want to put three bowling alleys in.*

—Ken Sparling, Dad Says He Saw You at the Mall

LITERATURE

## The Down-and-Out

*Monday Night Man* and *White Lung*, **Grant Buday**
These Vancouver books are the saddest, ugliest tales to ever make you laugh out loud. Follow the adventures of Buday's finely honed characters as they deal with everything from the closing of their bakery as a result of free trade to an accidental overdosing in a tenement bathtub. Buday portrays the invisible, grudging friendships that keep these down-and-out characters clinging to life.

*Can You Take Me There, Now?*, **Matthew Firth** Garbage men, disaffected convenience store clerks, and other urban figures lurk not on the margins but in the centre of this virulent collection. The morality of city life—or lack thereof—has never been more apparent than in these psychological explorations.

*The People One Knows* and *1978*, **(Daniel) Jones** Eight years after his suicide at age 34, the work of this truculent poet and fiction auteur seems increasingly relevant. His austere and unfairly dismissed autobiographical short story collection evokes an anti-literature that acutely prefigures the current sensibility of many young writers; solitude, substance abuse, and the soul-deadening day-to-day are at the very core of an emerging urban Canadian literature, and the sparse, confessional style of this book echoes through the margins of a new generation's prose.

*A Drifting Year*, **Dany Laferrière** A poetic, wry, beautiful account of this renowned Haitian writer's first year

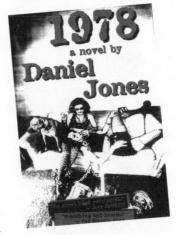

in Montreal. Laferrière is sarcastic, despairing, but never, ever, bitter. A fabulous read enhanced by its recipes for urban animals—pigeon, cat, etc.

## The Hip

*Titanium Punch*, **Yashin Blake** You don't often come across a novel with acknowledgements thanking Bolt Thrower, Brutal Truth, Cryptopsy, "and, of course" Motörhead. But, then again, books exploring the particularly un-literary world of Toronto's heavy metal/thrash scene are pretty scarce.

*Baroque-a-Nova*, **Kevin Chong** Saul St. Pierre, the 18-year-old narrator of Kevin Chong's accomplished first novel, has a lot to deal with: the suicide of his mother, a former folk icon who abandoned him as a baby; a recalcitrant father; the pseudo-Marxist German techno group Urethra Franklin; and the two luscious co-ed groupies who decide to spend their vacation visiting this bleak Vancouver suburb.

*The younger fans brought along their mothers. They wore their hair stylishly, slicked back or highlighted, and took turns peering at their watches. One little girl was staring at me. "Are you native?" She said this with a serious look on her face. I nodded. "When I grow up, I'm going to be native, too." A hyperactive man wearing a Molson Canadian T-shirt and sunglasses was standing among the reporters. As he talked, his elbow caught the girl in her eye. She began to cry silently, her mouth yapping*

*open like a little bird, ready to be fed. "Shit," the reporter said. "Shit." He pulled out a twenty dollar bill from his wallet and tried to fold it into her hand.*

—Kevin Chong, *Baroque-a-Nova*

***Darkness Then a Blown Kiss,* Golda Fried**  Fried is a surreal stylist whose prose straddles the Montreal-Toronto axis. Here, pizza becomes a box of jewels, every band is the next best thing, and every boyfriend leaves an invisible, enduring scar.

***Lenny Bruce Is Dead,* Jonathan Goldstein**  Oh Goldstein! Montreal's newest and bestest anxiety-ridden comic novelist slipped out of the country before this book was even published. Jewish neuroses meet a keen eye for the activities in diners and girls' bedrooms.

***How Insensitive,* Russell Smith**  This might have been the first truly urban novel to win a Governor General's award for literature. Smith documents the upscale producers, writers, artists, and poseurs that haunt Toronto's eight-dollar-a-drink bars.

***The Pornographer's Poem,* Michael Turner**  Coming of age in a 70s Vancouver suburb. The narrator is as compelling as he is disingenuous. Turner mixes the seedy with the tender and pulls everything off with a tour-de-force rollicking plot that surprises and shocks at every turn.

***A Grammar of Endings,* Alana Wilcox**  A librarian struggles to write the proverbial letter that serves as the tombstone at the end of many relationships, constantly failing to do so while dispassionately cataloguing the gut-wrenching depths of her own despair. Wilcox's

### STRANGE FUGITIVE

*Canada's first-ever urban novel,* Strange Fugitive *by Morley Callaghan, is a hard-boiled tale of 1920s Toronto under siege by "wops," "chinks," "niggers," and "kikes." When Callaghan's truculent anti-hero Harry Trotter isn't mixing it up with effeminate Jews and burly Italians, he's off wandering through the city, ruminating on his inability to get along with his wife. F. Scott Fitzgerald was a big fan of this book, probably because, like his own work, the protagonist is hard to love and spends an awful lot of his time in a milieu of speakeasies and bootleggers.*

*The book ultimately did well in New York, but was a failure in a Toronto the Good not ready to be portrayed as a haven of immigrants, seedy behaviour, and violent types like Callaghan's Trotter. Writing about the book,* the Mail and Empire *crowed: "One book dealer even went to the length of returning his copies to the publisher with the remark that the style was not for him."*

beautiful, brutally honest, meticulously crafted words are like a hail of razor-sharp icicles.

# Poetry and the Broccoli Theory of Literature (a Rant)

Canadians have a decidedly ambivalent attitude toward poetry. Almost no one buys or reads it—not even poets, in many cases—yet many people still believe that poetry is somehow the finest distillation of the very essence of a person's deepest feelings, poured out onto the page. Accompanying that belief is the nagging, guilty feeling that we should somehow be incorporating poetry into

LITERATURE

our daily lives because it's good for us to be exposed to it, even though *we don't really like it.*

This is the Broccoli Theory of Literature: Shut Up and Eat Your Poetry. It has resulted in, among other atrocities, the "Poetry on the Way" campaigns that place short, poorly typeset, seemingly arbitrarily selected nuggets of verse in the advertising spaces of the buses, streetcars, and subways of the nation. Poetry on the Way is like a multivitamin: small enough to be inoffensive yet appearing regularly enough to make transit riders feel righteous in their support of "culture" without having to actually buy any books.

On our frequent transit trips across Toronto, we've seen everything on Poetry on the Way banners from sonnets by William Shakespeare—a noted Canadian poet—to poetry by schoolchildren, but nothing systematic that would suggest that, say, someone has sat down with a list of Governor General's Award–winning poets, or even one of the country's better poetry anthologies, let alone a working knowledge of the nooks and crannies of the Canadian small/literary press since the 60s.

The resurgence of interest in having Poet Laureates for various cities and provinces is a related phenomenon, with the added distasteful mustiness of colonial anxiety. Poets Laureate are relics of the Empire, trotted out to perform on occasions that the state deems appropriate. The fact that they're beginning to reappear is not so much a sign that we as a nation are growing to love poetry but that we're longing for visible signs of our cultural legitimacy and power.

To recap: the misconception that poetry is somehow the product of "inspiration" in the minds of a few gifted souls is a hangover of English Romanticism, and is unadulterated, fertilizer-quality Bullshit. Poetry is a craft that can (and should) be studied carefully by those who wish to practise it. As our friend the poet Christian Bök is fond of saying, poetry is one of the only professions that can be entered by those who gleefully declare an absolute ignorance of its tools and contemporary context.

Following is an entirely subjective and utterly biased list of some of our favourite urban contemporary Canadian poetry:

*EUNOIA,* **Christian Bök**  By this point, quite possibly the fastest-selling book of poetry in Canadian history. *EUNOIA,* a book in five chapters, sequentially exhausts all the words in the English language that use only one vowel. This book blows the doors off the poncy European avant-garde by *actually delivering readable content* despite its mind-blowing conceptual constraints. Read it out loud or, if you get the chance, listen to Bök doing it; he's one of the best poetic performers of his generation.

***Days into Flatspin,*** **Ken Babstock**  The most carefully crafted Canadian book of lyric poems in ages. Babstock resets the wings of broken sonnets and makes them fly again. Not as good as new, but different … which is what we really needed anyway. "The expected has finally gone wrong."

**Objectionable Perspectives: Poetry & Other Objectionable Materials, jwcurry** A rare perfect-bound collection of concrete and visual work from the undisputed master of small-press, handcrafted poetry books made of recycled materials and assorted urban detritus. Scandalous, savage, meticulous.

**Comp, Kevin Davies** Post-Kootenay School of Writing (KSW) writing, too smart and too funny for its own good, but more than good enough for you. "You can more or less count on being part of the control group."

**But Could I Make a Living from It, Jeff Derksen** One of the cool things about Jeff Derksen is that it's hard to tell whether he's a genuine shit-kickin' redneck or actually the kind of good-for-nothing smartass punk that rednecks would sooner stomp all over than talk to. *But Could I Make a Living from It* is a series of Marxist bumper stickers from the most irreverent theorist of what's fucked about globalism. "He carefully explained his 'I'm so privileged that now I'm marginalized' position to me." Watch for Derksen's third full-length collection, *Muscle Cars,* coming soon.

**Ninety-Seven Posts with the Heads of Dead Men, Nancy Dembowski** White-hot anger put to use by cool intelligence in the forging of a sharp and dangerous feminism. Dembowski takes on the Big Boys of modern Western literature, plundering and rewriting Pound, Henry James, and T.S. Eliot with grace and fury. "The creative are no rulers."

**A Velvet Increase of Curiosity, Lise Downe** The lyric poem as the language of emotional and mental survival, but oddly impersonal, twisted into something resembling alien jewellery. "Instil us a queer cocoon."

**Last Instance, Dan Farrell** One of the precursors of the current wave of conceptual poetry, Farrell is now making videos, but we hope he'll return to poetry sometime soon. A series of re-examinations and re-presentations of the "innocuous" discourses that surround us, *Last Instance* will make you feel alienated even in your comfiest chair. "Who will remember when I'm delayed, a butcher, a baker; not me either."

**Debbie: An Epic, Lisa Robertson** A new kind of epic from Vancouver's Virgil, this lushly written, beautifully designed book was shortlisted for the 1998 Governor General's Award for poetry. "Because we are not free / my work shall be as obscure / as Love! unlinguistic!"

**Kingsway, Michael Turner** A long poem about a space between places, writing back through the work of Vancouver's own poets as the best route to the heart of the city, *Kingsway* is Turner's best book of poems to date. This is the book the TISH poets *should* have produced. "now people get on / just to get off"

**Spiral Agitator, Steve Venright** The third book of vertiginous delights from Sarnia's only native psychonaut, in the tradition of Henri Michaux, Terence McKenna,

LITERATURE

and Christopher Dewdney. "We're all going down the rabbit-hole. And that's an order."

Anyone *really* interested in contemporary Canadian poetry should go to the source—the publishers themselves. The Literary Press Group of Canada represents over 40 Canadian small presses (listed on their website <www.lpg.ca/publishers.html>). If you don't buy these books, you'll get the culture you deserve.

# How to Gracefully Exit a Poetry Reading

*The gods of poetry, small and quibbling, envious, slouch over the round table at the rear of the bar, their faces (twisted) half-lit by the yellow light of an uncovered bulb.*

—*Ron Silliman,* What

The key nugget of information to keep in mind when attempting to extricate oneself from a poetry reading is this: no one really wants to be there, *not even (especially not even) the poets who are actually reading* (they'd much rather be hanging with cool, fun people somewhere, but such is not their birthright). The practical upshot of this is that your exodus will produce either (a) collegial sympathy or (b) the foulest resentment in each person present, according to their various dispositions and current moods.

A few possible scenarios:

(a) *Reader sucks, audience sympathizes with you.* The most likely turn of events. Since poetry readings tend to take place in bars, it's usually possible to pretend that you're an unsuspecting patron who has wandered into the reading inadvertently, in the same way that one might inadvertently tread in something that a large dog has left in the street. Remember: there is strength in numbers. If people are leaving in droves, down your drink, grab your coat, and haul ass.

(b) *Reader sucks, audience resents your escape attempt.* Most likely to occur if you're in the front row of a small, crowded, overheated venue when you decide to leave. Spilling beer or cigarette butts on your neighbours will only make matters worse (though, in dire circumstances, you can always pretend that you're about to vomit, which will do wonders in terms of clearing a path). Note: It is entirely possible that some benighted souls in the audience may think the reader does *not* suck; your departure may be creating a contradiction in their world-view and sense of self large enough for them to do something as extreme as, well, giving you a dirty look. The likelihood of anyone being strong enough to physically harm you is extremely low … unless it's a spoken-word crowd, which may well be chock-full of aging heavy-metal musicians, suburban gangsta rappers, and other species of testosterone-laden postliterate thugs.

(c) *Reader sucks, resents your escape attempt; audience sympathizes with you.* Poets are drawn from the ranks of the socially challenged. On occasion, particularly insecure but extroverted poets may, in the middle of their readings, challenge your right to vacate the premises, or even to carry on conversations with your friends *sotto voce*. If this occurs,

# Common Exit Plays for Poetry Readings

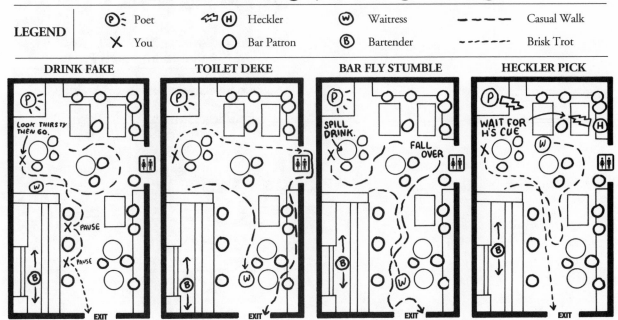

**LEGEND** | (P) Poet | (H) Heckler | (W) Waitress | - - - - Casual Walk
| X You | O Bar Patron | (B) Bartender | - - - - - Brisk Trot

**DRINK FAKE** | **TOILET DEKE** | **BAR FLY STUMBLE** | **HECKLER PICK**

don't fight it; the person with the microphone always wins. Instead, draw on your finest high-school method-acting moment—recall the single most humiliating thing that has ever happened to you. Burst into tears and run sobbing from the establishment (this will present more of a challenge if you have to wait for your credit card to be approved first).

(d) *Reader sucks, resents your escape attempt; audience also resents you.* Shoot your way out. This one is strictly Butch and Sundance.

(e) *Reader sucks, but nevertheless sympathizes with you.* Not as rare as you might think. Poets are an empathic lot—even the late, legendary guy's guy Al Purdy claimed to be "a sensitive man." What the hell: take the reader with you. It could be the start of a beautiful friendship.

## The Cheese Poet

James McIntyre was born in Forres, Scotland, in 1827 and immigrated to Canada at the age of 14. He first worked as a hired hand, but later became a furniture dealer in St. Catharines, Ontario. McIntyre was also a poet—the worst, in fact, in Canadian history, with the possible exception of Sarah Binks (but she wasn't real, so she loses by default). McIntyre's poems ranged over a great variety of topics, but he's best known for his writings about cheese. Here's a little slice:

**Ode on the Mammoth Cheese**
*(Weight over seven thousand pounds.)*

*We have seen thee, queen of cheese,*
*Lying quietly at your ease,*
*Gently fanned by evening breeze,*
*Thy fair form no flies dare seize.*

LITERATURE

*All gaily dressed soon you'll go*
*To the great Provincial show,*
*To be admired by many a beau*
*In the city of Toronto.*

*Cows numerous as a swarm of bees,*
*Or as the leaves upon the trees,*
*It did require to make thee please.*
*And stand unrivalled, queen of cheese.*

*May you not receive a scar as*
*We have heard that Mr. Harris*
*Intends to send you off as far as*
*The great world's show at Paris.*

*Of the youth beware of these,*
*For some of them might rudely squeeze*
*And bite your cheek, then songs or glees*
*We could not sing, oh! queen of cheese.*

*We'rt thou suspended from balloon,*
*You'd cast a shade even at noon,*
*Folks would think it was the moon*
*About to fall and crush them soon.*

For more on "the Chaucer of cheese," see <www.inforamp.net/~ihooker/cheese.htm>.

## Indie Publishers: Small but Mighty

After a close friend died of AIDS, Beth Follett gave up her career in social services and decided to try something completely different—she founded Pedlar Press and started publishing books. "I thought: Life is short. Am I doing what I need to be doing? Am I close to the things that I love?"

# LEGENDS
### of the Canadian Small Press
## COLLECTIBLE TRADING CARDS

These **HIGHLY COLLECTIBLE TRADING CARDS** are a delightful evocation of the ephemeral nature of Canada's Small Press Industry. Imagine the thrill of owning the "**Margaret Atwood 'First Book of Poetry' Rookie Card**" (for 'Double Persephone', Hawkshead Press, 1961) or the *Commemorative* "**First Chapbook to Share a Governor General's Award**" Card (for bpnichol's the 'True Eventual Story of Billy the Kid', Weed/Flower Press, 1970)!

**Over 50 in the Series!**          **Collect them all!**

Originality, attention to craft, excitement, and, most of all, commitment describe the current renaissance in Canadian independent micropublishing. While not all of the newest crop of fledgling publishers took on the task of publishing books as dramatically as Follett did, they share with her the conviction that what sets them apart from both the big publishers and the established small presses is the fact that they come to publishing not as a job but as a passion. Halfway between the small press and the evanescent zine (eccentric photocopied periodicals—see *Zines*) and buoyed by accessible technology and a young reading public hungry to see their words scribbled in the margins of a new generation's prose, Canada suddenly has more micropublishers than ever before.

"I wasn't very happy with the books I read," says the Montreal-based Andy Brown, brain child behind Conundrum Press. "So I bought a computer after a tree-planting cycle and I just started playing around with that. For me it has to do with the love of the object of the book, wanting to explore what a book is besides just pages and binding. We publish people, not books."

Similarly, over the last 10 years Toronto's Pas de Chance has published limited edition, handmade books of incredible beauty and intricacy—everything from novels to collections of lost pet posters from around the world. The books abound with wonderful flourishes: bulging plastic eyeballs, dogtags, and lockets that have been sewn, glued, or otherwise painstakingly attached. "Something that is handmade—someone can own an original piece of art for a very small price. That's the main difference between what we do and other presses," explains Pas de Chance publisher Ian Phillips.

But independent micropublishers don't always work in nontraditional formats just to push the boundaries of the aesthetic relationship between form and content. Some formats, particularly the chapbook, are popular because of their cost effectiveness and their appeal to younger audiences who feel more comfortable with literature that has the slim girth of a magazine as opposed to the heft of a book.

As an industry, it's an incongruous one, producing books that aren't always supposed to look like books for a generation that isn't supposed to have the attention span to read them. This new sub-industry has responded to the overall indifference of bookstores by, for the most part, appealing directly to their audience, launching titles and holding events in clubs more attuned to the deafening feedback of amplified instruments than the quiet murmur of a single voice.

"I produce a 100% homegrown product, bringing artists, musicians, and writers together, and it works

brilliantly," says Vancouver's Brad Cran, mastermind behind the Smoking Lung series of chapbooks and the 2001 anthology of Canadian poets *Writing the Blues*. "I've had people come up to me at our launches and say they've never been to a poetry reading or bought a book of poetry and they're leaving with a full set of books. You can make money off publishing. You just need relentless self-promotion, good writers, a competent soundman, a solid venue, and three kegs of beer."

# Folded, Stapled, Mutilated: The World of Canadian Zines

Louis Rastelli couldn't find a magazine he wanted to read.

"I used to spend whole evenings perusing the magazine racks checking things out," he says. "But gradually, over the last few years, I started doing it less and less. It just seemed like there was so little out there that spoke to me, to my generation. There were all these magazines trying to plug vacuous content into the same old formats, but I couldn't find anything to read. So I started my own zine."

The result is *Fish Piss*, an irregularly published, visceral collection of comics, fictions, and commentaries on underground culture in Montreal. According to Rastelli, issues of *Fish Piss* can sell as many as 1,000 copies—he once sold almost 50 at a single downtown Montreal Chapters. "All those people who bought *Fish Piss* were obviously hungry for something to read. And they didn't choose to buy any of those slick 20-something mags. I think it has to do with people wanting to find their own voices and also looking for communities they can be involved in."

At any given moment, there are hundreds of other underground periodicals with similar ideas. Zine titles come and go, but their spirit and intention remain, reminding us that younger generations of readers might just grow up with a whole new conception of periodical publishing—one that has more to do with reflecting urban Canadian life as they know it than with being passive vessels for mainstream entertainment.

That's not to say the goal of zine publishers is to encourage younger generations to stop reading magazines. Paul

Corupe, a Toronto zine veteran responsible in his younger days for such B-culture classics as *Ground Control* and *Radio Slack*, puts it this way: "Kids who are exposed to zines won't necessarily stick just with reading zines, but they'll be more skeptical of the big mags. They'll realize that there are many different viewpoints as a result of their exposure to zines."

In Edmonton, visual artist Lynette Bondarchuk (who runs the Edmonton small press association and was once the editor of *Errata*, a giant zine compendium of comics, feminist dialogue, and fiction) agrees with Corupe, and comments on the way she and other zine creators hope to transcend their own modest goals by, eventually, educating new readers in the possibilities of zines:

> *I envisioned mainly reaching people at first who read zines, but there's always the ulterior motive of hoping that other people will see it—that's what keeps us dedicated… The idea that anyone could see it, be challenged by it. It's an issue of respect. The artists and writers in it have the chance to be respected.*

Zines exist in Canada in numbers that dwarf all magazines put together. Sure, people have reservations about their often banal content (reservations, incidentally, that are also extended to the banal content of the majority of mainstream magazines), but for the most part, Canadian zines are impressive. They're interesting to read, well edited, and only about as radical as your average trade union: all these people want is a voice in their own present and future; a chance to shape their own stories, and, in the process, their lives.

The strength of Canadian zine publishing has to do with young people feeling shut out of their own culture. After all, we're talking about a country where it's extremely difficult to find Canadian magazines on many newsstands. Those Canadian magazines that *are* visible to younger readers are often little more than conduits providing information about the latest US movies, television shows, and rock stars. The writing is as dull as the subject matter. If you're looking for publications that genuinely reflect the trials and tribulations of the Canadian cities where they're made, then zines are definitely the way to go.

## Great Urban Canadian Zines

*Kiss Machine* Toronto zine known for its great writing and wacky themes, like Sex and Aliens. ($4, 18 Virtue Street, Toronto, ON M6R 1C2)

*Otaku* Ottawa's premier depressive Jeff wanders the underbelly of Canadian culture and reports back to us via a series of spot-on diary musings. (114 Canter Boulevard, Nepean, ON K2G 2M7)

*Hip Static* Kate's take on women's issues is grounded in the reality of (sub)urban life. Whether she's reporting on the myth of maturity or the bogusness of Judy Blume, she keeps it funny and forceful. (kate.zieman@utoronto.ca)

*45 Degrees of Separation* A delightful collection in which a group of young writers muse on the enduring conflict between East and West Canada, i.e., between Toronto and Vancouver. (1125 Pacific Drive, Delta, BC V4M 2K2)

*Pocket Gopher* "So what's so great about Regina?" asks one of the editors. Well, for starters, this excellent

grab-bag of interviews, miscellany, and Saskatchewan urban tidbits. (G-1550 14th Avenue, Regina, SK S4P 0W6)

*Tart* Occasional Winnipeg arts and culture roundup, including dumpster diving and leftie politics. (200-63 Albert Street, Winnipeg, MB R3B 1G4)

*Fish Piss* The essential guide to Montreal underground culture. (Box 1232, Succ. Place d'Armes, Montreal, QC H2Y 3K2)

*Synonymous to Anonymous* Adam's whimsical, spare, autobiographical zine is a time-out from the everyday, the work of a promising young writer, the tale of a horny young Halifax man, and the familiar story of lost generations who aren't quite sure they want—or need—to be found. (6015 Willow Street, Halifax, NS B3K 1L8)

CANADIAN ZINES

Darren Wershler-Henry

Graffiti off Bloor Street, Toronto

# Canadian Graffiti: Signs of the Times

**B**ombing, piecing, and tagging boxcars and walls—over the last decade, graffiti has come to Canada big-time, carried along with other aspects of hip-hop culture as it converts the globe to an infinitely funkier place. And what we've seen in Toronto, Montreal, and Vancouver—and on railway cars from Winnipeg to PEI—is often a lot more interesting than the tags decorating the Big Apple (see *Politics, "World Class"*).

If you're nowhere near the big smoke, or just not interested in venturing into any of the dubious locales where graffiti can be found (alleyways, abandoned buildings, tunnels, freight yards), there are some fine examples to be found online. One of our faves is Bombing Science <www.bombingscience.com>, a Montreal-based page that features sketches from artists' "black books" and videos of taggers at work as well as shots of the finished pieces. If you're interested in getting your hands dirty, you can also order paint, custom nozzle tips, and sets of markers from their online store (they've also got books, magazines, and videos for inspiration as well as stylin' toques and shirts so that you can tag in warmth and style …).

And then there are the boxcar shots. Painting boxcars is the Canadian cognate to spraying subway trains—and though there's no evidence that the practice began here (people started tagging boxcars after subway trains were redesigned with paint-resistant finishes), it certainly is flourishing in a nation that was built on its trains. It's also interesting to consider how new-school boxcar tagging is a revival of sorts of the old hobo tradition of marking cars with secret signs so that other hobos would know where to find food and shelter and where there were hazards to avoid.

An article from *Saturday Night* claims that there are about 35 people across Canada who regularly tag freights (probably a conservative estimate). "Every artist dreams of having a show in Chicago," one says. "Well, I have a show in Chicago every day, and in New York, and in all the small towns along the tracks."

# Sculpture/Public Art: A Plague of Moose Upon Your Houses

Toronto did it with moose, Calgary tried it with cows (a direct copy of the original Chicago cows concept), and Vancouver had … well … salmon. We hope you aren't put off public art and sculpture forever .

The idea was, like many of the various roads to hell, spawned by good intentions. The point was to create tourist-friendly art by mass-producing generic fibreglass animal shapes that artists could paint or otherwise decorate to reflect different regions of the city. Then the objects could be placed around town before being sold to corporations or rich people in exchange for a tax writeoff.

In Toronto, sponsors paid about $4,500 per moose, but the scheme was mocked by citizens who toppled the moose, ripped off their antlers, and gave them more idiosyncratic "decorations" than were intended. (In fact, the city employed two guys all summer solely to repair the damage—mostly by replacing stolen antlers.) Undaunted, the mayor (dubbed "Mel Lastmoose" by playwright Darren O'Donnell in his award-winning political satire *White Mice*) recently mused about doing it all again— this time with unicorns.

Despite the general lameness of the concept—which produced sanitized corporate-friendly art—public art and sculpture are important for the city. Outdoor art is fun, interesting, and unexpected—it gives the city unique charm that can't be duplicated by cheesy campaigns.

The best public art comes in all shapes and sizes. There's the famous Henry Moore sculpture in front of the Art Gallery of Ontario, a smooth, almost jungle-gym item that kids love to run around, through, and over (at least one of your *Almanac* editors has snoozed inside its warm, hammock-like confines on several summer days). And on the other end of the spectrum, before the current heyday of tagging (see *Graffiti*), someone scrawled the phrase "Fix Signs" or "Phony Karma" on the back of nearly every street sign in downtown Toronto.

One season in Toronto there was a more subtle form of public art: a group of used car lots agreed to have brightly lit banners strung across their tarmacs. The banners said things like "OKAY" and "ALL RIGHT," and were just hokey enough to be noticed and subtle enough to get us all wondering. Fleeting moments of public art are not unique to Toronto—Halifax had a downtown graffiti wall for a while, and Jonathan Dueck has been known to wander Calgary with a "suitcase gallery" he shows to anyone he can get to stop for a few seconds. Montreal has the Distroboto Zine Vending Machine, a converted cigarette machine installed in hipster performance space Casa de Popolo that rewards your change with bit-sized bits of literature and homemade cassettes.

We've decided to single out Winnipeg in this discussion, mainly because it deserves it. For starters, it has the ugliest outdoor sculpture in a Canadian city, that monstrosity of fake wheat and metal stuck in the middle of the Norwood Bridge. The priciest public art commission in Winnipeg's history, it looks like a UFO crashed into a field.

SCULPTURE/PUBLIC ART

Then there's the whole Louis Riel situation. A statue of the great Métis rebel who founded the province, the work of architect Étienne Gaboury and sculptor Marcien Lemay, was unveiled on the grounds of the Manitoba legislature in 1970 (albeit around the back of the building, in an area frequented by hookers and junkies, not up front with Queen Victoria). It depicts an agonized Riel, his naked muscled body twisted into knots—no doubt as result of the federal government deceit that led to the derailment of his dreams for the Métis people and his eventual execution.

Reaction to the statue was always mixed, but evidently, even the nine-metre-high concrete half-cylinders that rendered the statue invisible from all directions except the immediate front and side weren't discreet enough. Sometime in October 1991 vandals chiselled the penis off the statue; opinion was split about whether the vandalism was perpetrated by racists or by members of the Métis community, many of whom had always disapproved strongly of the statue and had been negotiating for its removal since its installation. Alas, in 1995 the statue was replaced with a handsome, dull, statesman-like Riel dressed in a suit and tie. Lame! The original work was moved across the river to the grounds of St. Boniface College, where it sits facing a small parking lot. The artist and a supporter actually chained themselves to the original in a losing bid to prevent the transfer. It remains, in our opinion (though no one seems to be asking for it), one of Canada's most compelling works of public art.

Well, Winnipeg isn't *all* bad when it comes to public art. It *is* the only Canadian city with an amateur website devoted to outdoor sculpture. Check it out at <http://home.cc.umanitoba.ca/~robh/pubart.html>.

# Winnipeggers vs. Public Art

Man oh man, does Winnipeg ever hate its public art. Check out these reactions from the citizenry to various projects over the years (we could probably have found similar dirt for other cities, but we were on a roll):

**Louis Riel Monument, 1970** Public sculpture, grounds of the Manitoba legislature, Winnipeg; installed c. 1970, relocated 1994.

> *The unveiling of this grotesque monstrosity will successfully perpetuate the controversy that has existed for a hundred years ... Riel's detractors must be smirking in smug satisfaction over this unexpected and unnecessary windfall to their prejudices.*
>
> —*Warner Jorgenson, Progressive Conservative MLA,* Winnipeg Free Press, *January 5, 1972*

> *... [for] the average citizen of this province who will cast his eyes in the direction of this brutally misshapen blob ... the reaction will be "now what the hell is that supposed to represent."*
>
> —*Warner Jorgenson, Progressive Conservative MLA,* Winnipeg Free Press, *January 5, 1972*

> *[Lemay's sculpture] is a dark and painful stain upon the memory and accomplishments of Riel and Métis people.*
>
> —*Billyjo DeLaRonde, president, Manitoba Métis Federation,* Winnipeg Sun, *July 28, 1994*

> *[The sculpture represents] a grotesque man with no pants on and his testicles hanging down. Can you*

## ZAK MEADOW

by Marc Ngui

...AND ON OUR LEFT WE HAVE A CONTEMPORARY INTERPRETATION OF THE ARCH AS A CIVIC MONUMENT...

...UNLIKE THE HEAVY STONE ARCHES OF ANTIQUITY, WHICH COMMEMERATE THE PAST, THESE SLIM, SOPHISTICATED 'GOLDEN ARCHES' STAND AS SYMBOLS OF THE CITY'S GLORIOUS FUTURE...

...REGARDLESS, THE ARCH CONTINUES TO BE A PHYSICAL CELEBRATION OF PUBLIC SPIRIT...

UH, YEAH, I'D LIKE MY FRIES SUPER-SIZE WITH EXTRA BACON.

imagine if John Diefenbaker was portrayed with no pants—or John A. Macdonald?

> —Jim Durocher, president of the Métis Society of Saskatchewan, Globe and Mail, *May 13, 1996*

**Justice, Gordon Reeves, 1986** Public sculpture, Winnipeg Law Courts Building, installed 1986.

*A crop of dandelions would have been nicer.*

> —Hymie Weinstein, lawyer, Winnipeg Free Press, *April 6, 1986*

*I think it looks like a giant mosquito with all the pincers and things.*

> —Anonymous, Winnipeg Sun, *Sept. 12, 1985*

*It's gross. It doesn't do anything for me except make me walk farther around the building to get to the front door.*

> —Anonymous, Winnipeg Free Press, *April 6, 1986*

And finally, two less benighted opinions:

*Public art remains an easy target. If something doesn't feed us or shelter us, right off we question its value.*

*Then, if something's meaning is vague in the remotest way, our immediate reaction is outright hostility.*

> —Morley Walker, journalist, Winnipeg Free Press, *October 25, 1997*

*If it's to be moved, I'd want it moved as far away from Winnipeg as possible.*

> —John Nugent, artist, regarding his sculpture No. 1 Northern

# Urban Tunage

Obviously, it would be extremely difficult to reprise the history of Canadian music and its intertwined relationship to the city. From Glenn Gould to Joni Mitchell to Bachman Turner Overdrive, Canadian music has alternately been intensely creative and totally derivative. It has blasted out of the windows of alternative colleges and wafted like the scent of pot into the turmoil of the streets (see *Denizens, Rochdale*) and whispered its quiet complexity to the upper classes in venues like the venerable Massey Hall. In the Canadian city you'll find everything from wanky classical to skronk-jazz to klezmer, soca, and, yes, even rock and roll.

Julie Doiron

But let's face it. The authors of this book put in their time growing up on the fringes of cities like Winnipeg and Ottawa. In those environs, it wasn't the mellifluous jazz of Oscar Peterson that stirred up emotions; it was the more primal beat of heavy metal, punk, and later when we grew up and knew better, indie rock. And so we give you a look—backwards and forwards—into the musical make-up of not just the city but also what lodged in the minds of two white kids growing up in the 70s suburbs. Without apologies or gratuitous references to how much we hate the Bare Naked Ladies (who were once upon a bizarre time actually banned from performing in front of Toronto's city hall because of their offensive name), it's time to rock …

## Rocking On: Contemporary Can-Pop

**The Weakerthans** Winnipeg's quintessential leftie prog-rock unit with great lyrics and hooks. With only

The Weakerthans

two albums under their belt, they play to sold-out shows across Canada. Singer and lyricist Jon Samson croons about troubled relationships, apathy, and the seemingly hopeless task of believing in something. "There's a spectre haunting Albert Street …"

**Julie Doiron** Moody Moncton singer/songwriter got her start as bassist in Eric's Trip, one of a handful of Maritime bands to be signed to SubPop in the mid-90s. She then founded Sappy records and released her own solo album, *Broken Girl*, as well as discs by bands such as Snailhouse and Elevator to Hell. These days she's releasing poignant albums sung in a tenuous vibrato in both of Canada's official languages.

**Corpusse** This heavy metal satanic keyboard duo is fronted by the man who will hump absolutely anything on stage. One of Toronto's longest-running acts, Corpusse's high-schooldropout lead singer is six-foot-plus in height, extremely, well, *corpulent* in girth, and obviously influenced by Alice Cooper. You go once for the experience, you go back because it rules. Sample lyric: "Barbara Streisand: IT'S. TIME. TO. DIE!"

**Godspeed You Black Emperor!** "The car is on fire and there is no driver at the wheel and the sewers are all muddied with a thousand lonely suicides. A dark wind blows. The government is corrupt and we are all so many drunks with the radio on and the curtains drawn. We're trapped in the belly of this horrible machine and the machine is bleeding to death." So begins the career of Montreal's hottest underground sensation. With a quasi-orchestral big band perpetually on the edge of deconstruction and a penchant for

The Dears

brooding spoken-word moments that crescendo into string-infused collapse, this band redefined the city's sound for the new century. The Next Big Thing.

**Sloan** With its Beatlesque power pop that never quite fit into the early 90s Maritime grunge explosion, this band has, perhaps, the most fervent following in all of Canada. After more than a decade, and despite setbacks breaking into the American market, the little Halifax band that could is still touring, perhaps afraid of the hearts that would shatter like dropped lightbulbs if they ever broke up.

**The Beans** Experimental semi-melodic instrumental alt-rock jazz just doesn't get any better than this. This Vancouver act uses homemade percussion and string instruments, tape loops, and other tricks to create their dense, unique, foreboding sound. Here, urban decay and urban glory meet in diffuse opposition.

**Wooden Stars** Post-rock angst at its absolute best, the Ottawa nonconformists incorporate rock and punk and jazz in songs that defy expectations and refuse to fragment into a thousand pieces. "When I was just a little boy ..."

**Royal City** "Quiet acoustic songs are filled with urban imagery, but unwind at a rural pace" is how one eloquent reviewer put it. Folk and fucked-up lyrics evoke the brooding melancholy of Smog and Palace, but nope, they're our very own semi-depressed post-rock incarnation. At Rush Hour, The Cars ... could we think of a better name for a downbeat Toronto band?

**The Dears** Cello keyboards and emotions-on-the-sleeve lyrical non-ambivalence just wasn't enough for this britpop-influenced band. So they also perform with a 16-person string and percussion ensemble known as the Cosmopolitan City Orchestra. Only in Montreal! A remarkably honest pathos meets pop confection.

**The New Pornographers** Insanely catchy first single "Mass Romantic," featuring the lovely and talented Neko Case on vocals, was *everywhere* when it was released (the album has already sold 28,000 copies in Canada and the US and is about to be launched in Europe by Matador). The band is a thinktank of Vancouver's new indie musicians that will go a long, long way ... if they can keep it all together. These are busy people. PS: The name comes from a right-wing screed claiming that music is the new pornography...

**The Sadies** The musical equivalent of a Surf 'n' Turf meal, Toronto's sharp-dressed (black suits, skinny ties) band mix Dick Dale and Sergio Leone in chunky, satisfying proportions. Best quote: "We do killin' songs because they're mostly in minor keys"—Dallas Good, guitar.

URBAN TUNAGE

**Kittie** All eyeliner and piercings and teeny-tiny black clothes, they look like the teen witches from *The Craft* and they rock harder than a rec-roomful of beer-soaked, bonged-out metalheads on the May long weekend. This London, Ontario, outfit are a refreshing change of pace from the 24-7 Britney/J-Lo bimbo parade emanating from south of the border.

## Heavy Metal: Music for the Hard of Thinking

Heavy Metal is the colourful indigenous folk music of our people. Many moons ago (say, before 1985), before punk, grunge, hip hop, jungle, and alt- and indie rock, we roamed the suburbs of the nation in a great leather-and-denim-clad tribe, but now our numbers are diminished, our people scattered to the winds.

Many things led to the decline of metal—the decreased importance of the electric guitar and the rise of the turntable; the heavy toll excised by the mandatory metal diet (drugs, beer, whisky, and nachos); the dawning realization, even among metal's major practitioners, that the mullet (the official haircut of metal, aka "hockey hair") is an incredibly stupid-looking coiffure; and that Levi's 531 Super Slims (the official stovepipe-thin blue jeans of metal) are a lot less comfortable than baggies and the resultant lowering of their wearers' sperm counts may also have caused births of baby metalheads to drop to panda-like levels.

… and, oh yeah: the music started to suck.

When compared with the fresh, loud, and (gasp) danceable sounds of the late 80s and early 90s—hip hop, jungle, grunge, indie rock, industrial, goth, and techno—traditional metal just couldn't cut the mustard. (*Note from Darren:* During my stint as a wage slave at Canada's largest record store in the mid-90s, I remember accepting a returned copy of Metallica's *Master of Puppets* CD, a cornerstone of the metal canon. In the space on the Returns form where the customer was required to describe the reason for the return, he had written, "I can no longer listen to this album without laughing really, really hard." Fair enough.)

In the early 90s, metal venues became fewer and farther between, and metal guys began to behave like punks did in the early 80s—as the few defiant keepers of a tiny flame. At one gig, we remember seeing two huge, pierced, tattooed, bearded, leather-clad men hugging each other emotionally (unusual only because they were straight) as one said to the other, "I love you, man—you're a really important part of the scene."

If there actually was a hooded cabal of people who met in a secret underground chamber on every full moon to plot the course of Canadian metal, we'd bet our bottom dollar that Metal Tim Henderson and Martin Popoff would be presiding.

Metal Tim is the Charles Foster Kane of Canadian metal—he rules over a small but mighty self-constructed publishing empire, including both the print and online versions of *Brave Words & Bloody Knuckles* <www.bwbk.com>, the thinking man's metal mag, and Brave Radio, the magazine's streaming Internet audio companion. In addition, Tim is the news director at HardRadio <www.hardradio.com>, the metal supersite.

Knuckletracks, a fistful of metal on CD, comes with every issue of *Brave Words & Bloody Knuckles*.

*layering itself with heavier and heavier blankets of the earth's crust. The most decisive and deafening of the original four heavy metal records, above [Deep Purple's]* In Rock, *above the band's own* Paranoid, *and way above* Uriah Heep, Master of Reality *is a relentless and pulverizing mountain of power chords, in essence the original model for future torch-bearers* Trouble, *and the last thing Sabbath would ever really need to say to turn rock on its broken neck forever.*

Such is the energy that nursed metal through the lean years of the 90s. Like all popcult trends, metal is infinitely recyclable, and, as a reaction to generic boy/girl dance bands, seems to be enjoying something of a renaissance. Watch for T-shirts bearing names like Mudvayne, Slipknot, Clutch, Soulfly, and (Canada's own, all-girl) Kittie to be prominently displayed on a surly teenager near you.

Martin <www.martinpopoff.com> is simply one of the best rock critics this country has produced, in any genre. In addition to editing all of *Brave Words*, he writes stories and reviews for it, as well as for hardradio.com and hmv.com. And he's written some amazing books, the best of which is *The Collector's Guide to Heavy Metal* (Collector's Guide Publishing Inc.), which, in its first edition, had the much snappier title *Riff Kills Man!*. What makes Martin's writing so enjoyable isn't only the reviews (which range well into hard rock, southern rock, punk, and other genres as well as metal) crammed full of useful information, but also that they're written in a totally unique, OTT (metalspeak for "Over The Top") style:

*Constructed from pure throbbing guitar gone bad, a righteous wrecking ball that seems to just spill bass, drums and vocals out in some dense, effluent birthing, [Black Sabbath's]* Master of Reality *is a masterpiece beyond words and beyond compare with other music. An expulsion of glorious thick power, this definitive Sab statement wallows in primordial energy, simply*

## DJs: Wheels of Steel

Hip hop has now been a serious part of Canadian musical culture for long enough that new school is way, way old school (remember the Maestro and the Dream Warriors? That was a long, long time ago, my friends). These days, everybody is in the groove; there are an astounding variety of Canadian hip hop crews. Canadian Hip Hop Online <www.hiphopca.com> maintains the most comprehensive listing of Canadian hip-hop artists and their releases on the web, the stores that stock the music, plus lists of upcoming events and clubs that regularly feature the cream of this country's DJs.

But in your quest for urban hipster status, you can expand your music listening at least one step further

URBAN TUNAGE

than traditional DJ mixing. "Turntablism" is the use of stereo turntables as instruments for creating new music out of existing vinyl recordings. While the idea isn't new—musician, writer, and visual artist John Cage, for one, raised the possibility of this kind of musical creation as early as 1937, and hip-hop scratching has been around since the late 70s, when Jamaican/New York DJ Kool Herc invented it during a Bronx street party—the term itself is of recent vintage, coined by DJ Babu (of Beat Junkies and Dilated Peoples fame) in 1995.

There are more Canadian turntablists that you can shake a stylus at, and they're aiming for official recognition (read "funding eligibility"). At the 1999 National Campus/Community Radio Conference a motion was passed committing the organization to work on establishing turntablism as a unique musical form. thereby fostering continued Canadian explorations of this genre. (France was apparently the first country in the world to officially recognize turntablism at the governmental level.)

The king of Canadian turntablism is Windsor's own Richie Hawtin, aka Plastikman, aka Fuse. His elegantly minimalist website <m-nus.com> houses various projects, cumulatively demonstrating that "musical boundaries are minimizing" and that "this subtraction of sound and communication broadens the future of creativity." Visit for info on upcoming gigs, streaming audio, MP3s, merchandise, and more.

Of course, you can ditch the analog hardware altogether and get straight into electronica, mashups, and bootleg MP3s, like Billy Pollard, or, to use his nom-de-DJ, "knifehandchop." Pollard likes his music fast (160 beats per minute and beyond) and chaotic, throwing in everything from Eminem to Pokémon (look for his *Respect to All the Haters* in your local indie dance music

store, or on the web if you're lazy). CanaEHdian has a small but growing directory of homegrown electronica at <www.canehdian.com/genre/electronica.html>.

# Punk

Punk's not dead, it just smells that way.

Contemporary punk is a spectrum that ranges between two extremes. On the one end are the squeegee kids, antipoverty activists, peace punks, and other outsiders; on the other, the cuddly, commercial "fun punks" that swarm the Alternative sections in record stores nationwide. Both groups (as well as the motley assortment of skinheads, ska punks, goths, skaters, emocore, straight-edge, krishna punks, and hardcore kids that fall in between) strive to be annoying; the former, at least, have something resembling a good reason for doing so.

With many of punk's original practitioners either dead from the lifestyle's excesses (Darby Crash, Sid

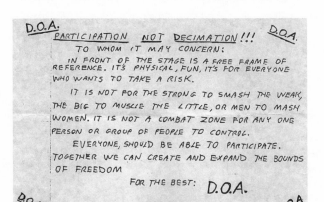

D.O.A. missive from the grand old days of Can-punk.

Vicious, Joey Ramone, Stiv Bators, and countless others have moved on to the big moshpit in the sky), ascended to the status of minor celebrity (from Henry Rollins to Lee Ving of FEAR, who went from being one of the scariest punks that LA ever produced to a character actor on *Blossom*), or locked firmly into the nostalgia tour circuit (most notably, the Sid-less Sex Pistols, but even Joey Shithead of Vancouver's mighty DOA has done the odd acoustic punk solo balladeer show), it's become increasingly difficult to see even the roots of punk as having any sort of integrity in its rebellious stance (possible exceptions: the Clash, Crass, Minor Threat). Glenn Matlock, who was turfed from the original Sex Pistols lineup in favour of Sid Vicious, once said that being in the Pistols was just like being in the Monkees. Sure he was pissed off because he missed all the fun, but he had a point.

Being punk in Canada was always very different from punk in New York, London, DC, and LA. The only people we can remember who could afford all the leather, Doc Martens, hair-care products, and hard-to-find albums that emulating New York and London punk required were the rich kids. Bruce Fletcher, editor of the infamous zine *Virus 23*, once said that Canadian punk was really all about vomiting all over your lumberjacket at a bush party while someone's crappy car stereo played a *Never Mind the Bollocks* tape. Being punk in Canada in the 80s also involved getting into a lot of fights—our friend, Mark Surman, at one point the only ska-friendly skinhead in Kenora (he claims that there was also a sole goth girl, but that she was really ugly), will attest to that, as he spent a good portion of his youth fending off attacks from mullet-headed jocks.

Nevertheless, there were a number of major Canuck contributions to the art form:

**DOA** Joey Shithead's mad crew of flannel-clad, guitar-toting BC woodsmen have always been the flagship act of Canadian punk: true supporters of indie art and foes of tyrants both big and small. *Bloodied but Unbowed*, their first "hits" collection (including punk anthems "Fuck You" and "I Don't Give a Shit"), still stands up to repeated listening <www.suddendeath.com/doa/>.

**Nomeansno** Four guys from Victoria created Nomeansno—a massive, crumbling edifice of sound that lurched back and forth between punk and a maddening, bass-driven mutant form of metal. Best album: *Wrong*. Scariest song: "Real Love," from *Small Parts Isolated and*

_Destroyed._ Their alter egos, The Hanson Brothers (sort of the Ramones of road hockey), are the slightly more cuddly purveyors of the uniquely Canadian subgenre "puck rock" <home.golden.net/~weboett/>.

**SNFU** Canadian punk rock and hockey go together like beer and nachos, especially if you're into Edmonton's SNFU. The band was once arrested in Texas for taking the entire audience on a bus to Ross Perot's estate and making them hum the theme music for _Hockey Night in Canada._ All their album titles have seven words in them; _If You Swear … You'll Catch No Fish_ and _Better Than a Stick in the Eye_ were veritable pickup trucks full of ugly fun <www.geocities.com/SunsetStrip/Cabaret/1299/>.

**Forgotten Rebels** Sick, fast glam from Hamilton perpetuated by lead-poisoned Iggy and Gary Glitter wannabes. _In Love with the System_ and _This Ain't Hollywood … This Is Rock & Roll_ are two fuzz-toned, amphetamine-drenched classics that will make you wonder how such sonic genius could stem from the minds of total idiots <www.forgottenrebels.com/>.

**Bunchofuckingoofs** Mohawked hardcore Kensington Market vigilantes who would have made Larry King

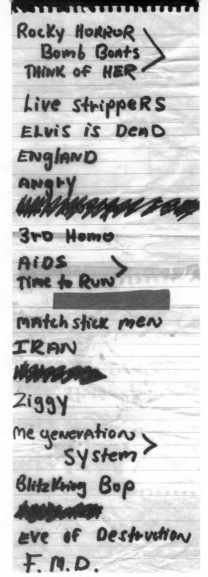

Forgotten Rebels set list

plotz if they ever came into his shop (see _King of Kensington_). The title of their album, _Carnival of Chaos & Carnage_, says it all.

**Slow** The best Canadian punk band that never had a chance. Shortly after the release of their debut EP, _Against the Glass_, lead singer Tommy Anselmi pissed onstage during a concert that was staged in conjunction with Vancouver's Expo 86, and that was pretty much all she wrote. More rock critics have touted "Have Not Been the Same" as a precursor to Seattle grunge than have actually held the record in their hands.

**Deja Voodoo** Not just a band featuring only a single tomtom and a beat-up bass guitar, not just the inventors of a signature sound ("sludgeabilly") imagine Jerry Lee Lewis whipped on NyQuil. Typical stage patter: "Hope you cats dug that last song 'cause we have 22 more that sound just like it"), not just two guys with the same first name ("Gerry"), Montreal's Deja Voodoo were the magnates of the semi-legendary Ogg Records label, which brought the likes of the Gruesomes and Chris "Baby Jesus" Houston (formerly "Pogo au Go Go" of the Forgotten Rebels) to the turntables of the nation. Their _It Came from Canada_ compilations are in desperate need of reissue on CD.

... But there were countless others—that was the whole point. And there will probably continue to be more Canadian punk than you can scrape off your shoe, as long as the original punk ethos ("Here's a chord. Here's another. Now go out and start a band"—from *Sniffin' Glue*, one of the original punk zines) survives.

A list of some other Canadian punk bands: <members.tripod.com/~canadianpunk/bands.html>.

## Elvis Impersonators

Among the people of Canada, we are blessed with the presence of many Elvii—those who carry on the legacy of the King by dressing, singing, and occasionally behaving like Him (Collingwood, Ontario, hosts an annual Canadian Elvis Tribute Convention, but the Elvii are always among us, spreading their sacramental hunks o' burnin' love). This is the story of one of them: Subway Elvis. (NB: this story has nothing to do with that Jared guy.)

In 1970, 16-year-old Michael McTaggart made the long journey from Etobicoke to become Toronto's Subway Elvis—the transit system's favourite busking clone of the King (in his Vegas incarnation) and arguably Toronto's first subway busker. During the height of his career, after the real Elvis's death, Subway toured in nostalgia shows with artists including Chuck Berry, Chubby Checker, and Jerry Lee Lewis.

But McTaggart's career was tragically interrupted by a tussle with the Man, and his life began to follow a path straight out of one of Elvis's films. He was arrested in 1986 at Kipling station, and in 1988, falsely convicted of committing a series of armed robberies and jailed in the Millhaven maximum security prison in Kingston.

When a new police investigation (spurred by the fact that the robberies continued while Subway was

## Two Kings Wrongfully Convicted

*Michael McTaggart meets Rubin 'Hurricane' Carter in a scene from the documentary film "Subway Elvis."*

in jail) convinced the prosecuting attorneys that the case against Subway was weak, the charges against him were stayed and he was released. In 1990 Subway discovered that the Halton police withheld evidence during his trial, evidence that may have biased the case against him. In 1991 he sued for wrongful conviction to the tune of $4.25 million. (In between these events, a small embarrassment: Subway forged a series of cheques at the

Greenwood racetrack on his mom's account, lost somewhere around $30,000, and did three months for fraud.)

A decade later (December 2000), Subway's case finally made it to trial. The judge ruled that the Halton cops had intentionally withheld evidence (notebooks containing statements from two bank employees who had identified another person as the bandit), and awarded our hero close to a quarter of a million dollars. But the Halton police appealed the judgment before Subway got a dime; he, in turn, cross-appealed for an even larger settlement. The Halton police finally offered to settle, but only on the condition that he drop the cross-appeal. Two weeks later, Subway got a cheque for $380,000. His first purchase: custom-made suits for his comeback.

Like the real Elvis, Subway had a fondness for prescription drugs and a tendency toward depression. And Subway's gambling jones came back with a vengeance (Greenwood racetrack told him at one point that his credit was good for exactly 67 cents).

So where's Subway now? In trouble again. In January 2002 he was charged with fraud over $5,000 and uttering a forged document, mere hours before his bio appeared on CBC's *Witness*. Like the King said, his middle name is misery.

# REAL estate

FINDING A PLACE TO LIVE in the Canadian city is like an elaborate game of musical chairs with millions of players. With each passing day, the music grows faster and faster, and there are more asses and fewer seats in which to put them.

This game has provoked a number of unforeseen responses in the players. Some of them try to secure a spot by waving around huge wads of money, paying off the referee, the other players, and anyone else who's in their way. Some dig in hard, refusing to leave their seats for any reason, restoring and renovating their chairs within an inch of their lives. Others try to wedge multiple asses into the same tiny seat, or to rent out temporary squatting rights on tiny, nasty portions of their seats for inordinate amounts of money. Some eventually get sick of the game and go someplace where there are more chairs and fewer players. And some simply give up, exhausted, and live on the floor in a cardboard box.

And, as a look at the archives demonstrates, in the Canadian city it was ever thus …

## Apartments

"**T**he exorbitant rate charged the very poor is the immediate cause of much suffering and too often of crime" announces a *Toronto News* headline from the early 19th century:

> *Overcrowding is made possible by the fact that the demand far exceeds the supply… Every room which is situated near the centres of employment is eagerly competed for, and the landlord is sure of tenants no matter how wretched the rooms may be. Repairs and improvements are, therefore, seldom, if ever, made.*

*Toronto News* reports that a sample house rented as follows:

> *4 rooms with 7 people: $9*
> *1 room with 2 people: $4*
> *1 large room with 4 people: $8*
> *2 small rooms of 6 people: $8*
> *2 large rooms with 2 people: $12*

**The slum is the city at its worst. It represents the sphere of congested housing, the lurking place of disease and impaired health, the hiding place of crime, the haunt of immorality, the home of poverty, the habitation of drinking and drunkards and, because of its lesser rentals, the colony of the foreigner in our midst.**

—S.W. Dem, superintendent, Methodist Union, delivering a 1914 address called "The Slum and the Church"

> *1 large room with 2 people: $8*
> *Shop and room, 5 people: $19*

Twenty-eight people in 13 rooms. With that rent, the *News* argued, the property was worth $20,400 a year, though it was assessed at only $1,500. "Owing to conditions like this," the article concluded, "speculators are buying up these properties."

## Landlords

> *Such a thing as "repairs" is never dreamed of, for the rent can be obtained all the same, and to fix up looks like unnecessary extravagance. The household refuse, slops, dish water etc. are thrown outside the door, to sow diseases that daily attack the inmates … These places are owned by well-to-do citizens who sin against their own city from avaricious motives and live in luxury on the exorbitant rents imposed on the poor and the comfortless occupants.*

> —*J.J. Kelso,* Saving the Canadian City

So writes the leading Toronto anti-poverty advocate in the last two decades of the 19th century. We can only imagine Kelso's dismay were he to discover how little has

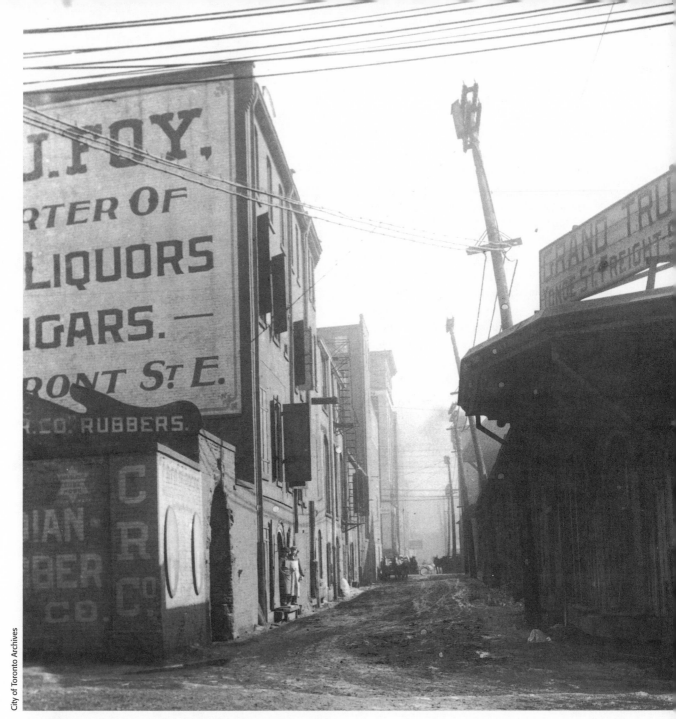

Yonge Street looking east, first lane south of Front Street, 1904

LANDLORDS

actually changed: landlords still get rich off the poor and do as little as possible to maintain their properties.

Those who rent know intrinsically that this is true. Those who are lucky enough to live in their own homes—well, you don't have to take our word for it. Headlines and tales of hard luck are replete. For instance, the *Saint John Times Globe* tells us that in Saint John, New Brunswick, "215 dilapidated and unhealthy buildings pockmark the South End." According to a complainant: "The sorry-looking buildings in [his] neighbourhood are contributing to an atmosphere of lawlessness and killing property values …" The city, he said, "should put more money into bylaw enforcement and come down harder on slum landlords." Sounds like good advice to us. Will it ever happen? Still in Saint John, we come across the sad story of tenants living in a building in winter for three days without heat. When an inspector showed up, families had to be evacuated because "the wiring in the building was too dangerous to let tenants stay inside."

Here's a little exchange that occurred on CTV National News just before the holiday season:

*PETER MURPHY (Reporter): Hi. I'm Peter Murphy with CTV News. What is happening now?*

*FRANCINE DAWKINS (Evicted Tenant): They're evicting me.*

*MURPHY: Francine Dawkins, escorted by Sheriff's Deputies, is among the thousands of people evicted from their apartments every month in Toronto. But for this single mother of three, being homeless at Christmas time is devastating.*

*DAWKINS: I know I'm being evicted. My locks are being changed. My children have nowhere to live and neither do I for the Christmas holiday and I don't know what I'm going to do. I don't know where I'm going to live.*

*MURPHY: And so as the lock is changed, a lone Christmas tree sits in a corner. There will be no presents under it this year. Dawkins was ordered evicted by the Ontario Rental Housing Tribunal after she fell behind in her rent. But the order says she should not be evicted if she paid*

---

**Little praise has been sung for the lowly landlord, who seems to achieve minimal expense through the creative use of cheap and shoddy materials. This landlord aesthetic has blessed Montrealers with many fascinating treats to the eye.**

1. **Brown metal industrial siding. Why use expensive siding, when siding normally reserved for industrial warehouses is cheaper and just as good?**
2. **Brightly coloured aluminum awning over doorways always adds a touch of class to that otherwise dull facade.**
3. **Impossibly cheap railings available in lovely gold and white. It's not as if anyone's going to lean on them.**
4. **Cut rate bath fixtures can be combined with the ever popular plastic shower stall and rubber/vinyl "tiles."**
5. **Paved or cement space instead of hard-to-maintain lawn.**
6. **Linoleum!**

—*Vince Tinguely*, Perfect Waste of Time, Montreal

---

*the rent in full. Dawkins paid the back rent and has the cancelled cheques to prove it, but was still evicted.*

A recent article in the *Hamilton Spectator* featured a young fellow discussing his search for an apartment.

*The vacant places were vacant for a reason. One place I saw had one bathroom for a floor of five or six rooms. And it looked like the last time Mr. Clean came here he must have been mugged 'cause he ain't been back since. The landlord or super, or whoever the heck he was, offered to show me the rooms. Out of politeness I agreed, knowing that I would sooner sit on hot coals than live there. He opened the door and I noticed it was not only a small and filthy room; it also came with a resilient pet—a cockroach. And this hole was $300 per month.*

Things are so bad in Toronto that they actually had to put a landlord in jail after one of her tenants died in a fire because she neglected "to maintain smoke detectors." As Ontario fire marshal Bernard Moyle told the *Toronto Star*, "This will be the first time in Ontario that an individual will serve time in jail for failing to provide or maintain working smoke alarms."

Woe to the renter, whose life is in danger because the landlord doesn't want to spend six bucks on batteries.

Of course, landlords can do more than just threaten health and safety and cause bankruptcy. They're also known to arbitrarily refuse pets and children, impose byzantine requirements and credit checks, and make moral assumptions about their tenants. In the great Montreal zine *Fish Piss*, editor Louis Rastelli recounts various landlord–tenant struggles. Recalling the ongoing tension between his roommate Scott and one landlord, he writes:

William James, City of Toronto Archives

Slum house in Toronto's infamous Ward District, 1911

*Not long before my old roommates got evicted, Scott had a fistfight with the landlord... Holy shit, did that landlord ever hate all of us. He threatened to call the cops once when Scott put his cross out on the porch. "Blasphemy, blasphemy!" he cried. Now what's wrong with a cross? So what if it's full size? (He used it for bondage photos; he's a photographer.)*

Perhaps you're thinking that Louis and his pals deserved what they got from their offended landlord? If you are, put down this book and go join the Tory party. Go ahead, future slumlord in waiting. If you realize that tenants should live free of their landlord's religious beliefs, then you'll probably realize that there is NO SUCH THING AS A GOOD LANDLORD. If they're nice to you, it's only because you're paying a rent so outrageous that you've

LANDLORDS

even managed to buy their kindness. Landlords are universally evil. There can be no middle ground. If you're a landlord, you should hate yourself with a passion. And you might as well, 'cause no matter how much you pretend to care, you won't be able to resist fleecing your tenants. How could you? With vacancy rates of 1% or less in many major Canadian metropolitan areas, people are desperate enough to pay anything and put up with anything. Landlords have a bad rep not because they get a bum rap, but because they absolutely and totally deserve it. So save your pity for, as J.J. Kelso so eloquently put it, the "poor and comfortless occupants."

# Condos, Lofts, and the Unlikely Act of Downtown Home Purchase

Look, every city is not Manhattan. So why is it that everyone now wants to live in a loft? It's not as though all the people purchasing lofts in the downtowns of the nation need the room so that they can more easily produce huge oil paintings and sculptures. But most of those who want lofts aren't even playing at being artists. Lofts (or, more accurately, the tiny condos that are laughably called "lofts") represent the conspicuous consumption of huge amounts of space, an increasingly precious commodity when apartment vacancy rates in our largest cities are frequently below 1% and houses and condos consistently sell for tens of thousands of dollars above their list prices.

And, more and more, what people are getting for their money is garbage—in Vancouver, especially, where the "leaky condo" phenomenon was born. Leaky condos aren't just badly constructed—the problem stems from an experimental building technique that sealed the building walls so that no air was allowed in. Instead of creating a higher insulation value, the water was sucked into the airspace, didn't evaporate, and began to rot the wooden frame of the buildings.

Repairing leaky condos involves opening up the walls, replacing the rotten wood, and recladding the building. In many cases, condo owners are dinged with up to $30,000 for repairs, and have little prospect of selling the unit to an increasingly wary public. And the scale of the problem is vast—over 50,000 units are affected. The total cost of repairs is estimated at $1 billion, with an additional $2 billion in indirect costs. And here's the punchline: as the lawsuits and bankruptcies continue to spread like a bad rash, the costs filter out to the taxpayers. It's been estimated that BC's leaky condos and soaked homes could all be repaired for the same cost that's being incurred through litigation, bankruptcies, and foreclosures.

Other downsides to the condo/loft phenomenon include paper-thin walls and once ornate, cool-looking factory buildings gutted and turned into 1001 jail cells with high ceilings, granite countertops, and no parking (not that you should be driving anyway; see *Transportation, Bikes,* etc.). A 2002 loft conversion plan put forward by the owner of an empty factory on Dovercourt Road in Toronto includes adding two floors to a large heritage building already several storeys higher than anything else in the neighbourhood. The plans also state that a whopping 38 parking spaces will be provided for 87 residential units and their visitors. No word yet on how small the cubicles, shiny the countertops, and over-the-top the price tag.

Naturally, those tired of living in rented dives, wary of signing up for the loft lifestyle, and capable of saving some cash will be looking to the downtown house-buying market. To you, we say a hearty good luck. The agents are usurious, the competition even more virulent than apartment rental, and the various taxes, bank charges, and miscellaneous fees no one bothers telling you about are staggering. While your landlord paces the sidewalk insisting that you must leave by midnight, you're being dragged around by a ReMax lady with big hair (a friend of your mom's friend you signed up with as a favour) who doesn't seem to realize that half a million dollars is just slightly above your price range. When you finally find something you think you can live in, there'll be four other bids and pressure from all involved to agree to a deal without any sort of house inspection by a qualified engineer to make sure the idling of the moving truck's engine isn't going to bring down the roof.

By the time it's all over you'll be a nervous wreck—and the discovery that your next door neighbour keeps three attack dogs in his backyard isn't likely to soothe your nerves or improve your empty bank balance. But, in the end, those lucky few who manage to buy their own homes in the city, those privileged bastards who have separate rooms for guitar, computer, stove, and futon—they know it was all worth it.

They're home owners now, they can act as surety when their activist pals get arrested for squatting in abandoned buildings and even invite those friends over for back-yard barbecues, regardless of the dangers. (See *Attractions, Parties and Zeitgeist, Community*.)

# Suburbs

Immortalized in the photos of Bill Owens <www.billowens.com>, especially in his 1973 collection *Suburbia*, the suburbs are the distillation of organized ennui, a space

> *Up to a quarter century ago citizens of Toronto charged, with some reason, that their city was being allowed to grow in a haphazard way without thought for the future, and indeed without solutions to the pressing current problems. It was sprawling across a widening area, so it seemed to them, without proper attention to health, appearance or convenience ... highways leading out of the city were wholly inadequate. A maze of overhead wires defaced the streets. No substantial steps were taken to eliminate slums. Land that could have been reserved for parks was allowed to be used for other purposes. The waterfront was shut off by railway tracks, commercial buildings, and smoke. And yet if the city had been judged by the quantity and quality of paper plans it would have been seen as one of the most advanced of its time.*
>
> —G.P. Glazerbrook, The Story of Toronto, 1971

SUBURBS

Always plenty of parking in the burbs.

characterized by fear and anonymity, and the epitome of everything the urban hipster professes to hate.

Large cities everywhere are starting to resemble the layout of Disney World: giant doughnuts of asphalt and suburban sprawl semi-organized around shopping malls, airports, industrial parks, and other local conveniences, with the city's once-vital financial core reduced to a nocturnal magic kingdom for adults. Suburban "edge cities" accrete along strips of road rather than circular cores. With the boom of high-tech industrial parks like Kanata that are usually well outside the city proper, most people don't even have to go into the core to work any more; in fact, many people choose to live downtown and work in the suburbs, reversing the migration pattern established in the mid-20th century.

But maybe it's too easy to hate the suburbs.

In *Architecture Must Burn* (Gingko Press, 2000), one of those incredibly sexy-looking, borderline-incomprehensible-postmodern-architecture-as-art coffee-table books, Aaron Betsky asks us to take a second look: "Sprawl may be good. Sprawl may be our destiny." (*Architecture Must Burn* has no page numbers; such are the wages of cool.) Yes, sprawl is ugly and wasteful, but it may not be as costly to maintain as its opposite extreme, megalopolises like San Francisco, New York, and Hong Kong. "The issue is not how to stop sprawl but how to

use its composition, its nodes and its leaky spaces to create a new kind of architecture. We have to build a new kind of home on a new kind of range."

So how do we do that? To return to the theme park analogy, Betsky wants to take a page from Walt Disney and "imagineer" our suburbs. Public spaces, in other words, need themes—"temporary environments that make up complete stage-sets in which we can appear and see at least one version of the world making sense, if only for a moment."

While Betsky's idea may be a brave attempt to work around an unavoidable problem, it's unlikely that hip urban deconstructive architects will get to have a say in the ongoing development of sprawl. With imagineering come the rules established by the imagineers, as in the town of Celebration, Florida. Built by Disney, it served as the setting for *The Truman Show* and operates in a way that's depressingly similar to the film's plot. Celebration isn't really a town so much as a mall shaped like a town; everything is owned by a company, and ultimately, the company governs. Yes, your neighbour has to keep her lawn mowed and her house painted certain colours … *but so do you*. You say utopia, I say nightmare.

At least in the Canadian suburbs built in the 60s it was possible to find the wild places in between the developments. Growing up in suburban Winnipeg in the

70s, you could be on the open prairie after five minutes of bike riding, or in a forest that appeared in the heart of the city, or in the empty guts of abandoned or half-completed buildings. There were spaces to drink stolen beer, to smoke surreptitiously, to fumble awkwardly while attempting to undo your first girlfriend's bra strap without both of you catching frostbite. In an imagineered world, will there still be room?

# Architecture

Alfred Holden has been commended by Heritage Toronto and nominated for a national magazine award for his writing about architecture and the urban past. He holds a master's degree in Historic Preservation, is the regular essayist for both the literary journal *Taddle Creek* and the community newspaper *The Annex Gleaner*, and is currently an editor at the *Toronto Star*. We contacted him to find out how Canada is doing in preserving its architectural heritage. His articulate and knowledgeable replies make us look like the immature brats we are, and we reprint them here with pleasure.

*Why should people care about the architectural heritage of their cities?*
I may surprise you when I argue that "heritage" or "preservation" or whatever you call advocacy on behalf of buildings that are old, not so old, or even close to new in cities is not primarily about aesthetics or history.

Yes, old buildings can be pretty, but caution here—beauty is in the eye of the beholder. And sometimes you can argue that a building should be saved because some historic event or person is connected to it. These can be very useful arguments if a battle is raging and public support for a building is needed.

But I believe those are side issues. The real value of "heritage" is simply the contribution of a wide mix of buildings to the actual functioning of cities. We need old buildings because they help make the city work.

Jane Jacobs has pointed out that old buildings can offer cheaper rents than new ones; one result is that new businesses and budding industries are usually found in them, and not in new skyscrapers, which play a different role. So obviously we need both. Old buildings, perhaps ironically, are one of the keys to renewal, to the future.

Old buildings force us to innovate, to adapt; we adapt to them, and adapt them to serve us. It can be challenging, but the result is a much richer, more desirable, more valuable, and often more humane environment. These are very tangible, important things. A good illustration is the choice sometimes made by small towns to renovate or restore their old city hall versus building a new one out on the highway somewhere, as is often done in the United States. Adapt the old one and you keep your town's focus; you avoid throwing away resources and real estate and keep a scale that, while mostly used by drivers now, is also walkable if need be; you avoid using up farmland or greenspace; you often get a beautiful building. Build out on the highway, and even if you get a beautiful building it's disconnected; you drive there, do your business, and leave. You'll never get Paris this way, never get an environment that satisfies in much more than strictly utilitarian ways.

Old buildings, as they exist in many cities, also define streetscapes in ways that are hugely useful as we struggle with sprawl and concerns, at least among some, that

ARCHITECTURE

sprawl is a form of waste in which ugliness conquers the landscape to the detriment of people's happiness, the environment, the future.

That's because many old buildings, whether in neighbourhoods or business districts or mixtures of these, were built to a smaller, tighter scale, and are not so oriented to roads. This includes very large buildings, like skyscrapers, whose walls are built to the sidewalk. These forms remain wonderful for humans, because although technology has evolved our bodies remain much the same; if a restaurant is across the street we're glad to walk to it, glad to stop in the bookstore on the way, if the urban environment's scale is in proportion to us.

There are many buildings I love, and most people who like cities and communities, be they dense downtowns or spread-out sprawl, have some favourites. This in itself is a reason we may defend them. But there's a bigger picture, in which the stewardship of "heritage buildings" (which may include something built just yesterday) is one of the prerequisites to maintaining a viable city. There are other things that work in conjunction; "heritage" infrastructure, such as Toronto's streetcar system, is one of these. The streetcars truly shaped the city into the modern age, "preserving" its smaller business districts and neighbourhoods. This is thus not an aesthetic or historic thing, primarily; this "preservation" is the very underpinning of the modern city. Ironic, perhaps—the future depends heavily on the past, not for its glory or its historic interest, but for the shapes and economic opportunities the whole existing city offers us.

*Is architectural heritage under siege in the Canadian city? What can people do to preserve their city's heritage?*
Our "heritage" is certainly not doing well. We're very good at demolition, and when we do keep a building we often do a poor job with it. My own pet peeve is the popularity in Ontario of the "bottom slider" replacement window, which to me symbolizes our overall philistinism when it comes to architecture. Bottom sliders consist of a single insulated pane at the top of the opening, with the bottom part of the window divided into two parts. To open the window, you slide (though they often stick) one of the squares across, overtop the other. To insulate properly you usually need two sets of these panes. The whole mechanism is complicated and ugly and the actual openings very small, hardly enough to admit much air. Yet everybody has them; people take elegant homes in Rosedale with beautiful, functional, architecturally interesting windows and think somehow that they need these bottom sliders. They're often lured by the prospect of saving on heating bills, though I've never seen a shred of real evidence that actual savings materialize.

Such indifference to detail is a characteristic of Canadians' management of old buildings. Citizens often reflexively "gut" (the term is proudly used and sums up a widespread general attitude toward old buildings in Canada) old houses and apartments. Ironically they're building chateauesque "monster" homes, new-old homes that are usually ill-proportioned and made with expensive materials poorly used. I realize I'm being harsh here; I accept that that's their taste, and that free speech lets me criticize it. I'm not for rules or controls of any kind. In my own writing I try to enlighten people to old buildings and things that may look tired but do work well and may be masterpieces. I am forever stunned by the poor layouts of new homes and condominiums that reflect hunger for costly-looking features such as granite countertops but lack real luxuries such as big windows (rooms in many new Toronto condominiums have no windows at all) and good room layouts.

This has a lot to do with heritage. We just don't see the possibilities in the buildings and homes around us; we feel pressured in many cases to destroy good work and replace it with bad; we're not good at adapting and reusing; we have value systems that distort realities, that make us want things that don't really improve our lives. Why do we want those granite countertops, gilded-frame mirrors? They speak to deep yearnings, I suppose. In my writing I try to counter these with stories that shed light on how alternatives are there, how they came to be, and how people might like them. I tend to put things more diplomatically than I'm putting them here.

A developer I know who likes old buildings and had done good things with them feels that the problem with heritage here is rooted very deep in the Canadian psyche, that it's connected to our long-felt self-loathing and

sense of underachievement. We're not proud of what we've done, don't value it, get a measure of satisfaction from destroying it. In contrast, the Americans are a prouder, more patriotic people, and they embrace their heritage in all its forms, including architectural.

So here we have a huge dichotomy: in Canadian cities, anything is fair game for the demolition crew, but the cities as a whole have survived and done well, including their downtowns; in the US, sprawl and racism destroyed cities, and in their wrecked state Americans awoke to the value of historic buildings and sought to preserve them.

It's hard to reconcile, but it's reality. I would say that in Canada no building is safe—not New City Hall in Toronto, whose public square will soon be "updated" to some soon-dated design; not Place des Arts in Montreal, made a white elephant by the stroke of a pen creating a new concert hall nearby; not the Toronto Dominion Centre, Mies van der Rohe's Canadian masterpiece, whose underground shopping mall is being made over to look like any mall, anywhere. I'm not saying these buildings must be frozen in time. But I've lived long enough to see generations of fashions come and go, and become frustrated when architecture that is also art is treated with disrespect. Sometimes people are simply ignorant; in my writing I have tried to bring people around by revelling in the glory of the city as we find it. Often enough I see the Canadian dilemma being played out in major alterations and demolitions—our loathing for everything these buildings stand for. We loathe their beauty, the achievement they represent. It's very sad.

*What are your favourite Canadian city buildings?*
I very much like some of the banner buildings—the TD Centre, Commerce Court, Place Ville Marie in Montreal.

ARCHITECTURE

169 St. George Street, a virtual glass box with some of the brightest apartments in Toronto

I love Habitat 67, and Expo 67 was, I think, Canada's finest architectural moment. But my favourite of all time is a mere apartment house on St. George Street in Toronto, where I once lived. 169 St. George Street was built around 1957 and designed by George Boake and James Crang, two young U of T graduates who became blue-chip architects. Their later work is considered rather bland.

The building has been treated poorly in recent years—a good case study of my complaint that Canadians just don't have an eye for good buildings. Its original windows were partly changed, and landlords have tried to "early it up" with classical furniture in the lobby of a very stark postwar modernist building.

But as I remember it, 169 St. George is a virtual glass box; it has no exterior walls. Windowsills are just above knee level. It has the brightest, most beautiful apartments in the city. The design was such that every corner apartment had windowpanes right to the corner of the room; the pillars that hold up the perimeter of the building are placed outside, on the balconies.

The windows themselves were in rolled-steel frames of a type commonly used in Toronto in the 1950s. Only there were acres of them—they were used as a curtain wall across the whole building. No, they don't insulate well, but who cares? They had big casements that cranked open, picking up the breezes. The window structure itself was, on the inside, almost flush with the glass; it gave rooms a wonderful sheer, modern look. Balcony doors consisted of thin steel frames and three glass panes. It was like the building was made of glass. Light would fill these apartments, reaching into every corner. They had spacious hallways. Nice galley kitchens. All units had very thoughtful layouts. Everybody who lived there seemed to sense the building's integrity; tenants fought and halted the window replacement project; the building stands today, scarred but proud and still loved by me and many, many others.

## CN Tower

Three hundred and fifty metres above Toronto, we diners pat our lips with our cloth napkins, sigh, and look longingly out the window. The sight is exhilarating, unnerving—we can, as the CN Tower slogan goes, see it all. The miniature world blurs below us, a miasma of ceaseless speed reduced to a nonchalant creep, the entire greater Toronto area nothing more than a live-action diorama. Slowly, we revolve, our food and our plates and our table and our chairs situated on a doughnut-shaped platform that spins us gently around our world.

Beneath us, hidden by dim lights and matted carpet, is a hatch that, when thrown open, allows access to another world—the world of mechanical feats that underlie our predetermined amusements. Four hundred and eighty-four eight-inch wheels support the 60-ton platform we dine on. The platform is rotated with the friction of just two sets of two 18-inch wheels powered by two lone 2.5-horsepower motors. We're just in the middle of dessert; by the time we get the check, we'll almost be back to where we started, a 72-minute rotation timed to coincide almost perfectly with the arrival of the bill.

We put a credit card on top of the check, and stare at a view that hasn't changed much in an hour and 12 minutes: a never-ending loop of vehicles rolling off the Gardiner Expressway, spiralling around and down to Bay

CN TOWER

Rick/Simon's poster depicts the radius of destruction should the CN Tower fall.

Street. We imagine we're floating, swaying, falling. We imagine we can feel the roll of 492 wheels propelling us past a scene we can't escape, we can't quite take in. Maybe we're not imagining. Maybe we do feel the gentle irrepressible torque, a slightly unpleasant sense of orbit, a Ferris wheel inevitability, a revolution that leaves us exactly where we started. Shrugging, we sign our name on the dotted line, nod to the waiter, stand up. We stumble, unsteady just for an instant.

That's the view from *inside*, though. From outside, things look a lot different.

Photographer and designer Rick/Simon, a long-time resident of Toronto's Ward's Island, put it this way: "Nobody asked us if we wanted that thing messing up our view of the skyline." And then he went a step further … well, a whole bunch of steps further, actually. While the tower was under construction, he designed a poster signed by the suitably bureaucratic and anonymous rubric of the Ministry Without Portfolio (Zone Definition Section). The poster, which reads "CAUTION: ENTER AT OWN RISK," depicts the radius of destruction that would result if the tower, um, *fell over* in any given direction (this was decades before 9–11)—a circle that extends from Spadina on the west side to Adelaide on the north to Bay on the east, then down to the Island ferry docks on the lakeshore to the

south. He then posted copies of the poster on lampposts all around the circle's perimeter.

It wasn't long before the newspapers and TV stations got wind of this and began to run stories across the nation. CN Corporation was hopping mad, and tried their best to find the instigator, but he was allowing TV cameras to film only the back of his head during interviews, Gouzenko-style.

Rumours persist that *someone* actually managed to affix a laminated copy of the poster under the tower's skin, at its highest physically accessible point (standing on half of a closed gullwing door while hanging on to a lightning rod for balance in the high wind), before work was completed, sealing it inside. The National Gallery of Canada's collection includes a Greg Curnoe drawing of the CN Tower with an arrow pointing to a tiny speck on the top; a nearby caption reads "Rick/Simon."

# Infiltration

"**N**injalicious" is the *nom de guerre* of a nerdy suburbanite hailing from Pickering, Ontario, one of Canada's most uninspired industrial pseudo-cities. In person he is small in stature, anonymous, even bland. If you passed him on the street, you wouldn't notice. If you ran into him in the bowels of a closed-down nuclear power plant, you'd figure he was the night watchman. But don't feel bad for Ninj. That's the way the publisher of one of the world's premier zines on the subject of illicit tourism wants it.

"When you infiltrate," he says, "people will assume you're supposed to be somewhere if you act like you're supposed to be somewhere. Clichéd but incredibly true. I want to learn more about the subtle ways to send off 'I'm supposed to be here' signals."

Ultimately, Ninj hopes to become the master of an endeavour that's as dedicated to subterfuge as it is to the visceral thrill associated with activities like mountain climbing and skydiving. Jeff wants to be an authority on the growing pastime he calls "infiltration." And just what exactly is infiltration? It's an amorphous sport-hobby, sometimes called "reality hacking," that involves penetrating urban spaces marked off-limits to the average citizen. It's the kind of do-it-yourself, no-money-down leisure activity that's sure to take off as our cities continue to crowd and crumble and consume our capacity for individuality.

Inscrutable anonymity is the ironic premise behind Ninjalicious's antics, as documented in his popular *Infiltration*, the zine about "going places you aren't supposed to go." Ninj's dedication to the blend-in is ironic, since it's exactly this conversion of the bulk of the earth's population into faceless drones skittering blindly through and past an ever-expanding grey, formless urban space that his vocation challenges. And yet, the infiltrator—having thrown off the mantra of blind acceptance and mass invisibility that, increasingly, society demands—ends up becoming, well, invisible. In fact, Ninj's own formative experience of exploration came from a tenure of recovery in a giant hospital where he was just another sick lump of flesh occupying a bed:

*To fight off the boredom, I took to exploring the building's darkened hallways in my bathrobe at night. I had a lot of morphine in me at the time, so travelling down to the morgue and up onto the roof seemed like reasonable things to do. The sense of danger and the rush of adrenaline those explorations provided was such a welcome antidote to the boredom of lying in my bed all day that it seemed to be just about the most fun I'd ever had. After that, I was hooked ... on infiltrating, not morphine.*

Readers of *Infiltration* will also quickly develop the addiction. The appeal of the zine isn't just the excitement of surreptitious, even covert, tourism. It's the way Ninj documents his exploits—with precise, methodical notations of where he's been and how you can get there too. Upon opening up an issue, it's immediately clear that the author isn't just another bored teen who happened across an unlocked door. His explorations are serious, in-depth, and, more often than not, dangerous:

*I do try to avoid death. But the chance is there. In sub-way tunnels, you face the obvious dangers of getting run over by the trains or electrocuted by the third rail. In steam tunnels, you can touch the wrong pipe and*

INFILTRATION

*give yourself a third-degree burn. In drains, you can get drowned by a flash flood or pass out from inhaling poisonous vapours. On rooftops, there is often a significant danger of falling off. In abandoned buildings, you can fall through a rotted-out floor, or cripple yourself lots of other fun ways, and be left there to moulder until the next explorer happens along. There are also less obvious dangers, like live wires or lack of guardrails, which make every journey into the off-limits world a little riskier. My fingers are still blistered from the electrified pole I accidentally grabbed for support while exploring this weekend, though I'm pleased to report my nose has finally stopped tingling.*

There are, of course, dangers that transcend the mortal. On this subject, Ninj is even more glib, shrugging off the ever-present possibility of being charged with trespassing or worse. Part of this comes from the fact that *Infiltration* advocates a socially conscious urban exploration, one that never crosses certain boundaries. Ninj doesn't do damage, doesn't steal, and always respects the privacy of others. He preaches a kind of eco-trespassing: carry out what you bring in, and never sully the virgin wilderness of sewers and forgotten tunnels. The infiltrator must always take the moral high ground: it's not just about having fun; it's also about reclaiming the cities for the people who are actually stuck in them.

*Breaking into a house or a shop is not my kind of trespassing. But I don't think it's even debatable that too much urban space is cordoned off as private. Virtually every spot in the city is private property, aside from the occasional grudgingly conceded parkette. Malls have replaced public squares. I don't really have a problem with this, as I'll take a building over a park any day; I just hope no one seriously expects me to suppress my natural human urge to explore my environment, simply because I live in the city. I see big things for the hobby of urban exploration as the world fills up with more urban space, more abandoned buildings, more tunnels all eagerly waiting to be discovered and explored.*

So look twice at that geeky little guy sitting primly in your hotel lobby. It might be Ninjalicious, on his way to one of his dream infiltrations of, say, "the tunnels under Moscow, the drains under Melbourne, or the luxury hotels of Las Vegas." Hey, that anonymous, benevolent figure might just be your guide to an ever-expanding hobby whose bible is called *Infiltration*, and whose 10 commandments go something like this: "Not all the sites have an admission price and a gift shop."

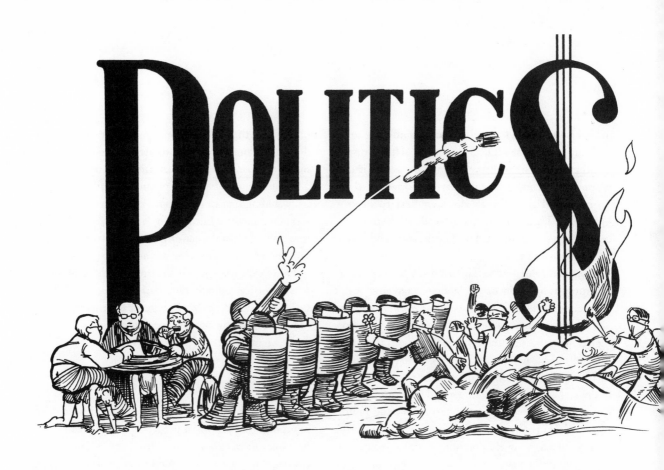

# POLITICS

**P**OLITICS. THE MERE MENTION OF THE WORD and our eyes glaze over. We start looking for the exit, the sports pages, the nearest emporium for pedicures and aromatherapy. Anything to relieve us of the tedium of polls, position papers and, worst of all, politicians. Despite the fact that cities are known to be generally left of centre compared with the rest of the country, those who live in the city would like to believe that they're somehow above politics—with the exception of Ottawa, naturally, a city that exists solely because of it. (See *Zeitgeist, Beginnings*.) This largely unspoken sentiment maintains that the city has its own kind of interpersonal politics, a politics that has nothing to do with supporting the NDP candidate for school trustee. In other words, it's what we do and how we do it that matters, not who we vote for. Let the Tories try to gut Toronto and the Liberals do their best to destroy Vancouver. The city is the city, after all—indestructible, ceaseless, an entity governed only by the spirit and potential of its myriad citizens.

Alas, if only this were so. Though many of us don't vote and most us have concocted elaborate strategies for not getting involved (see *Zeitgeist, Angst and Alienation*), we're vulnerable to politics, which is, after all, an abstract, boring, esoteric practice unless it has to do with providing more affordable housing and you're on the waiting list.

What follows is a look at some of the political realities of the Canadian city—from past and present mayors to the city as a haven for lies and corruption and radical protest. We may be able to lose ourselves in the city's charms for a day, a week, a month, or even a decade. But eventually, politics catches up to us—the decisions made on high spiral down to us lowly denizens and, if we weren't at the table, we end up saddled by a suburban rule book that has our squeegee kids crowding the jails and our condo entrepreneurs dining with the mayor.

# Mayors

According to research by three Brock University professors, the typical Canadian big-city mayor is male, with an average age of 60, a university education, and a background in business. Of course, what the Brock study *doesn't* tell us is that the average Canadian city mayor is much more than a middle-management type who accidentally attained executive status. To the contrary, our mayors are ornery, idiosyncratic, and unpredictable. They also tend to be bitter, paranoid creatures, perpetually chafing against restrictions that give the provinces too much power while keeping a wary eye on the electorate who, though seemingly content to re-elect the same figures year after year, are notoriously fickle.

Despite the drab picture the Brock study paints of the mayor's office, Canada can boast some pretty "colourful" figures presiding over its big cities. Here's a sampling of just a few of our best and brightest leaders.

# Fighting Joe Clark

Mayor of Edmonton five times and an eight-time alderman, Fighting Joe was a perpetual mayoral candidate ever since he roared into town from the Yukon in 1908. Among the notches on his résumé: he played slam-bang lacrosse for teams in small-town southern Ontario, including Brockville and Prescott; joined the North West Mounted Police in Regina in 1892, but soon deserted (he got off with a $100 fine because the judge was his uncle); and attended the University of Toronto law school, where he began his lifelong friendship with future PM William Lyon Mackenzie King.

Joe Clark was a scrapper, and got his nickname from the many times he was unable to control his temper. Famously, while biding his time as an alderman and plotting a new mayoral campaign, he lost his patience and started a fistfight with then-mayor Bill McNamara (obviously no slouch himself). The match spilled out into the street and ended up a draw.

When he finally reclaimed the title, Fighting Joe Clark was so comfortable with the mayor's mantle that he was known to sit in his office with his feet up on his desk and growl at people coming in: "Well what the hell do *you* want?" Perhaps his most ignominious moment came when a man, coming before the judge after a drunken spree, was asked how he ended up in such a deplorable state. "I was drinking with Mayor Clark," the fellow explained. Clark happened to be in the courtroom at the time, representing a client of his own. "You're a liar," he yelled—for which he was fined $10 for contempt of court.

## Médéric Martin

Populist French-Canadian mayor Médéric Martin came to power in 1914, at a time when language issues were just beginning to tilt the balance of power away from English Montreal. Martin won his first election by polarizing French voters against the English candidate. He won again in 1926 using the slogan "No more English mayors!" All in all, he would hold the office five times.

A Montrealer by birth and residence, Martin made much of his working-class upbringing, and was the first Montreal mayor to come across as being outside the business oligarchy. But the poor-man schtick didn't last once

---

*I wish the British Government would give you Canada at once. It is fit for nothing but to breed quarrels.*

*—Lord Ashburton*

---

he was safely ensconced in office. Apparently, Martin wore a special mayoral toga of mink and ermine and had his own rallying song: "The Martinaise."

## Louis D. Taylor

Mayor of Vancouver five times between 1910 and 1934, Taylor's policies were liberal and progressive for the period and earned him plenty of enemies. These included the Vancouver Board of Trade, which tried desperately to shut him out of a reception with former US president Teddy Roosevelt and his wife. Taylor's support for organized labour also earned him the ire of BC Electric, which is said to have caused him to lose an election. Apparently, on election day, all power to the poor East End region mysteriously failed, leaving his constituents unable to travel by streetcar to the polls. BC Electric later produced a singed woodpecker that they claimed was the culprit.

Taylor rebounded and reclaimed the mayor's spot. But more bad luck was to come. In 1928 he was struck on the head by an airplane propeller at the inauguration of BC Airways passenger service. He was forced to preside over council meetings partially paralyzed and in a wheelchair. Later he would make a full recovery—evidenced by the fact that he almost drowned at age 72 while on a five-week canoe trip in the BC interior.

## Hazel McCallion

First elected mayor of Mississauga in 1978, Hazel McCallion has clung to the top seat in Canada's seventh-largest city come hell

MAYORS

staggering 94% of the vote (though only 21% made it to the polls). Most people in Canada and Mississauga seem to love the mayor, and why not? She surely meant to make a positive contribution to the debate on immigration policy when she let slip that she thought Canada was letting in too many "unacceptable and unproductive" people.

Like many ridiculously popular politicians who rule seemingly by acclamation, McCallion has her detractors. She even has the distinction of being the only mayor in Canada who has an entire website devoted to chronicling her evil misdeeds (we won't direct you, but Google might).

## Mel Lastman

No account of oddball Canuck mayors past and present would be complete without a nod to Mayor Mel, the longest-serving mayor of any major city in the world, according to his official bumpf and the Guinness Book of World Records. (This is based on Mel's 10 straight terms as mayor of North York, where he presided with an autocratic McCallion-esque style until "the city above Toronto" was forced to amalgamate with TO.)

Although Lastman's 20-plus years as head of North York were relatively smooth, his reign as head of the fifth-largest city in North America has been a bit, well, bumpy. In support of the Olympic bid, Lastman was nervous about his trip to Africa and worried aloud to reporters that he might be boiled in oil and eaten or something. This prompted various groups to call for his resignation. Lastman apologized. And apologized. And apologized. His apology speech was so completely, utterly, bizarrely lame and insincere that the incredulous staff at *Harper's* magazine (who are professionally droll, and thus not

or high water. She's going on 80 years of age, but has no plans to retire. Under her rule, Mississauga has been dubbed MissCorp, reflecting her staunch pro-business, no-nonsense agenda.

Subject of many flattering profiles in the Mississauga press (part of which her family owns), McCallion only rarely undergoes serious scrutiny. But she was famously described in *Toronto Life* as looking "like a netsuke bulldog, a discontented heel-snapper in a chenille jacket, until her smile locks into place in a most experienced way."

McCallion is said to govern mostly by fiat: "She's put this cast on her council, this pall," Toronto councillor Howard Moscoe told *TO Life*. "They're sort of clones. They walk and breathe like Hazel … Hazel's the closest thing to divine right in this province that I've seen." Moscoe might not like her, but she won the 1997 election with a quick to rise to the bait) printed a transcript of it. Despite Lastman flying all over the world and racking up $3 million in expenditures, Toronto didn't even come close to getting the Olympics.

This left Mel feeling like he needed some new friends, so, while hanging out with the Hell's Angels at their hotel conference in Toronto, he did a handshake photo-op, which prompted various police and law enforcement types to call for his resignation (evidently, the bloody Hell's Angels–Rock Machine war that's been raging in Montreal for the last decade, never mind the half-century of malfeasance attributed to the world's most famous outlaw motorcycle club, didn't register on his radar). Lastman apologized. Again.

Lastman has even managed to be sued by a woman claiming to be an ex-girlfriend, who wanted payments because he failed to support the two now grown-up sons she claimed he fathered. We can't remember whether or not Lastman apologized, but we're thinking of beginning an "Illegitimate Sons of Mel" club. Who does it better? Evidently, Nooooooooobody.

Speaking of family, Lastman once also threatened a city hall reporter: "Leave my family alone. If you don't leave them alone, I'll kill you." Lastman later apologized.

Through all of this, the mayor has managed to cut social services in the city; consistently raise taxes despite promising not to; fail to negotiate with unions, thus prompting a massive stinky garbage strike, and blame it all on the provincial government. Lastman's negotiating technique with the province of Ontario is, by the way, a model for any cunning kindergarten student. Fed up with provincial Tory lies, he lashed out at Labour Minister Chris Stockwell, calling him a "trained monkey" for "organ grinder" Mike Harris. Stockwell retorted

with what remains the ultimate Mel putdown: "I'm not sure anyone five feet tall with curly black hair should call anyone a monkey." Hey, what kind of way is that to talk about the longest-serving mayor of any major city in the world?

# Graft

Despite what we may think of today's city politicians, the heyday of municipal corruption came around the turn of the *last* century. In Montreal, city corruption was so bad

GRAFT

that the provincial government set up a Royal Commission to conduct an inquiry into the administration. The 1909 report was a devastating indictment, describing the city as "saturated with corruption" and leading to an overhaul of the city government. What kind of stuff was going down? Well, in 1894 Herbert B. Ames, president of the Montreal Volunteer Electoral League, had this to say:

> *During the past 2 years, matters have gone from bad to worse ... While Toronto annually receives $125,000 from her street railway privileges, the council of Montreal recently granted similar privilege for 30 years to a company this year paying the city only $25,000.*
>
> *Although there were 3 other lower tenders, the contract for electric lighting was renewed with the old company at $124.10 per arc light annually, and the tenders of the other companies offering to save the city $25,000 a year were not even opened.*

Of course, corruption was hardly limited to Montreal. Canada's other great metropolis at the time harboured one Samuel Thompson, a city election returning officer. When accused of stuffing the ballot boxes, he claimed that he was guilty only of ardent friendship: "I just had an insane desire to do kindness for people I took a fancy to." Later, though, he confessed to being employed by a candidate for alderman looking to better his chances.

Then there was John Chambers, commissioner of parks, who resigned in 1908. Apparently he'd been selling Parks Department surplus material and retaining the proceeds. He also had his employees raise vegetables, which he sold to a St. Lawrence market vendor.

But our favourite graft king of the turn of the century has to be E.N. Carter, zookeeper. He was found to have been stocking his larder with bread and meat destined for the Riverdale Animal Park critters. He also ran an exotic pets business on the side and was known to make a bit extra selling the bodies of deceased animals to a rendering company.

Of course, nothing like that goes on *these* days.

# Saint John vs. St. John's

*Saint John, New Brunswick: population 126,000 (largest city in province)*
*St. John's, Newfoundland: population 171,000 (largest city in province)*

*Saint John: claims to have had its harbour discovered on June 24, birthday of St. John the Baptist*
*St. John's: claims to have had its harbour discovered on June 24, birthday of St. John the Baptist*

*Saint John: claims to be Canada's oldest city*
*St. John's: claims to be Canada's oldest city*

*Saint John: ravaged by fire in 1877*
*St. John's: ravaged by fire in 1892*

*Saint John: fishing port and home to large Irish community*
*St. John's: fishing port and home to large Irish community*

There's often confusion when travelling to one of these two cities, though we can't imagine why. A busload

Water Street, St. John's, Newfoundland, 1886

of Honduran soccer fans once flew to Saint John to take in a soccer match. "Where is the stadium?" they asked. Uh, Saint John doesn't have a stadium. They really wanted St. John's, but it's a 14-hour drive plus a long ferry ride to get from Saint John to St. John's. "They missed the tournament," commented one Bruce Tilley, manager of the St. John's board of trade. Another time, an Italian skating team ended up in St. John's by accident. "They called us from the airport in St. John's and said, no one's here to meet us," a Skate Canada competition official told the *Globe and Mail* about the incident.

# Megacity

In Quebec, it went all the way to the Supreme Court of Canada. In Ontario, 13,000 amendments and a filibuster in the legislature were last-ditch attempts to stop it. But in the end, nothing mattered: Canada's two largest cities were forcibly amalgamated despite vocal protests from residents and politicians losing their jobs.

The last decade has seen cities across Canada amalgamate, including Halifax, Montreal, Ottawa, Toronto, Hamilton, and Charlottetown. In many cases, the process was long and acrimonious. Frankly, the wounds may never heal. In Hamilton, Stoney Creek MPP Brad Clark vowed to "fight to the death" any municipal reforms that would swallow Stoney Creek into a supercity. But a few years later … guess what happened? In Montreal—forcibly amalgamated by the province on January 1, 2002—former Westmount mayor Peter Trent still refuses to accept that it's over and he lost. "There's a chance that maybe one day Westmount can regain its former status," he said in an interview.

Alas, it's unlikely that anybody is going to come along and return Canadian cities to the hodgepodge of boroughs, towns, and fiefdoms that existed before amalgamation. So it's time to look at how things are going so far. Well, the general rule seems to be that the smaller the city, the smoother the amalgamation. This is hardly surprising, considering:

- Cities with a population of more than 1 million people are 21% more expensive per capita to run than cities of 500,000 to 1 million people.
- Counties with a population of over 1 million are 42% more expensive to run than smaller counties.
- School districts and transit districts become more expensive per unit of service as they grow larger.

MEGACITY

Charlottetown amalgamated in 1994. By 1997 it could boast three balanced budgets and was sitting pretty. In Halifax, with an amalgamated city of 340,000, there have been calls for reconciliation between the original city and Dartmouth, Bedford, Cole Harbour, Sackville, and its other newly acquired parts. "Let's now accept that we are all Haligonians (gulp)and take pride in our new strength" wrote one commentator in a 1999 article in the *Halifax Daily News*.

But in Montreal and Toronto, with populations in the millions, there have been deficits and scandal since amalgamation. Montreal's post-amalgamation months have included "a bribery scandal. Conflict-of-interest allegations. An alleged violation of municipal-election laws," as an article issued by the Canadian Press put it. In Toronto, which has been plagued by ill luck since amalgamation, there were immediate budget shortfalls, prompting the newly elected mega-mayor Mel to attack Mike Harris, architect of all the Ontario amalgamations, at a press conference: "Mr. Premier you lied. You screwed Toronto Mr. Premier. You are cutting the heart out of this city."

The final legacy of the amalgamation decade remains to be determined. A cursory cultural inspection, however, suggests that the megacity has not had the hoped-for effect of bringing downtown cool to the suburbs. For instance, one might wonder why it is that most of the top-level references to "megacity" on Google point to lame shit in Toronto. Web hosting services, choral groups ("MegaCity Chorus—Toronto's Exciting New Male A Cappella Group"), model car contests—it's as though the amalgamation of our cities has brought the worst aspects of suburban idiocy to the fore rather than the longed-for spread of urban hipness.

We at the Almanac believe there's still time to untangle the massive messes that result when politicians resort to cookie-cutter solutions for highly individual urban cores. Here's an idea: Why don't we try making the suburbs survive on their own for a while? We can relocate them *en masse* to remote northern locales … the result would be something a lot like Pinawa, Manitoba. Let's see how long people last on a recreational diet that consists exclusively of dinner at Hooters, drinks at the local Elephant & Castle faux-Brit franchise, and your choice of *Police Academy* instalments (including the unnumbered seventh episode, *Police Academy: Mission to Moscow*) at the local megaplex.

# "World Class"

*"Wow, I just couldn't believe it!" cheered the new Regina Mayor, "We're millions of dollars in debt and don't have any means to pay it off! Do you know what that means?*

*"We're one of the Big Boys now! We are officially a World Class City!"*

—*"Regina Challenges Toronto for 'World Class' Bankruptcy," from www.saskabush.com, satire Saskatchewan style*

In the context of Canadian urbanism, "world class" is a code phrase that signals a major inferiority complex on the part of our mayors. Usually, they seem to believe that becoming "world class" involves spending an inordinate amount of money on spectacles that will irrevocably mess with the city's infrastructure for years to come: world expositions, the Olympic Games, new domed stadiums for expensive sports franchises, and so on.

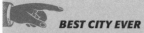

### BEST CITY EVER

There's a dizzying array of claims for best Canadian city. Lists, charts, reports, and surveys come out every year. So what's the best city in Canada? Depends on whether you're looking to raise a family, start a business, or get a lap dance. Also depends on what century you're living in. Here are some of the "bests" we've uncovered.

**Cleanest City (world):** Calgary (based on a 1998 Mercer survey of the world's 215 major centres, which put Calgary at the top of the environmental rankings and 31st overall. Vancouver came in second overall and Toronto came in 18th overall)

**Best City for Ambience (world):** Victoria (according to Conde Nast's 1998 Reader's Choice awards, which gave the sleepy BC city top marks for "environment and ambience")

**Best for Civic Beauty (Canada):** Winnipeg (the national Communities in Bloom contest 2001 ranked the Manitoba capital #1 for civic beauty, its second win in the seven years the contest has been running)

**Best City to Do Business In (world):** Toronto (according to Fortune magazine in 1996, but the city didn't even make the top 10 in 2000)

**Best City to Start a 500-Person Company (Canada):** Fredericton (according to Canadian Business magazine, which hired Boyd Company, a major US location consulting firm, to look at nine different cities and see which would be the best place to set up a business with 500 employees. Fredericton's bill came in at $39.67 million in annual operating costs, ahead of Edmonton with $40.89 million and Winnipeg with $41.28 million)

**Best City to Live In (world):** Vancouver (1997 annual city rankings compiled by Corporate Resources Group, which gave Toronto the #2 ranking in a tie with Auckland)

**City with Hottest Lap Dancers (North America):** Montreal (according to a 2001 article in New York-based men's magazine Stuff. The introduction to the piece states: "We even included Canada because the women are really loose up there")

**Best City to Raise a Family In (Canada):** Quebec City (according to the 2001 Parent Magazine ratings, Winnipeg was fourth; a Winnipeg newspaper article about the rating began: "Winnipeg may not be the best place in Canada to raise a family, but it's better than Calgary and it puts Edmonton, Toronto, and Vancouver to shame, according to a magazine survey")

But these grand projects often seem to lead to folly. For years after Expo 86, Vancouver's False Creek was a huge asphalt parking-lot–like scar. Hong Kong billionaire Li Ka-Shing eventually bought 200 acres of it, with zoning to build over 50 buildings to house 15,000 people in about 9,000 units, but you can bet that none of the estimated 500–950 poor and elderly people who were dislocated from downtown Vancouver prior to Expo could afford the fancy new digs. (See *Attractions*,

*Olympics* for more on residential displacement and the dangers of giant stadium/parking projects.)

When "world class" status is the impetus to host huge events or build extravagant structures, they've basically been a bust for the Canadian city. Toronto, the city most often cited as desperately seeking to attain said status, is more likely to be made fun of by its urban peers than acknowledged for its global stature. When you're constantly striving to be world class and you can't even get

"WORLD CLASS"

# World-Class Vancouver?

**by Dominic Ali and Paul Razzell, from *Geist* magazine**

Ever since Expo 86, city boosters have touted Vancouver as a "world-class" city. In a continuing effort to explore the Vancouver identity and to discover what the term "world-class" might mean, Dominic Ali and Paul Razzell (both Vancouverites) offer this exercise in comparing and contrasting the megalopolis in Lotus Land with other densely populated urban areas.

| | New York City | Paris | London | Vancouver |
|---|---|---|---|---|
| **Major Historical Event** | Wall Street Crash | Storming the Bastille | The Great Fire | Doug & the Slugs records first album |
| **Best-known Shop** | Macy's | Au Printemps | Harrods | Mountain Equipment Co-op |
| **Famous Citizen** | Woody Allen | Coco Chanel | Prince Charles | That guy from The Beachcombers |
| **Leisure Activity** | Shopping | Making love | Pub-crawling | Not smoking |
| **Nickname** | Big Apple | City of Lights | The Big Smoke | Vancouver |
| **Local Anthem** | "New York, New York" by Frank Sinatra | "La Vie En Rose" by Edith Plaf | "London Calling" by The Clash | "Cuts Like a Knife" by Brian Adams |
| **Favourite Souvenir** | I Love NY T-shirt | Perfume | London Underground map | Dime bag of homegrown |
| **Status Symbol** | Penthouse apartment | Season tickets to the opera | Country estate | Kayak roof rack |
| **Spiritual Sanctuary** | St. Patrick's Cathedral | Notre Dame Cathedral | Westminster Abbey | Wicca drum circle on Wreck Beach |
| **First Date Activity** | Gallery hopping in SoHo | Debating existentialism on the Left Bank | Picnicking at Kensington Gardens | Driving down to Seattle |

the garbage picked up, you've got some major problems. As one newspaper commentator wrote about the 2002 summer garbage strike in Toronto: "I can't wait for the Toronto tourism spin doctors to start telling us how Toronto is finally a truly world-class city, complete with the exotic smells and appearance of far-off lands."

"World class" aspirations not only open your city to justified abuse, but expose the egocentrism and wasted opportunities that have swirled around the concept. For fat-cat business types, Ottawa politicos, and big-city mayors, world class means lots of attention and long, lavish lunches. For the rest of us, it might just mean something entirely different. It could mean a city where no one sleeps on the streets, where day care is subsidized, the buses come on time via their own high-speed lane, and the restaurants aren't a health hazard. Once you've got the basics down—a rarity in this day and age—the word will get out: a livable city. Now *that's* world class.

# Youth Subculture

When most people think of youth rebellion and protest, they think of the unrest of the 60s—of flower children and nonviolent protest. But the image of a unified mass of young people standing together against racism, war, and oppression while smoking a little pot and engaging in the occasional bout of free love is a far cry from the reality of the diverse pockets of bohemian youth culture that populate our cities. Today's counterculture kids are much harder to pigeonhole. They don't all dress the same, think the same, or live in the same area of the city. Their interests are diverse and, more often than not, surprisingly narrow—the artists don't necessarily talk to the anarchists

who in turn ignore the punks who wouldn't be caught dead with the poets or the goths. (See *Denizens.*) At the same time, such divisions are counterintuitive. There are anarchist goth poets, queer punks, and anarchist artists. The city allows the youth subcultures to make connections even as it demands that the groups maintain their separate identities so as not to be lost or dismissed as just another bunch of urban poseurs trying to glom on to an identity they didn't earn.

Despite the complexity and endurance of today's youth culture, many tend to think of the city's hordes of bohemians as one big mass of ephemeral and silly subculture. Academics James and Robert Simmons, writing about urban Canada in the late 60s, put their disdain quite artfully:

> On the margin between the cheap housing of the decaying central city and the 20th century affluence and newness of the high-rise areas, live what the early urbanologists called the Bohemians, and modern journalists identify as hippies. Perhaps near the university, but within range of downtown, and surrounded by their own bookstores and coffee shops, are those who can temporarily ignore their native affluence and play it poor for a few years, with the comfortable (or uncomfortable) feeling that when necessary they will cop out to the suburbs.

That kind of putdown may have made sense at a time when increasing numbers of middle-class flower children rejected their 50s upbringing and sought refuge in the libertarian havens of Yorkville, Commercial Drive, and Halifax's art college. But that attitude does little to help us understand today's postmodern 21st-century bohemian. Today, events like the Montreal Anarchist Book Fair and

# The Enigma of Youth Culture
## A Diagrammatic Analysis Based on Derfla's Developmental Model of the Human Psyche

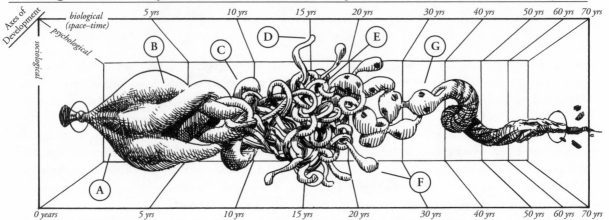

This Glandular-PG (Peer Group) mapping of Derfla's Model indicates several significant morphological developments during the 10–20 year period. The gently furrowed cone of early childhood [A] differentiates into several independent exploratory tentacles [B] during late childhood (5–10 year period); further polifurcation [C] follows with the onset of pre-pubescence, reaching maximum complexity in the 15–20 year period. The manifestation of this psycho-social hydra may be seen in the characteristic mood swings and uncertainty-motivated social curiosity of adolescence. In an effort to contain this veritable explosion of identity-seeking egopodia [D], the adolescent will move through various phases of group affiliation (identified in this diagram as the **Squirming Mass [E]**).

In the diagram, certain egopodia can be seen terminating with gentle buds (representing the end of a particular phase)[F], whereas others can be observed developing tumescent sacs [G] indicating the beginning of a maturing identity. The maturation of these identity sacs can be seen in the the 20–30 year period. The difficulty of tracking the phases and trends of adolescence may be attributed to several factors: 1) The fluid nature of the transformations 2) The secretive behaviour associated with the transitions and 3) Any attempt to study an earlier period from a later period will suffer from standard space–time refraction. The average researcher will be in a more compressed iteration of the s–t continuum, thereby distorting his/her view of the adolescent experience.

Toronto's widely attended Active Resistance Conference in 1998 show us, for starters, a serious side to youth sub-culture—a capacity for organization and dedication to a variety of causes that would seem to go well beyond mere posing and eventual flight to the suburbs.

Active Resistance events were meticulously organized, from the surreal opening press conference to the 50-plus seminars. The press conference began and ended with a spokesperson lecturing the gaggle of journalists about displaying their "corporate media" pass at all times, warning them not to try to conduct interviews in Symptom Hall, a dilapidated downtown meeting place/safe zone where conference participants could chat informally over a free meal. One primly dressed reporter stepped up to ask for an explanation of the conference's hostile attitude toward mainstream media. The kids in the crowd demanded that the reporter explain to them why the press consistently distorted their opinions. The reporter contended that he was at a press conference—here to ask questions, not to answer them. "This is an *anti*-press conference," an onlooker jeered.

The attendees of the conference were unwashed, pierced, studded, and battle weary. They were to be the same people who would gather a year later in Seattle and a year after that in Quebec City, where 1,200 metres of chain-link fence and thousands of canisters of tear gas were employed to keep dissent off the globalization agenda. And yet the cynical attitude exhibited at Active Resistance made it obvious that the new generation of loosely linked bohemian activists lacked the innocent fervour of yesteryear, when it was believed that you could join hands, put together a few banners and chants, and make everything right.

Karen Manko came from Manitoba to listen and participate. "It sounded interesting," she says, shrugging off the distance she travelled to be at the event. She was part of a radical-left youth coalition operating out of Winnipeg and, despite her affected disinterest, she seemed to be getting a lot out of the conference. "Street theatre is really good to get the media's attention. Most people hear about demonstrations through the media, so if you can get their attention …"

But today's subcultures can never agree on whether they want to repel or attract the media and public attention. Billboards are secretly defaced and joke communiqués are faxed to the press even as protests are choreographed for maximum effect. A few days after Active Resistance, the kids had dispersed and you'd be hard pressed to find evidence that the gathering had ever taken place. The minutes weren't published, no manifesto was issued, and even Symptom Hall was soon to be demolished.

So why gather at all? Perhaps because in the scattered post-60s bohemian terrain of urban Canada, there are no real meeting points: Commercial Drive has gone, well, commercial. Yorkville is probably the best place for street kids and loitering punks to get arrested fast. The inner city is coveted territory these days, and those who don't work at white-collar 9-to-5 jobs are finding themselves pushed farther and farther from the core so that yuppies can live closer to their fave sushi bars. As a result, bohemia is everywhere and nowhere—cropping up in a coffee shop, bar, or record store and disappearing as quickly as it arrives.

Perhaps the most successful bohemian focal point in all of Canada is Winnipeg's Mondragon Café—collective restaurant, coffee bar, and leftie bookstore. But even the Mondragon doesn't encompass every youth movement in the city, speaking mostly to the same loose grouping of semi-punk anti-globalization types who gathered for Active Resistance. For years the goths of Winnipeg apparently preferred to hang out in the Valley Room Restaurant, aka Eaton's fifth-floor cafeteria. But like most subculture youth groups intent on using the city as a staging point for unconventional lifestyles, the Winnipeg goths have, no doubt, moved on to some other strange dark cranny of the city most of us don't even know exists. (See *Denizens, Goths.*)

The fact is, the anti-press-conference attitude of Active Resistance embodies a bigger anti- attitude that the so-called underground or bohemian youth subcultures have cultivated over the years as they've watched their ideals and ideas get slowly co-opted and consumed by cool. Being part of a recognizable scene the media can anthropologize and the public can gawk at is no longer the point—the point now is to live the way one wants to live, free of apologies and asinine observations of mainstream society. Though they might gather to protest or meet their peers from around the world, underground culture has, in effect, been driven underground by its own cliché. You can't find it in any particular urban neighbourhood any more, and if you know where to go, you're probably going to keep it to yourself. And yet the underground haunts our cities—Toronto's Rochdale College is now an old people's home. The McGill ghetto is now coveted real estate. Where once the hippies frolicked and announced their emancipation, pockets of subterranean rebellion look on in disgust, emerging only to stage disinformation campaigns in forms as varied as a fake press conference or a fake edition of the *National Post* (see *Arts & Entertainment, Newspapers*), forms that leave the mainstream's emissaries as confused as a bank executive trying to find out why a homeless punk won't just get a job.

With that, we'll leave you to ponder the absent presence of bohemia in the Canadian city, but not before quoting from *the Salivation Army*, a now-defunct Toronto zine of gay punk culture whose creator, Scott Treleavan, just happened to pen the final word on the lost world of youth subculture:

YOUTH SUBCULTURE

*Once and for all: There is No Scene: There is no*
*membership activity. We've all done our time with*
*the punks, the Goths, the crusties, the club scenes, art*
*scenes. Galleries, grebos & factories. You name it.*
*We've done the tattoos, the hair-dos, the scars, and*
*the steel till we all looked alike. Communist meet-*
*ings, anarchist rallies, potlucks, back rooms, witch*
*circles; all the underground credentials you could*
*want… Having now safely returned to the helm we*
*can report: there wasn't really anybody there.*

# John Clarke:
# Menace or Messiah?

Described on *The National* as "one of the country's most
aggressive anti-poverty activists," John Clarke is a Toronto
organizer and the spokesperson and leader of the Ontario
Coalition Against Poverty. There are those who hate his
methods, those who tolerate his ornery, outspoken presence as a necessary evil, and those who believe he's a public menace. He's been arrested, harassed, and publicly
lambasted by everyone from right-wing proles to his own
leftist allies. And yet John Clarke soldiers on, the seemingly lonely leader of a seemingly hopeless battle to meet
indifference with attitude and make a difference for the
poor on the streets of our cities.

Hero or menace—no matter how you see him, Clarke
is difficult to ignore. As the *Toronto Star* once wrote,
"Though many are involved in the fight against poverty,
it's him that the public most associates with it. It's his
voice on the nightly news, his militant language, his
perpetual rage, that most unsettles people—when it isn't
driving them up the wall." The fact is, Clarke and his
Toronto-based OCAP have been involved in some of

the most memorable anti-establishment activities of the
last decade. It was Clarke and OCAP who attempted
to bargain at Loblaws after an Ontario government minister, offering advice in the wake of a 21.6% cut to social
assistance rates, suggested that the poor could haggle
for the price of their tuna fish. Sadly, the minister's suggestion seemed, in retrospect, not to accommodate grocery store protocol. As Clarke told the court after the
group's subsequent arrest, "When we attempted to bargain about the prices of various food items, the Loblaws
staff insisted they would not bargain. A number of us
informed Loblaws that we were acting on the advice of
Minister Tsubouchi, and we reminded them of the
nature of that advice. This did not appear to have any
impact on the staff."

Charges were later dropped, and Clarke and OCAP
moved on to bigger fish, including a massive and, ultimately, violent protest at Queen's Park (for which Clarke
would get arrested months later as an instigator), the
trashing of an Ontario MPP's constituent office to demon-
strate what it's like for the poor to be forcibly evicted, and
more recently the widely reported "Pope Squat" in which
an occupied building—taken over to coincide with the
Pope's summer visit to Toronto—served to keep the lack
of affordable housing on the media agenda.

Though some may question his tactics, none question Clarke's commitment to bringing the issues of
poverty and homelessness in the big city to the forefront.
Since 1990 he's been earning a pittance of $20,000 a year
and agitating tirelessly on behalf of those whose voices
we rarely hear in cities awash with the rich (see *Denizens,*
*Millionaires*), the clueless (see *Denizens, Cats*), and the
frivolous (see *Attractions, Parties*). Is he getting tired? He
doesn't seem to be. As Clarke once told the *Toronto Star*:
"I'm paid a wage to organize something I consider to be

OCAP poster announces The Pope Squat, the occupation of an abandoned building in Toronto

**THE POPE SQUAT**

Building takeover for cheaper rent, higher wages, and more housing.

OCAP

**THURS JULY 25 7 PM at MASARYK COWAN PARK**

(In Parkdale - Queen St. West at Cowan Ave., WEST of Dufferin, EAST of Lansdowne, beside the Masaryk Cowan Community Centre)

vital. I can fight these bastards. I get immense satisfaction from what I do."

We caught up with this anti-poverty crusader and asked him a few questions.

*We keep hearing—through the media and statistics—that there's more poverty and homelessness on the streets of the Canadian city than ever before. Is this true in your opinion? What are you seeing out there?*

That poverty and homelessness have exploded in the last few years is, as the question suggests, statistically verifiable. The removal of federal support for social programs has combined with provincial cuts to income and housing to mean that hundreds of thousands of precariously housed people keep a roof over their heads only by cutting back on other necessities, especially adequate and nutritious food. A vast destitute population has been put on the streets. Two thousand a month are evicted and the homeless shelters are not meeting the standards set for refugee camps by the UN. People are also facing massive police sweeps to "socially cleanse" them from areas of upscale residential or commercial development.

Before he was premier, I once heard Bob Rae observe that "the politics of poverty are only the reverse side of the politics of wealth." While his subsequent behaviour raises issues as to which side he's on in this matter, I'd have to say that this is a most insightful statement. It's the demands of a cheap labour economy and the redevelopment of Toronto as city where working-class and poor neighbourhoods are pushed out to the fringes that drive this agenda.

*A lot of people turn away from what they see on the streets, perhaps thinking that the problem is too big and that they can't do anything about it anyway. What can the average*

*Canadian city dweller do to help alleviate the problem of poverty in the big city?*

The average person is probably quite unsettled by large-scale homelessness. The polls register great concern on the issue. I can't, however, offer much hope in responding to this question. Passive discontent is not going to stop developers from putting up condos and having the police force that serves and protects them drive out the homeless. The real point, I think, is that the agenda that puts families into shelters and food-bank lines is the same one that seeks to gut health care and education and take back the gains of the labour movement. We need social mobilization to turn this back and, if the poor have the sharpest and most immediate interest in this struggle, many others have a huge stake as well.

YOUTH SUBCULTURE

*Your own organization, Ontario Coalition Against Poverty, goes far beyond what the average person might do. Can you describe briefly how the organization works and some of its major activities?*

OCAP has a membership made up, overwhelmingly, of people directly affected by homelessness or poverty. We organize on two levels. We take action to defend people being denied income support, facing eviction, threatened with deportation. We will use collective action or the threat thereof to give those who are intended to be helpless victims some clout. We also campaign on broader issues. We've won housing by occupying it. We've prevented the passage of regressive zoning legislation by invading meetings set up by local politicians. We've challenged organizations that introduce exploitive workfare programs with picket lines. We think the issue is to pass beyond protest, in the sense of applying moral pressure, and to find the means to disrupt the institutions that deal out misery.

*OCAP has been fiercely criticized for some of its tactics— like trying to shut down the Bay Street downtown financial centres for a day, storming the office of a politician, attempting to disrupt the visit of the Pope to Toronto. Can you talk about those types of actions and what you hope(d) to achieve?*

The three examples you give are all cases in point that take us back to my reply to the last question. To gather outside a finance minister's office and make speeches is to appeal to deaf ears. To retaliate against the 2,000 evictions a month by giving that person a taste of his own medicine disrupts his political functioning and inspires resistance as opposed to passive discontent. Rallies at Queen's Park are 10 a penny, but to shut down the operations of a right-wing government by hitting the cash registers of their corporate backers is another matter. That thinking underlay the march on Bay Street. Similarly, the Pope Squat. People die on the streets of this city while buildings are boarded up for speculative and parasitic purposes. That won't end until people start to take the buildings and make it cost-ineffective for them to continue this practice.

If OCAP has not yet built up its size and strength to the point where our disruptions have become an acute threat as opposed to a major concern, it only shows that we must go on growing and convincing many others to give up bleating out futile indignation and to "fight to win."

*What is your most optimistic vision for the future of the Canadian city? What do you think needs to happen to have that vision realized?*

Canadian cities are being devastated by the whole neo-liberal agenda; that is, removal of social supports, allowing infrastructure to decay, and pushing the ugly problems being created under the rug or out to the fringes. At present, I can only say that we're trying to find the means to stop the advance of this regressive tide. In the future, however, the development of the city as a place for all to live in and be part of will be a task of boundless possibilities. Once the planning of economic development, housing development, transportation systems, social services, and so forth can be viewed from the standpoint of democratic planning, community participation, and equal benefit and access, an unlimited field of work will open up. For the present, however, it's a matter of organizing the excluded to demand a place at the table.

# DENIZENS

**B**IG CITIES ARE LIKE DISNEYLAND FOR ADULTS, from the bizarre architecture right down to the weirdos in costume that roam the streets. Only they're not in costume; most of them dress like that *all the time.* And they may not be all that interested in coming up and giving you a big hug … or, conversely, they may be *too* interested in coming up and giving you a big hug. Most of them are completely harmless and some are even beneficial, but most are merely ineffectual, desperately attempting to capture your attention like so many purple-assed baboons grooming and fighting on a hot rockpile. What the hell: it's better than TV (see *Arts & Entertainment, TV* ).

Part of the fun of living in the city is the rapidity with which these groups mutate, evolve, vanish for long periods, or disappear completely. For example, you're not as likely to bump into a hippie these days as you were 20 years ago (though in isolated parts of BC there are still nests of them that haven't been wiped out), but the headbanger, once thought to be nearly extinct, is re-emerging in both its classical form (the mullet and leather jacket forever!) and in the guise of "nü-metal" fans who look like the misbegotten hybrids of punk, metal, goth, hip hop, and skate culture (which they basically are). Sadly, the only section of the urban population that seems to be growing at a steady rate is the panhandlers and street people.

The following is a sort of field guide to help you sort out the denizens of the Canadian metropolis. We wanted to make Pokémon-style trading cards for them all (five yuppies and a goth for a mint-condition cyborg, anyone?), but it wasn't in the budget. Read on.

# Kooks

What's a kook, then? Donna Kossy, author of the infamous eponymous book on the subject (*Kooks: A Guide to the Outer Limits of Human Belief.* 2nd ed., Feral House, 2001), says this:

> The word "kook" was coined by the beatniks, as a pared-down version of "cuckoo," as in "going cuckoo." A kook is a person stigmatized by virtue of outlandish, extreme or socially unacceptable beliefs that underpin their entire existence. Kooks usually don't keep their beliefs to themselves; they either air them constantly or create lasting monuments to them.

"Kook" in this usage is not necessarily a pejorative term. Whether or not they choose to act on it, kooks sincerely believe in some essential "truth" that differs from the ones that motivate the bulk of society. Sometimes history even vindicates them (Galileo was a kook in his time; so was Nikola Tesla).

It should come as no surprise that Canada has a long and proud tradition of kooks. Louis Riel, the great statesman and founder of the province of Manitoba, had his kooky side, wanting to rename various constellations after members of his family. Former prime minister William Lyon Mackenzie King talked to the spirit of his dead mother through his dog and built English romantic ruins in the Gatineau Hills (see below). But these are the kooks we all know about; following is the dirt on a few of our nation's more colourful (but definitely outré) thinkers, past and present.

## Brother Twelve and Madame Zee

Brother Twelve and his consort Madame Zee were Canada's first prophets of the new age, preaching that "destruction cometh upon many" and claiming that they would personally be selecting the next president of the United States.

Brother Twelve's origins are clouded in mystery: he may have been born Edward Arthur Wilson ca. 1878 in England or Wyoming (where he may have been banished for knocking up a young lady), or he may have been born Julian Churton Skottowe, son of a church missionary and an East Indian princess.

The Brother was a bit of a womanizer, dumping his wife for one Myrtle Baumgartner, a doctor's wife he'd seduced on a train from Seattle to Chicago. The Brother preached that he and Myrtle were the reincarnations of Osiris and Isis, and that they would bring the next

## IVAN & AKIKO

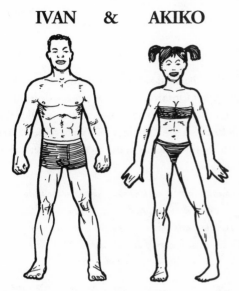

*They're young and beautiful ... and in the Big City!*

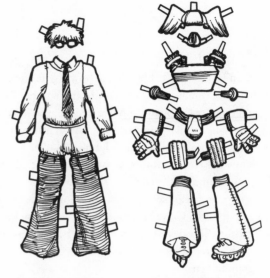

**INSIDE OUT IVAN**
He wears his underwear
on the outside!

**SAMURAI ROBOT AKIKO**
She thinks she's
a superhero!

saviour into the world (note for calendar watchers: this saviour was supposed to rise up in 1975. The clock is still ticking …).Together, they set up a "City of Refuge" on Vancouver Island and nearby De Courcy Island, convincing prominent people (including Group of Seven painter Lawren Harris and *Saturday Night* magazine's literary editor William Arthur Deacon) of the veracity of their beliefs.

But all didn't go as planned. They had a girl instead of a boy (apparently, saviours in the Brother's world had to be male), and Myrtle went crazy (crazier?), only to be replaced with Mabel Skottowe, who reinvented herself as the bullwhip-wielding Madame Zee. The oppressed believers in the City of Refuge soon grew tired of their own poverty in the face of the Brother's luxurious living, and Madame Zee's bullwhip didn't help much either. They took Brother Twelve to court, but he used his evil magic to make a witness vanish without a trace, cause others to

vomit to the point where they couldn't take the stand, and render the prosecuting attorney (literally) speechless.

The Brother had had enough. He removed his $430,000 fortune from the bank in $20 gold coins, placed them in Mason jars, and supposedly buried them all over Vancouver Island. (Treasure-seekers are still looking for them.) After blowing up the City of Refuge, he departed Canada for Switzerland, where he apparently died. All he left behind, in the cult's vault on De Courcy Island, was a piece of tarpaper with a chalk inscription: "FOR FOOLS AND TRAITORS—NOTHING!"

## William Lyon Mackenzie King

He was our prime minister for 22 years, including all of Word War II … and he may have relied on the advice given to him by spiritualists for his political decisions. Frightening? You bet. Throughout his life, King conducted séances with a few friends and, occasionally, a medium in attendance. He believed he was communing with his dead mother (frequently, through his terrier Pat), his grandfather (William Lyon Mackenzie, who led the 1837 Rebellion), Sir Wilfrid Laurier, British prime minister Gladstone, as well as Saints John and Luke.

When he wasn't communing with the dead through his pets or running the country, King was busy collecting stones to erect fake romantic ruins (or "follies") on his estate in the Gatineau Hills. These ruins include stones from Canada's and Britain's houses of Parliament, and in his fireplace are three stones from the house of his grandfather.

## ManWoman

On top of his appearances as the Mr. Peanut–inspired "Mr. Death" and his prolific output as a painter, Canadian pop artist ManWoman (born Patrick Charles Kemball in Cranbrook, BC) has taken on a difficult task for himself: rehabilitating the public perception of the swastika. His chosen vehicle for this mission? Tattooing the symbol on himself, over and over and over…

You can read all about it on his websites, <www. gentleswastika.com> and <www.manwoman.net>, or in his book, *The Gentle Swastika* (Flyfoot Press, 2001):

> *For thousands of years almost every race, tribe, and religion on earth has revered the Swastika, using it in a variety of shapes and styles, associating it with the hammer of Thor, the footprints of Buddha, the emblem of Shiva, Apollo, Jupiter, and even Jesus Christ.*

Hitler chose (and reversed the direction of) the swastika as a good luck charm, but dishonoured it in the process. Now ManWoman and the other Friends of the Swastika are trying to rehabilitate it. The book is chock full of weird facts: until World War II, there was a town called Swastika, Ontario. ManWoman has found evidence of at least three Canadian hockey teams called the Swastikas (there's a team photo, too!). Want to help? You can sign the online Friends of the Swastika Declaration of Independence:

> *We, the undersigned, declare the swastika to be innocent of the crimes perpetrated in its name under Nazi banners. Five years of war cannot be allowed to wipe out five thousand years of sacred history. We declare that the swastika has an independent life.*

Chief Dan George himself has praised ManWoman's rehabilitative efforts, so you know it's gotta be good … and Mark Mothersbaugh of Devo says: "The masses are asses who need ManWoman glasses!" Make sure you also check out ManWoman's paintings of transcendental consumer goods like "Truthpaste," "God Is My Foundation," and "Spiritual Chips."

## Pocketman

Don Bell's novel *Pocketman* (Dorset Publishing, 1979) tells the story of a "holy fool" who, like the 13th-century Sufi, Mulla Nasrudin, is the subject of numerous teaching parables. Pocketman wanders the streets of many Canadian cities, especially Montreal, dispensing wisdom from his voluminous pockets on scrawled pieces of paper or posters.

Pocketman is based on Roy McDonald, who's been wandering the college campuses and downtowns of many cities in Ontario and Quebec for over 40 years, selling photos of himself standing under a lilac tree with flowers in his hair and beard. Though he's battled alcoholism and depression, McDonald is still around,

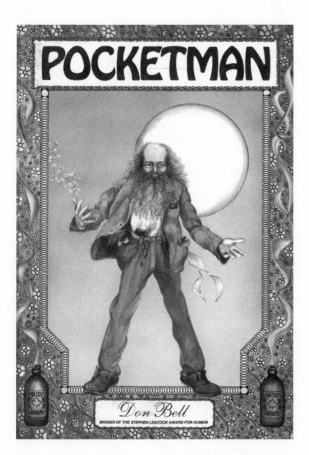

**POCKETMAN**

*Don Bell*

WINNER OF THE STEPHEN LEACOCK AWARD FOR HUMOR

last seen on the streets of London, Ontario, selling three books of his own: *Beard, Living: A London Journal,* and *The Answer Questioned*, all available for under 10 bucks from <theatreshop.bizhosting.com/beard_by_roy_mcdonald.html>, and a bargain at that.

# Intellectuals

**Y**ou can't swing a dead cat in Canada without hitting a public intellectual. Our universities, think tanks, and nonprofit organizations are full of vibrant and engaging thinkers of all sorts. The next time you feel

The story of a "holy fool" who wanders Montreal.

like flexing your head, try the writing of one of these folks on for size; you won't be disappointed.

### Derrick de Kerckhove

The director of the McLuhan Program in Culture and Technology and professor in the Department of French at the University of Toronto is a busy guy. When he's not off consulting for the government or the media, he's writing books in several languages, including *The Skin of Culture* (Somerville House, 1995) and *Connected Intelligence* (Somerville House, 1997).

### Northrop Frye

The late great granddaddy of Canadian literary criticism (Companion of the Order of Canada, member of the Royal Society, yadda yadda yadda) took Biblical and archetypal criticism and turned them on their heads to create *The Bush Garden* (House of Anansi, 1998)—a solid basis for the first interesting manifestations of contemporary Canadian literary identity (books like Margaret Atwood's *Survival* and *Surfacing* are a direct result of engaging with Frye's thought). Greatest hits include *Anatomy of Criticism, The Educated Imagination, The Critical Path*, and *The Great Code.*

### George Grant

The author of *Lament for a Nation* and *Technology and Empire* was a tireless champion of the notion that the corporate culture of the US is the greatest threat to our ongoing well-being. Grant's writing chiefly concerns the fraught relationship between technology and contemporary society. He believes that we've interpolated technology into ourselves in order to extend our mastery over the world, and, nihilistically, that we would rather "will nothing" than have "nothing to will." A depressing notion, but thought-provoking.

## Harold Innis

Another famous U of Toronto professor, Harold Innis was an economist educated at McMaster and the University of Chicago. His early studies of the Canadian railroads and fur trade helped him to grasp the necessity of transportation and communication systems in building and controlling political and economic systems. Innis's book *The Bias of Communication* is a key text in modern communication theory; Marshall McLuhan's slogan "the medium is the message" is essentially a snappy rephrasing of Innis's key idea.

## Jane Jacobs

Without any professional training as a city planner, Jane Jacobs has nevertheless managed to become a leading authority on the health of contemporary cities. Though she was born in the US, Jacobs has lived and worked in Toronto since 1968, producing books such as the classic *The Death and Life of Great American Cities* (her first book), *Cities and the Wealth of Nations*, and *Systems of Survival: A Dialogue on the Moral Foundations of Commerce and Politics*. Unlike many city planners, Jacobs believes that a high level of population density is essential for the growth and prosperity of a city. She's a strong advocate of diversity, eclecticism, and spontaneity in cities, believing that there should be little or no separation between residences and businesses, or old buildings and new ones.

## Alberto Manguel

Writer, translator, editor, and anthologist Alberto Manguel is a citizen of the world. Born in Argentina (where he read to Borges after he went blind), he's lived in Italy, England, and Canada, and currently resides in France. He's the author or editor of, among other things, *A Dictionary of Imaginary Places, A History of Reading*, and two anthologies of fantastic literature, *Black Water* and *Black Water 2*. By focusing on the literature of the impossible, Manguel makes us expand our notion of the possible.

## Marshall McLuhan

Once merely the director of the Centre for Culture and Technology at the University of Toronto, Marshall McLuhan is now, for all intents and purposes, the patron saint of the media-saturated contemporary milieu. McLuhan welded the modernist verbal and typographic fireworks of Wyndham Lewis, James Joyce, and other experimental writers to the history and sociology of ideas, producing a singular, aphoristic style of philosophy whose effects are still being felt. Try *Understanding Media, The Medium Is the Massage, War and Peace in the Global Village*, and *The Mechanical Bride* for starters—once you're hooked, you'll want to read it all.

## John Ralston Saul

Novelist, doctor of economics, and consort to the governor general, John Ralston Saul has written five novels and four major works of nonfiction. Each of Saul's novels deals with conflicts between the individual and the power structures of contemporary society; his nonfiction examines the same themes. For fiction, try *The Next Best Thing* and *The Paradise Eater*; for the nonfiction, start with *Voltaire's Bastards: The Dictatorship of Reason in the West* and *The Unconscious Civilization*.

## David Suzuki

Geneticist, environmentalist, professor (at UBC, until he retired in 2001), and broadcaster David Suzuki has

**GOTH PUNK IVAN**
His python is albino!

**MISTRESS AKIKO**
She'll read your tarot!

been patiently explaining science (and how badly we're messing up the environment) for over 30 years now, most visibly as the host of CBC TV's *The Nature of Things*, CBC Radio's *Quirks and Quarks*, and various and sundry TV miniseries. He has 15 honorary doctorates and has been formally adopted by two Canadian First Nations tribes in recognition of his work on behalf of Canada's First Peoples. He's also written over 30 books, including *The Sacred Balance: Rediscovering Our Place in Nature*, *Earth Time*, and *Wisdom of the Elders*.

# Goths

*The Valley Room Restaurant (aka Eaton's 5th floor cafeteria) is the buffet that time forgot. You can walk through Eaton's (for years) and not even know it's there. There are only two types of people who hang out at the Valley Room: really cool old people and goths. The cool old people remember when it was glamorous to shop at Eaton's. The last time I was there I saw a woman that looked like an ancient Bette Davis. She was smoking a cigarette and looking very bored with the world. Why do the goths hang out with these old people? They like the ambience—the sense of faded grandeur. So meet us for lunch at Eaton's—where you too can eat mashed potatoes with the undead.*

—*Clystemstra,* Spooky Winnipeg *zine*

We have a soft spot for goths. They're the subculture that time forgot, lost somewhere between punk and industrial, trapped in a Phantom Zone between worlds … and that's just the way they like it, because it's all the more tragic. (Seen on a T-shirt in Toronto: "Vampires aren't real. Grow up.")

It's amazing that goth has persisted as long as it has, given the molecule-thick (or thin) cloth out of which it was shaped: a couple of really good albums by Joy Division and Bauhaus, some silly ones from the Sisters of Mercy, Bram Stoker's *Dracula* (and all of its derivatives, including those stupid Anne Rice books), a jar of black nail polish, and lung-choking clouds of hairspray. It's even harder being goth in Canada, because people who are *really* that sick normally just die from the cold.

Goth received a much-needed boost from the piercing and vampire crazes and *fin-de-siècle* decadence in general, which may explain why it's still around. Times are tough for the goths, however. Many goth boys have recently jumped ship to Norwegian death metal, because it's scarier and has better music. And many goth landmarks have disappeared, such as the Toronto club Sanctuary, which was replaced by a Starbucks (oh, the ignominy of it all).

Another club, called Ilyich's—one of our fave watering holes for years—has also sadly gone to the grave for good. Founded by Ukrainian immigrants, Ilyich's was an amazing exercise in post-Soviet chic: a five-foot-across brass head of Lenin with red glowing eyes and devil's horns presided over an upstairs bar lit primarily by three video screens, which were usually showing something like Eisenstein's *Battleship Potemkin*, Syd and Marty Krofft's psychedelic kids' classic *H.R. Puf 'n' Stuf*, and White Zombie videos. Downstairs was the worst pool table in the city, a ceiling covered with bones, and (the crowning touch) a glass coffin/bar containing a wax effigy of Lenin. (You can't make shit like this up—no one would believe it.) What's a goth to do? Well, there's always the Bovine Sex Club (whose motto is "Milk me and eat my young"), but it's been overrun with tube-sock-and-base-ball-cap-wearing people from the suburbs for at least five years now, so times are grim indeed.

But here's the thing—no matter what you might think of the quality of the art that inspires them, at the height of their glory, *goths always looked great*. They were like a kind of cultural heatsink: with them taking care of looking fine (there *is* a minimum quota of "really, really good-looking people" for all cities, you know), the rest of us could slouch around in our jeans and skip shaving on alternate mornings. But hard times have fallen on the goths; the few remaining ones look increasingly ratty. The recent popularity among goths of giant platform

shoes, garish drunken-sailor-style tattoos, and multiple facial piercings aren't helping much, either. We should declare goths an endangered species and set up game preserve–like areas for them immediately; it'd be just like having your own personal Addams Family.

# Yuppies

… are almost too easy to hate; it's like shooting fish in a barrel.

Thankfully, yuppies are not quite the scourge that they were in the 80s, when they choked the cities with vast fleets of BMWs and Audis, yammering into their cell phones (see *Tools, Cell Phones*) and swilling fancy coffee (see *Tools, Coffee*) at 70 kph. At the dawn of the new millennium, most of them have either consigned themselves to a career of soul-deadening busywork "with opportunities for advancement" or have settled into spawning behaviour in the remote suburbs.

Now that the yuppies have reached child-rearing age, they're faced with an interesting conundrum. All their lives they've been trained to think that career advancement is the only thing that matters. In the corporate world, for the young and ambitious, families are a liability and the drive to reproduce smacks of the evolutionarily regressive. The choice is, for them, a difficult one: big salaries, peer respect, and job satisfaction on the one hand, and dirty diapers, screaming, and stains on the Beemer's upholstery on the other.

It's especially tricky for female yuppies, since "having it all" usually entails putting

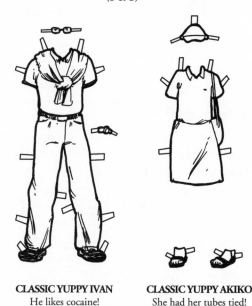

**CLASSIC YUPPY IVAN**
He likes cocaine!

**CLASSIC YUPPY AKIKO**
She had her tubes tied!

*like all the other commodities they encounter. Children, unlike contentment, cannot be bought. Children are the Yuppie Achilles heel.*

All the high-quality educational toys in the world won't change the fact that what kids need the most is their parents' time, the one thing that yuppies are most loath to sacrifice. While most yuppies are pretty smart, recognizing intellectually that this problem exists doesn't seem to help matters much. Sullivan leaves us with a depressing testament to his own helplessness: the image of his own son playing with a Speak and Spell—the only adult friend who will talk to the boy for as long as he wants, providing the moral support that his parents can't: "You are Correct. Perfect Score."

off pregnancy until the last possible minute, and then having to deal with possible biological complications during pregnancy, not to mention the disinclination of one's partner to stick around and be supportive through the early child-rearing years (the time when men are most likely to have extramarital affairs). Paul Sullivan, a TV producer from Winnipeg, put it succinctly:

> *The Yuppie couple believes the secret to life is buying quality. Not ordinary quality, but exotic quality. Yuppies have children the same way they have cars, the smart way.*
>
> *In this respect, Yuppie is just a new word for fool. Because the Yuppie will find out that children cannot be solved like other consumer dilemmas. It doesn't matter how many books you read, or how much money you have, or what kind of baby car seat you buy, or what Montessori school you send them to, children are not*

# Artists

Artists are strange urban creatures. They haunt bars, hardware stores, and gallery openings (particularly when there's likely to be free cheese). They have paint in their hair and leave five-minute spaces between their sentences. Though most of them won't get famous or even noticed, they persist. The effect is an odd one: a strange collective but usually invisible imprint on a city's consciousness.

To explicate and add further mystique to the artist persona, we sought out Drue Langlois, member of the infamous Royal Art Lodge, a collective that includes, among other great talents, the eponymous Marcel Dzama. Langlois, like most of the Art Lodgers, is a Winnipeg artist savant who does everything from publishing his own comic book to drawing irreverent pop-culture-savvy

ARTISTS

The Things You Never Forget, a collaborative drawing by Winnipeg's Royal Art Lodge.

*When we think about Canadian art, we usually think about the Group of Seven and paintings of the outdoors. But most of us live in the city now. Should everyone be sculpting skyscrapers?*
I think, instead, we should think back to a time before human beings came into existence. There were a lot of funny stages the animals of today had to go through during evolution. There were elephants with hair all over their bodies and I think they may have had two trunks for a while. The horses were like little dogs.

*You live in Winnipeg. What's that like? Does where you live cause you to make different kinds of art?*
I spend most of the time ignoring where I live … so the art I make tends to avoid any reference to Winnipeg or Canada or the fur trade.

*How does the RAL make the city a happier, better place to be?*
The RAL doesn't improve the city in any noticeable way. What Winnipeg really needs is a place where you can buy fresh walnut cakes. They're these little cakes with red bean or almond paste inside of them. I buy them in Toronto when I'm there. I've never had anything like them.

*If you had to devote an entire show to one particular urban Canadian person, who would you choose? Why? What would the show look like?*
I think I would like to dedicate a show to this Sears catalogue model that I've been collecting photos of for the past couple of years. I use the pictures to draw one of my comic book characters, Radiana Bluestocking. I didn't see the model in this year's fall catalogue … I wonder what she's up to. She usually had about three pictures in

scenes of cartoon surrealism to fashioning his own noise-making kite. In the interview below, Drue presents some shocking truths about himself, the art world, and his unhealthy obsession with the Korean walnut cake. He is honest to the extreme, telling us in an e-mail, "I hope some of these answers are okay. I found the first one to be very difficult. I was going to compare art to sports and talk about how they're equally unnecessary but decided to write something closer to what I'd actually say to someone." Take it away, Drue:

*Most urban residents say they don't really get art. What would you tell those people?*
I would tell them that I don't understand a lot of it either but that once in a while you come across things that you can relate to or things that are visually appealing … or appealing in a sad or funny way.

*Lola,* an excellent source for accessible commentary on the arts in Canada.

the whole catalogue and often only modelled jackets or hats. I think I have a picture for every angle of her head now so I don't really need any more, but I liked that the character would age along with the model. The show would exhibit paintings and sculptures of the Radiana character, and maybe I'd get the model to dress up as the character and fly around the room on strings or something.

## Where Are the Artists?

If you want to find artists, you have to look in the right places. Two places to start are *Lola* magazine and the Instant Coffee mailing lists.

*Lola* was born in the summer of 1997 when artist Sally McKay, curator John Massier, and arts writer Catherine Osborne vowed to create a Toronto art magazine on the cheap that was a genuine reflection of the art and of the people making and showing it. The editors had little interest in tautological art jargon, which to them, while on occasion "nerdishly sexy," was mostly boring and impenetrable. In December 1997 the first issue of *Lola* saw the light of day, and there's been no looking back.

One of *Lola*'s strongest features is the Shotgun review section, a collection of dozens of short-short reviews of various art exhibitions and events written by people from all over and from all walks of life. Hundreds of writers have contributed to this section; about 270 exhibitions are reviewed every year. This is art criticism for the real world.

Instant Coffee <www.instantcoffee.org>, a series of local, national, and international arts-events-related e-mailing lists, is the brainchild of co-founders Jenifer

Papararo and Jinhan Ko. Instant Coffee began (and continues to operate) as a curatorial enterprise, with its members curating and hosting events at various venues, and making their own art in the process. The concept behind the mailing list is simple: you send them an e-mail a minimum of a week before your event, and they add it to their mailing. Instant Coffee comes in three yummy flavours:

**instant events:** local toronto/ontario announcements + inter/national posts + Saturday Edition. events@instantcoffee.org

**instant national:** inter/national posts (shows, calls, www, jobs) + Saturday Edition. national@instantcoffee.org

**instant halifax:** news of interest to haligonians/ maritimers + inter/national posts + Saturday Edition. halifax@instantcoffee.org

ARTISTS

# Jason Dunda's Top 10 Art Clichés You Can't Do Any More

1. Faux controversy: Please stop trying to shock your audience unless you're sure you can get a government official to take away all of your funding, or at least a cease and desist order from someone's lawyer. People who go to galleries aren't easily offended anyway.

2. Words: Words officially suck, especially words like Diaspora, dialectic, edgy, vocabulary, rhetoric, virtual, transformative, interactive, and identity. Perpetrators: Anybody who has applied for a grant in the last twenty years.

3. Artists' statements: See #2. Folks, let's leave the writing up to the writers.

4. Dolls: Cheap, cute, and chock full of meaning, dolls are the ideal thing to make a redundant statement, especially if there's weird sex stuff involved. Toys are a related banned topic particularly close to my heart. Perpetrators: Me and half of Toronto's emerging artists.

5. Piles of stuff: It's time to put to rest the "if one is good, dozens are better" formula. Perpetrators: Katharina Fritsch, and everybody profiled in that *Lola* spread a few issues ago.

6. Hair: We all have it someplace, so when you think about it hair isn't really all that exciting to begin with. Related banned items include bodily fluids, fingernails, and belly button lint. Leave 'em at home.

7. Big photographs of small stuff: Don't make me confiscate your macro-lens and train set.

8. Painting: I'm jumping on the bandwagon: painting is for 20th century hayseed suckers. From now on I'm going to take pictures of my crotch and you better damn well like it.

9. Food: Let's keep it in the kitchen from now on. Perpetrators: Me, Rirkrit Tiravanija, Jana Sterbak. Felix González-Torres is acceptable because you're allowed to eat his work.

10. Irony: See #8. No, really. ●

---

*Cheap, cute, and chock full of meaning, dolls are the ideal thing to make a redundant statement, especially if there's weird sex stuff involved.*

---

# Secret Jane: Portrait of an Artist as a Young Posterer

For Shaan Syed, the culmination of his 2001 urban art project came nine months later—with a call from Nike.

"They wanted to use me to do an advertising campaign that would be like the Jane campaign," says the soft-spoken 27-year-old Toronto painter and provocateur. "It was for a sneaker they were planning on marketing to the artsy neighbourhoods in Canada."

For three months, Syed, who is known primarily as an up-and-coming painter, trolled the empty late-night streets, putting up 1,000 silk-screened posters featuring the sketched face of a woman and a single word: "Jane."

"It was a project about the personal, about the ego of the individual. I wanted this face to be everywhere at once, and people would come to know her as Jane. The posters would get ripped down eventually, but the images would still stay in people's psyche."

Jane is pictured as young, winsome, with just a hint of what Syed describes as a "Mona Lisa smile."

"Jane is a real woman, a friend of mine, and her name is Jane. The sketch came from a two-minute drawing I did in my sketchbook."

The Jane campaign follows a similar experiment Syed conducted in 2000, also featuring a sketch of a woman identified by first name.

"Margarita had a sad expression. This time the posters are a bit more upbeat. I think they attracted more attention because of that."

Syed put up far fewer posters of Margarita, and because he timed it to coincide with a solo exhibition of his paintings, he was accused by some in the art world of simply conducting a PR campaign for his work.

"People thought I was advertising the show. I wanted to do it again, do it so it would be taken more as a project in and of itself."

Nevertheless, reactions to the second effort have been mixed. Syed refers to those who were intrigued by the project's grassroots ability to evoke everything from advertising campaigns to missing persons posters. But some continued to accuse him of "blatant self-promotion," which he cites as his least favourite interpretation of the Jane campaign.

If Syed is sensitive to charges of self-promotion, it is with good reason. The poster campaign got him the kind of notice and attention that young painters don't usually experience, including articles in several major newspapers and a national radio interview on the CBC.

"You put something out there, you have to come to terms with how it's taken," says Syed philosophically about the small cutesy articles that appeared on the project. But Syed insists that it wasn't about promotion. "I looked on it as an experiment—I put out all these posters to see if they would really stick in people's heads. And they did. They got noticed."

The success of Jane can be directly attributed to what the posters were not: part of some slick corporate scheme.

"They were noticed because they're not advertising. They're not designed. People thought it was the start of an ad campaign, but when nothing came after, they were forced to think about it in a different way."

In a city deluged with advertisements, anything that wedges itself into the populace's collective sensibility the way Jane did is notable. Thus the call from Nike which, in many ways, represented a conclusion to a project as ambivalent as Jane's coy smile. With that call, Syed was faced with a difficult dilemma: could he—or should he—apply the ambiguities and subtleties of Jane to a Nike sneaker ad campaign?

"They said that the Jane project was a success. That's a huge compliment, coming from these ad executives. But in the end they went in a different direction. I was relieved. I didn't want to have to make the decision."

ARTISTS

# Window Washers

"The first thing I thought when I got to the city was: look at all the glass," explains Bill Peddle, a 10-year veteran of window washing in Toronto. "It's like a lot of things," he says, shrugging. "You start and you just kinda keep at it."

But it isn't like a lot of things. How many other jobs are there where a wrong step can kill and the wind can ruin two hours of hard labour? "You have to play the wind," Bill admits. "You're moving along the wall and then the wind'll switch up on you and splash dirty water all over what you just cleaned. And you don't get paid to clean them twice."

"Poor fella ..."

Still, a grizzled veteran like Peddle is rarely surprised—by the weather or anything else. He's had at least one dangerous moment on the job, but he doesn't want to talk about it. Instead he wants to give this message to architects: "They design buildings that are nice to look at, but it's not always easy to go in and clean them. They should think about us poor bastards." But few do think about the souls who keep our towers gleaming. "That's the thing I hate most about the job," Peddle says. "Nobody notices you. You'll be working and people will walk right underneath where you've got signs up saying it's dangerous and they'll stop right there and talk."

Peddle finally relents and confides that once, while cleaning some windows angled in, he leaned out just a bit too far and stumbled off his platform. "I fell through [the rigging] and I was hanging by my armpits. First thing I did was look around to make sure nobody saw me." A consummate professional, the last thing Peddle wants is for the denizen of some cozy office to see him slip up. He takes far too much pride in what he does.

"You have to be a climber. You're outdoors. Nobody bugs me, and I'm not strapped to a desk all day." Peddle downs the last of his beer. "*That* would be a nightmare."

# Squeegee Kids

All through the 90s there were squeegee kids all over Canadian cities. A natural result of the collision of punk culture and panhandling, squeegee kids took the high road under impossible circumstances, offering a useful service in exchange for your change.

But times changed in the summer of 1999, when Mel Lastman and the Toronto *Sun* declared "war" on the squeegees. Gregory Boyd Bell of *eyeweekly* made an astute observation: "Look at Toronto newspapers of the late 1960s and substitute 'squeegee kid' for 'hippie'—sure enough, there is a parental culture complaining about weird-looking, smelly, dirty kids with no jobs and no ambition. When today's reporters make clever remarks about 'multiple pierced' kids with brightly coloured hair, funny names and odd musical tastes, they perfectly imitate the squares of 30 years ago."

When the actual crackdown occurred, a task force of 175 police officers began to sweep squeegee kids from the streets. There were 54 arrests and 2,000 "noteworthy problems" during the program's first four days. There was even a "squeegee kid hotline" for people to rat out the punks working the local corner.

For some sense of what the squeegee issue looks like outside of the prism of law and order Lastman-style, we recommend taking a look through the RoachCam.

Roach is a squeegee punk who's been on the street since he was 14. In the best Canadian tradition of participatory documentaries (see *Arts & Entertainment, Public Access Cable*), filmmaker Daniel Cross gave Roach and his squeegeepunk buddies portable video cameras—and now you can see what *we* look like to *them* through the windshield.

The resulting documentary, *S.P.I.T.* (Squeegee Punks in Traffic, 2001, 77 minutes), presents a devastating dialogue between squeegee kids and the uncaring city they depend on. Roach's camera acts as the hammer: hard, forceful, direct; impacting with the force of an actual life. Daniel Cross's camera documents the impact: recording the reflections of individual lives, mirrored upon the shards of flying glass. Daniel Cross is best known for his feature-length theatrical documentary titled *The Street: a film with the homeless*, which won awards at film festivals around the world.

# Panhandlers

*The sky was an indecisive gray. The snowbanks were a few shades lighter. Snow that had blanketed the trees and lampposts the day before in a false Christmas Eve scene was now falling and smashing into the ground.*

*I sat on a bench on Barrington and waited for the 80 to come and take me home. A gutter punk sat on the next bench over. He wore the typical ripped combats, a sleeveless black jean jacket with a Dead Kennedy's patch hand stitched on the back over a black hoodie, and a fraying studded ballcap over his faded green mohawk. I chuckled to myself as I thought about how it would be funny to see him get hit by the chunks of falling snow. Then again, I grew up watching Bugs Bunny and America's Funniest Home Videos.*

*A man in a suit and a long trench coat walked by, and the punk feebly asked him for some spare change. Surprisingly, the man stopped and dipped his hand into the pockets of his pinstriped trousers. I figured he was looking for some loose change, but instead came out with what looked like an American fifty dollar bill. Slightly stunned, I watched as he gave it to the kid. The punk flipped out, and thanked the man repeatedly while shaking his hand with both of his.*

*The man smiled a selfless smile, muttered something to the punk kid, and then walked away.*

PANHANDLERS

weather is like? Why didn't he give it to that long-haired and bearded hippie who plays the flute in hope of making enough money to go to India? Why didn't he donate it to a food group or a housing group that deals with such situations?

My bus came from around the corner. I got up and walked towards the sign through the puddles of melted hail that had collected between the streets and sidewalks. Whatever the case may be, it must be a great day for that gutter punk.

—Adam Kelly, "Gutter Punk Panhandle," from the Halifax zine Synonymous to Anonymous

I twiddled my thumbs and stared at the gum and cigarette butt covered sidewalk. I was confused. I couldn't help question the kid's integrity. How will he spend his money? Maybe it'll be on some yummy food at a fancy restaurant. Maybe it'll be on liquor for another party. Maybe it'll be on a bus ticket home wherever home may be. Maybe it'll be on a Sex Pistols CD Box set. And it's just so rare to see someone being so generous to a stranger that I was skeptical of the man's motives. Why did that man give away so much money? Maybe he used to be in a similar situation. Maybe he was feeling guilty, and that fifty dollars was for all of the times he didn't give any money to pan-handlers. Maybe he lost a bet with a friend. Maybe he's extremely rich and has a huge heart. So why did he give so much money to just one kid? Why didn't he give it to Rob Lemon who stands at the same corner every day and plays his guitar no matter what the

# Wildlife

It's not just the people who have deserted the Canadian countryside for the city—it's the animals too. Raccoons, possums, deer, foxes, rats, skunks, mice, pigeons, Canada geese, peregrine falcons, and even the odd cougar or bear can be found living cheek-by-jowl with the humans in the midst of our most densely populated areas. The various types of rodents have always been city dwellers, but the size of the rodents living indoors keeps increasing. As if in a bid to outstrip the size of New York City rats (see *Politics, "World Class"*), we've jumped straight to the heavyweights: raccoons, skunks, and possums, who've grown fat and sassy on the rice and bread that old ladies frequently leave on boulevards for the pigeons.

Rats, at least, have the virtue of not smelling bad. Try living with a skunk inhabiting the space under your porch or in your crawlspace for a few weeks and rats will seem

## Who's Doing the Doo Doo?

seagull

pigeon

goose

small dog

big dog

duck

cockroach  mouse  sparrow  rat  squirrel  raccoon  skunk  cat  fly

*The size of the animal is directly proportional to the level fecal nuisance it presents to the urban environment.*

like bliss by comparison. In our colourful rural past, Darren's mother informs us, kids frequently got 25 cents per skunk carcass they could produce; this frequently meant setting leghold traps, killing the skunk, puking like sailors on weekend leave from the inevitable release of skunk spray, and prying the carcass out with a stick. But because we're evidently now a "humane" society, the only way to get rid of the little bastards is to stick a radio in their hole (skunks hate talk radio, so they can't be all bad) and have a pest-control company install a one-way door over the main entrance to their lair. Once the skunk is out of the hole they seal it up, and, hopefully, the skunk looks for an alternative residence. Unfortunately, this new residence is usually in the same vicinity.

Thanks to the wonders of global warming (just think: Thunder Bay as resort mecca!), many geese now refuse to migrate. Why should they? It's warm here all year

round now. So they continue to wander along the shores of ponds in our parks like so many drunken frat boys at a cheap buffet, eating and shitting their way through life. The only creatures who seem pleased about this are the innumerable dogs wandering the same space, gobbling up the goose grease and chasing the odd one into the water for amusement.

Vancouver Island is home to more cougar attacks than anywhere else in North America (big cats have even found their way into office buildings in downtown areas), though there have also been cougar sightings in Saskatoon. Helpful hint for surviving cougar attacks: do not make any sudden movements, and whatever you do, don't turn your back and run. Cougars kill by jumping on the backs of animals and biting their jugulars.

And just to make things interesting, every now and then a poisonous snake or two belonging to some idiot

WILDLIFE

with a fetish for dangerous reptiles will slither its way to freedom.

But even the pretty little animals can ultimately be dangerous to your health, so don't even bother trying to be nice to them. In 1997, 55-year-old Stefan Macko of Mississauga was standing on a wheeled chair, cleaning a bird feeder on the balcony of his condo, when he slipped and fell 23 stories to his death.

# Cats

*After pigeons, cats will be next, naturally. Their meat is soft but somewhat elastic. Boil it with papaya leaves to tenderize it. It tastes like skinny goat. Cat-hunting is difficult because the cat is the most protected animal in North America. Check out the neighborhood around the SPCA. There's always one or two hanging out there.*
—*Dany Laferrière,* A Drifting Year

### Sphynx Cats

There are fewer than 10,000 Sphynx cats in the whole world. They cost around $1,000 each, and the waiting list to get your hands on one of the precious felines is something like two years. What's the big deal about the Sphynx? Well, it's the only species of cat that's completely bald (a big selling point for nesting upper-class urbanites—see *Yuppies* and *Real Estate, Condos*). With their large pointed ears, wrinkled skin, and oval eyes they look like a cross between an alien and a reptile. Dr. Evil in Austin Powers holds one in his lap as he plots the world's destruction. Which is appropriate, because like Mike Myers, these peach-skinned creatures call Toronto their home.

That's right, the Sphynx breed is unique to Toronto. The first litter was discovered in 1963 in an alley near Roncesvalles Avenue. The new breed was the result of natural genetic mutation. Not only is the Sphynx the only urban cat breed to have arisen in a Canadian city, it is, in fact, the only cat breed to have ever originated in any city across the globe. We're proud to proclaim the Sphynx the ultimate urban Canadian pet, and urge our government to adopt it, alongside the wilderness clichés of beaver, moose, and loon, as one of our national animals.

# Dogs

Unlike cats (which we advocate, above, as either lifestyle accessory or important part of a healthy diet), dogs are all about sociability. Basically (to crib from poet Christopher Dewdney), a dog is a furry, detachable probe that allows people to make contact with others without risking too much of themselves in the process.

To understand how this works, all you have to do is visit your local "dog park." Every city has one, whether it's designated as such or not. Dog owners cheerfully gather at such places and let their pets do the introductions for them. What's odd is that people can and do remain on a nodding acquaintance for months or even years, cheerfully talking to people who they only identify as "the guy who owns Murray the golden retriever" or "the accountant lady with the terrier." Canadian dog parks have even been the subject of a feature-length film—Kid in the Hall Bruce McCulloch's *Dog Park* (1998), a goofy, mildly funny sex comedy starring McCulloch, Janeane Garofalo, Mark McKinney, Natasha Henstridge, and others. (See *Zeitgeist, Community* for more on the importance of dog parks in the neighbourhood.)

The major downside of having dogs in the city is, of course, the rate at which they produce dog shit. The staff here at Almanac Central (which consists of 50% dog owners) are strongly opposed to those who don't stoop and scoop. Especially in the summer, and especially during garbage strikes. So do your duty, dog owners, or we'll set the kooks after you (see *Kooks*).

# Cyborgs

Steve Mann is Canada's premier cyborg (man-machine integration). The Hamilton, Ontario–born electrical engineer sees through a computer in all his waking moments. The computer mediates his vision by filtering everything he sees through a hard drive and then projecting that view via laser beams into his eyes. As a result, Steve Mann is online 24–7, can zoom in and out on objects, and even see via freeze frame. Mann has been known to make a record of everything he sees (and, if he should so please, broadcast everything he sees live to the world wide web).

All of this has a point, which Mann articulates in his great book *Cyborg: Digital Destiny and Human Possibility in the Age of the Wearable Computer.* (Okay, we're a little biased since one of us Almanackers had a little to do with that tome…) In the book, Mann describes his cyborg coming-of-age in an 80s New Wave Hamilton, and articulates the need for personal and individual technologies that return to users the ability to control their own technological environment. A *Wired* magazine feature on

wearable computing describes him as a "counterpoint to the military-industrial complex" of "people designing computers as uniforms." Which is to say that Mann wants to reclaim the cyborg as a way to enhance individual freedom.

Whether you agree with him or not, he's definitely one of the more fascinating figures that can be encountered in the urban environment. If you're ever strolling around the University of Toronto campus, keep an eye out for him: he's the guy with the wraparound sunglasses and thinning hair who keeps walking into trees. Despite his general awkwardness, there seems little question that Steve Mann's time has come. As he once told an interviewer:

> Twenty years go there was no corporate interest in my work. Twenty years ago people called me Computer Steve, they called me Medusa with the wiring in my hair and everything. Twenty years ago this was all very weird; an ordinary walkie talkie was something really weird. Now the average businessman carries around a cellular telephone, he's got this antenna sticking out of his head and people don't think it's so weird any more.

# Rochdale and the Hippies

The topic of books, many articles, and a feature-length documentary by Ron Mann (*Dream Tower*), Rochdale College was an 18-storey concrete monolith that occupied the downtown corner of Bloor and Huron streets, blocks away from the University of Toronto. When it

Back in the day, you could mail order a Rochdale College diploma.

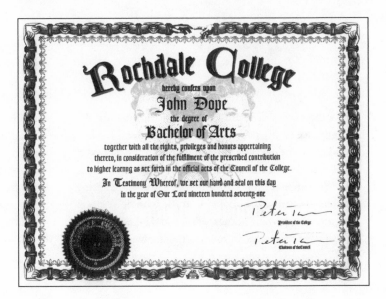

first opened its doors in 1968, it was the largest experiment in communal dwelling and alternative education in Canada and the world.

The College quickly became known for its quirky mix of high-rise living and hippie idealism. In fact, after the cops raided Yorkville and rousted out all the hippies, most of them moved straight into Rochdale, whether they had a room or not. People lived in the elevators, in the stairwells, and anyplace else they could manage. Rochdale developed a reputation as a haven for teenage runaways, suburban party-seekers, drug dealers, and deadbeats. Plagued by confrontations with the police and the community, internecine conflicts erupted about the need for security and financial accountability. At one point, the bikers had cordoned off a floor for the sole purpose of drug dealing. Governor General's Award–winning artist John Scott, a short-order cook in Rochdale at the time, recalls fearing to open his door because the bikers had hung a target on it and were using it for archery practice.

At its height, Rochdale housed US draft dodgers, bohemians thrown out of Yorkville, would-be revolutionaries, university students, and biker gangs as well as a clinic, health food store, recording studio, and even an illegal weekend pizza delivery business. It gave birth to or influenced some of Canada's most important cultural institutions, including Theatre Passe Muraille, Coach House Books, House of Anansi Press, and the Canadian Film Makers Distribution Centre. But it also served as impetus and venue for thousands of arrests, nine deaths (overdoses, suicides, and at least one murder), and millions of dollars in property damage. With its mixture of cultural urgency, deliberate anarchy, and accidental angst, Rochdale

was, and still is, the focal point of the 60s experience in Canada. A genuine icon, it is Canada's Woodstock and Altamont all rolled into one.

Rochdale closed its doors in 1975, amid riots, forced evictions, police raids, and bankruptcy. Built to house 900 people, it's estimated that more than 5,000 stayed in the building over its seven years.

# Queer Culture

"Right now," Jon Pressick, editor of the queer culture zine *Trade* tells us, the Canadian queer lifestyle "is without definition, and really is very fluid. The concept of the gay village (ghetto) is foreign to many queer people. Queer can now encompass so many seemingly disparate yet truly interconnected lifestyles that you cannot pin anyone down. Queer culture is in the financial district, the snob hills, the suburbs as well as the usual haunts of the arts crowds and student life."

When you want to write about queer life in the Canadian city, you run into a problem. As Pressick aptly notes, queer is not a monoculture, it is no longer located in a singular location, and it means more than bathhouses, drag shows, and pride parades featuring gleaming biceps and revealing (non)outfits. Queer is everywhere; it has slipped out of its ghetto and into the Canadian mainstream.

At the same time, queer still comes with a price, including prejudice, self-loathing, and gay bashing. In 2001 yet another gay man was brutally murdered in Stanley Park. One of the strangest true crime stories of 2002 was also a kind of gay-bashing killing. It happened in bucolic Victoria, where 33-year-old Gregory Thomas was sentenced for killing a 73-year-old Anglican lay brother, Lawrence Blakie. The murder happened after the two met in Beacon Hill Park and went back to Blakie's apartment. Blakie then spiked Thomas's drink with sedatives and proceeded to sexually assault him. Thomas woke up in the middle of all this, and ended up strangling and beating Blakie. Hardly an angel himself, he absconded with Blakie's valuables before running off.

Like so much that goes on in the city, there's a dark side to queer life that cannot be denied. Of course, much progress has been made in queer acceptance in the city and Canadian society. In 2001 Elaine and Annie Vautour become the first same-sex couple wed in Canada. The service was performed under the ancient Christian tradition of "the reading of the banns" and presided over by Rev. Brent Hawkes, who performed the marriage at the Metropolitan Community Church of Toronto. The marriage perhaps epitomizes queer culture in the Canadian city—at once accepted and on the fringe, secret and in-your-face, cutting-edge yet totally conservative.

What follows is a list of queer Can-city icons, personalities, and locales that don't define, but do describe:

- *The End of Gay,* Bert Archer: Conservative pundit Archer argues that the divisions between queer and straight are blurring and disappearing. Spiced up with memories of his early sex life!
- *Trade:* Toronto-based Queer culture zine with an emphasis on great writing and excellent interview subjects.
- *In a Queer Country: Gay and Lesbian Studies in the Canadian Context,* ed. Terry Goldie: Fourteen essays from established and emerging writers on the struggles, pleasures, and contradictions of queer culture and public life in Canada. Everything from queer black identity to lesbian park rangers.
- Buddies in Bad Times Theatre: Founded in 1979 by, among others, the prolific playwright and writer

QUEER CULTURE

Sky Gilbert, and located just outside of Toronto's infamous Church and Wellesley queer ghetto, Buddies in Bad Times is Canada's premier spot for cutting-edge performance with queer themes. Gilbert once described himself as "a pariah in the Gay community ... a thorn in the side of the conservative Gay community." The same, in a positive sense, can be said for the theatre he co-founded. (Famous urban gay playwrights include Montreal's Michel Tremblay, Toronto's Brad Fraser, R.M. Vaughan, and Sonja Mills.)

• *Jonathan et David,* Fr. Brumoy: This was one of the earliest books every published in Canada. It was originally a play that was performed in Montreal in 1776. The tale of the biblical friendship between Jonathan and David, it apparently includes a pronouncement of love between the two main characters. The priest who penned the play obviously wanted to make sure that his tale wouldn't be misconstrued. The work comes with a prologue warning us that the play is about "Tender friendship, holy friendship and not of [that friendship] which resides in the hearts of those who are slaves of crime."

• PrideVision TV: This TV channel was proudly launched on September 7, 2001. Based in Toronto, it's the only full-time queer cable channel in the world. Tune in to catch shows like *Locker Room*, a saucy comedy offering a half-hour look at the world of sports from a brand-new perspective. A really gay one!

What's queer life like in the urban Canadian city? We turned to the very smart R.M. Vaughan for elucidation of this matter. The Toronto-based writer and artist (orig-inally from New Brunswick) is the author of a fistful of poetry books, one novel, and a basketful of plays. Here, he tells us everything we need to know. Thanks, R.M. We get it now.

*How would you define Canadian urban queer culture?*
Perhaps the better question is: How would I de-claw Canadian Urban Queer Culture. Hey, that spells CUQC!

*What are the differences between the queer urban lifestyle and the straight urban lifestyle?*
Straight people who choose to live in Canada's cities are either poor, artistic, or students. Gay men spend every cent they have, think soap making is an art, and just never learn.

*How has urban queer life evolved and changed over the last 20 years?*
Generally, we are less likely to be killed. Generally.

*Describe your favourite urban queer hangout.*
"Urban queer hangout"? Why don't you ask me whether I'd prefer thumbnail screws or sleep deprivation?

*What is the future of queer culture in the Canadian city?*
Parades, tube tops, parades, tube tops, parades, tube tops, and, eventually, a Golden Labrador Retriever.

# Millionaires

Wanna be a millionaire? Well, you're not alone. Most urban Canadians—that is, most Canadians—have spent some time on the subway to the office, stuck in traffic, or cleaning up someone else's mess dreaming about what it would be like to be really really rich. Needless to say, the majority of Canada's wealthy types live in the cities, and it's in the city that evidence of gratuitous wealth is most visible in the form of lavish real estate, fancy cars, exclusive clubs and restaurants, blah blah blah, you get the idea even if you've never been able to afford the entrée.

There's something about proximity to the big money that leaves us wanting it so bad we can taste it. Some urbanites become dangerously obsessed with big money. So obsessed that they're convinced they're destined to be next. In a survey of Toronto accounting interns, only 25% thought they would *not* be millionaires one day. In other words, 75% of these *interns* were so addled by their proximity to wealth that they were positive riches were just around the corner.

Most of us never will be millionaires. The best we can do is hope to see millionaires on the streets of our cities as we go about our mundane, not-as-rich lives. But that's

not necessarily as easy as it seems. A portrait of the average millionaire in *Profit* magazine suggests that they "don't eat caviar and drink vintage wine, but stick to regular food." To add to the complicated issue of identification, apparently "most people who live in expensive homes and drive luxury cars do not actually have much wealth." So the real millionaire is frugal and, well, kinda boring.

How can we get our gratuitous thrills or our hooks into one if we can't even tell them apart from us plebeians? Luckily, the *Financial Post* comes to the rescue with this addled, lugubrious portrait: "When Canada's wealthy go on vacation, they head for a Four Seasons

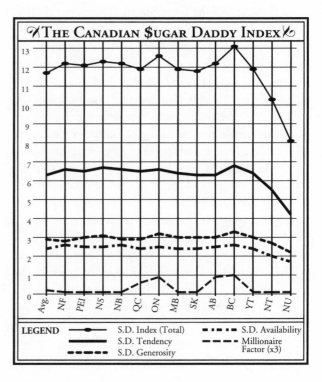

THE CANADIAN $UGAR DADDY INDEX

LEGEND
— S.D. Index (Total)
— S.D. Tendency
■■■■ S.D. Generosity
■ ■ ■ S.D. Availability
■ ■ ■ Millionaire Factor (x3)

hotel. When they shop for wheels, they look first at German luxury cars. And you're far more likely to find a millionaire on the golf course than the squash courts." So, okay, golf courses, Four Seasons bars, and Mercedes outlets are places you can expect to find "Canada's rich," who apparently "like the good things in life"—and have "earned the right to enjoy them." The *Financial Post* article, reporting the research of something called the Taddingstone Consulting Group, goes on to tell us that "most amassed their fortunes by working hard, investing shrewdly and saving scrupulously." So abandon all hope ye lottery players, Casino-Rama road trippers, and unscrupulous schemers.

If you're looking for millionaires to marry, abduct, or admire, you should probably try Vancouver. There were 56,218 millionaires living in British Columbia in 1999. That's the most of any province. Their average net worth was a cool $2.7 million. Among the more notable millionaires who've set up shop in Gastown is Rick Rockwell, the jilted groom from *Who Wants to Marry a Multimillionaire?* He finds the market in Vancouver to be "really ripe" and apparently picked up his downtown condo at a 30% discount from what it sold for seven years ago. Says Ricky: "There are values like that all over this city."

Canada's relatively young cities have always cared less about class and more about cash. Historian Max Foran tells us that "Calgary's elite tended to be imitative, and their upper-class trappings often appeared gauche … In the absence of tradition and heritage, entry to Calgary's upper class depended primarily on financial success." A fellow by the name of Pat Burns was Calgary's first bonafide millionaire. Described as "unprepossessing, chubby and uneducated," he cornered the slaughterhouse and meat-packing business out West in the late 1800s. He would later claim that he "made Calgary."

Millionaires are supposed to be mysterious and eccentric, but most of them, it seems, are cheap, dull, and obsessed with cattle and real estate. An exception, perhaps, was Simon McTavish, who was the richest man in early 19th century Montreal. As one of the heads of the North West Company, he secured a lovely lot with Mount Royal as a backdrop, upon which he planned to build a lavish castle. Nicknamed "the marquis," McTavish was an aloof figure who became obsessed with his grand manse. But he also found time to indulge in his passions: women, wine, and oysters. He even took a bullet in a duel after he slighted another fellow's rep. McTavis survived the duel but passed away unexpectedly before his mansion was even half completed. The partially built mansion was torn down, and a workman helping with the dismantling fell and died. This fuelled rumours that McTavish's ghost was haunting Mount Royal, where he was interred. McGill students cross-country skiing across the mountain late at night would stop by the site intent on taunting his ghost, which was said to make the occasional appearance.

What does this story tell us about millionaires in urban Canada? Not much, really. But the next time you see some flashy type counting his credit cards in his German automobile, keep in mind that being rich can be a sad, lonely, dangerous business. After all, millionaire brewer John Labatt was the first person to be kidnapped for ransom in Canada. Abducted at gunpoint on the way home from his cottage by three men who asked for a ransom of $150,000, Labatt eventually turned up in the lobby of Toronto's Royal York Hotel after his kidnappers panicked and released him unharmed. The *Financial Post* remains bewildered: Why didn't he check into the Four Seasons?

# Immigrants

"Immigrant" has become kind of a negative word in Canada, which is strange because, to evoke the cliché, Canada is a country founded by immigrants. This is especially true of Canada's cities, which exist only because of the immigrants whose fortunes and perils so closely mirrored the peaks and valleys of our urban history. Perhaps it's time to reclaim the word *immigrant*, to wear it proudly on our sleeves as a symbol of courage, industriousness, and Canadian city values (whatever those are). After all, at the heart of Canada's growth and maturity into a real country is the city's collective acceptance of different nationalities and backgrounds, allowing Canada to use the talents of our newest citizens and enrich all our lives—whether through bringing the cooking of Afghanistan to a local neighbourhood or conducting groundbreaking, world-renowned research at the local hospital.

Much rhetoric has been employed about the benefits of immigrant life to Canadian society, but in the end the diversity of our cities, their relative prosperity, their safety and accessibility, speak for themselves. Of the 3.3 million people living in greater Montreal, about 2.2 million are French speaking, there are around 400,000 anglophones, and *580,000 Quebecers consider another language as their first*. Toronto is home to people from 169 different countries, speaking *100 different languages*. There are few other cities in the world where you can move as quickly from a Little Lisbon to a Small Saigon to a Bit of Beijing, sampling delicacies and pop culture oddities all along.

Just as an example of the kind of inviting life that once-strange immigrant cultures carve out of the forbidding big city, let's look at the Polish community of Toronto. There are something like 150,000 people of Polish origin living in the Greater Toronto Area. They enjoy two daily newspapers, five magazines, three radio shows, four television shows, an amateur orchestra, a Polish Film Festival, and even an annual Polish Day at Ontario Place. This enriches not only their lives, but the lives of all Canadians who want to, say, sample a traditional Polish meal or check out a Polish movie. "There's no way a Polish city with that population would be as cultured," Wojciech Sniegowski, a Polish TV producer with CFMT and co-presenter of Polish Day, once told the *Toronto Star*. "It's because Canada gives us so much opportunity for self-expression."

Since just about all Canadians were immigrants to this country's cities, it's really impossible to cite particularly wonderful and laudable people who made a significant contribution to Canadian life. Timothy Eaton,

William James, City of Toronto Archives

Immigrants arrive in Toronto, 1910

IMMIGRANTS

*Dany Laferrière was a Haitian journalist before fleeing to Montreal out of fear for his life. In* A Drifiting Year *he describes his difficult first months in Montreal:*

This morning I went to the office on Sherbrooke Street that offers temporary help to immigrants. The guy looking after my file told me that if I was willing to declare I was an exile, he could give me sixty dollars instead of the usual twenty he hands out to ordinary immigrants. I wasn't an exile; I fled before they could kill me. That's different. He smiled and gave me an envelope. When I opened it in the street, I found one hundred and twenty dollars.

*Joanna Pawelkiewicz is a Toronto writer whose zine,* Giant Kielbasa, *deals with issues of body size and ethnicity. Here she charts her path from Poland to Toronto:*

1986, Greece: While on a "family vacation" in Greece, my parents inform me that we are never going back to Poland, and we are immigrating to Canada instead. I still remember the anger and fear I felt.

1987, Mississauga: The landlady was reluctant to rent to us because she had problems with people like "us" before. My uncle bought her a $100 gold chain and she changed her mind... The enchantment of immigration began to wear off soon. My dad, who is a pilot by trade, worked in a box-making factory, and my mom, a Polish-Russian translator, worked at the Dixie Value Mall.

2000, Toronto: Lately I've been feeling very homesick. I am not sure what it is I miss about the old country. I try to recreate "home" by renting Polish movies or catching up with my grandma ... If I go back home (for a month, a year ...) will I feel at home? Will my fat hips and dodgy Polish mark me as a foreigner?

a surly Irish immigrant, took his kick at the can in 1869 when he opened up his first dry goods operation. Ujjal Dosanjh came to this country in 1964 and ended up as the premier of British Columbia—the first Indo-Canadian to lead a province. Dosanjh, who didn't even speak English until he was 17 years old, spent the 80s as an outspoken, crusading immigration lawyer, and was attacked and beaten with an iron bar after he publicly condemned his fellow Sikhs for applauding the assassination of Indira Gandhi.

But not all immigrants to this country have to be outspoken power brokers in order to be remembered. Consider the legacy of Vancouver's Seraphim "Joe" Fortes, originally of Barbados. Through the 1890s, Joe lived in a shack on the shore side of Beach Avenue. When not working, he took it upon himself to manage the beach, teaching kids to swim and watching over them. Finally, he was officially appointed lifeguard of the beach and is credited with over 100 witnessed rescues. When houses were cleared away from the beach, the mayor personally saw to it that Joe's cottage be moved up to the park beside the bandstand, where it would stand as long as Joe lived. Joe died in 1922 of pneumonia, and the ensuing cathedral funeral was filled with sobbing admirers of all races, creeds, and classes. A plaque was subsequently erected in the park. It shows the head and shoulders of the Barbadian immigrant and bears the inscription: "Little children loved him."

# Endnotes

## Introduction
**p. viii** course outline: <mage.geog.macalester.edu/apgeogdemo/acity.html>.

## Zeitgeist
**p. 2 Peter Warren:** <www.blupete.com/Hist/NovaScotiaBk1/Part5/Ch04.htm>.

**p. 4 Margaret Ormsby:** Allan Morley, *Vancouver: From Milltown to Metropolis,* Vancouver: Mitchell Press, 1961, p. 210.

**p. 4 J.G. MacGregor:** J.G. MacGregor, *Edmonton,* Edmonton: M.G. Hurtig Publishing, 1967, p. 17.

**p. 6 Native Cities:** James and Robert Simmons, *Urban Canada,* Toronto: Copp Clark Publishing, 1969, p. 49.

**p. 6 Lorne Foster:** "Small Talk in the Big City," *City Magazine,* 1988, reprinted in *The Canadian City,* ed. Kent Gerecke, Black Rose Books, 1991.

**p. 6 William Teron:** William Teron, "A New Canadian Environment," *The City: Canada's Prospects, Canada's Problems,* ed. Lloyd Axworthy and James M. Gillies, Butterworth, 1973.

**p. 8 Lorna Bailie:** <www.canoe.ca/National Ticker/CANOE-wire.Mental-Health-Survey.html>.

**p. 9 Valerie Kalynchuk:** Valerie Joy Kalynchuk, *All Day Breakfast,* Montreal: Conundrum Press, 2001.

**p. 13 "…after Evelyn's discharge from hospital.":** Betty Nygaard King, *Hell Hath No Fury: Famous Women in Crime,* Ottawa: Borealis Press, 2001, pp. 61–77.

**p. 18 Bryce M. Stewart:** Paul Rutherford, ed., *Saving the Canadian City,* Toronto: University of Toronto Press, 1974.

## Transportation
**p. 25 "…only two biking-related deaths.":** Ian Edwards, "Cracking Down on Cyclists," *Financial Post,* September 18, 1998, p. D6.

**p. 27 Grant Buday:** Grant Buday, ed., *Exact Fare Only,* Vancouver: Anvil Press, 2000, p. 9.

**p. 28 "…increasing at a mere 1.5% annually.":** Dennis Bueckert, "Choking on Traffic Congestion," *The Canadian Press,* June 22, 2000.

**p. 29 "…three years more than desirable.":** <www.tc.gc.ca/programs/environment/urbantransportation/transitstudies/urban.htm#Current>.

**p. 32 "…UFO sightings that year.":** Scott Edmonds, "UFO Sightings Up in Canada," *The Canadian Press,* February 26, 2002.

**p. 33 "Official admonition from 1800 reads":** G.P. Glazebrook, *The Story of Toronto,* Toronto: University of Toronto Press, 1971, p. 27.

**p. 36 "…the non-linear behaviour of the system as a whole.":** Tracy Picha, "Physicists, Engineers, See Cause of Gridlock Differently," *National Post,* December 29, 2000.

## Tools
**p. 38 BAI global study:** *Lola* #7, Fall 2000.

**p. 39 Pink-N-Ink:** <rr.sans.org/authentic/ATM_theft.php>.

**p. 40 "…a teller machine at Yonge and Eglinton.":** <urbanlegends.about.com/library/blatm.htm>.

**p. 41 Zagat Restaurant Guides:** <www.getgirls.com/tips188.htm>.

**p. 41 Dr. Don Rendelmeier:** <www.cbc.ca/consumers/indepth/celldriving>.

**p. 42 *Canadian Medical Association Journal:*** Robert S. Remis, "HIV Incidence Among Injection Drug Users in Vancouver," *Canadian Medical Association Journal,* vol. 166, 2002, pp. 908–909.

**p. 42 Earl Berger:** <globeandmail.workopolis.com/servlet/News/fasttrack/20020302/UDRUGN?title=Sales>.

**p. 43 *The Straight Goods:*** <www.straightgoods.com/Boutin/010312.asp>.

**p. 43 *The Globe and Mail:*** <globeandmail.workopolis.com/servlet/News/fasttrack/20020302/UDRUGN?title=Sales>.

**p. 43 RCMP:** <www.rcmp-grc.gc.ca/crim_int/drugs_2001_e.htm#khat>.

**p. 43 "…known on the street as 'Cat.'":** <www.sas.upenn.edu/African_Studies/Hornet/qat.html>.

**p. 44 Tiffany Wong:** Tiffany Wong, "An (E)xperience," *Jook Sing Mui,* Mississauga.

**p. 44 "…dropped to the dance floor with seizures.":** Broadcast transcript, CTV NEWS, April 3, 2000.

**p. 44 "…by just saying no.":** Broadcast transcript, *The National,* CBC, May 8, 2000.

**p. 44 Drugs Seized in Canada table:** <www.rcmp-grc.gc.ca/crim_int/drugs_2001_e.htm>.

**p. 45 Captain John Smith:** <www.koffeekorner.com/koffeehistory.htm>.

**p. 45 "…we consume are coffee-based.":** <wwww.coffeeassoc.com>.

**p. 46 "…down to trendy neighbourhood-lite Queen Street.":** "Starbucks Cast as Villain," *Ottawa Citizen,* September 16, 1996.

## Attractions
**p. 54 "…gathered to talk things over in the summer evenings.":** William Coates Barrett, *Historic Halifax in Tales Told Under the Old Time Clock,* Toronto: Ryerson Press, 1948.

**p. 57 "…but always hit the mark.":** Alan Morley, *Vancouver: From Milltown to Metropolis,* Vancouver: Mitchell Press, 1961.

**p. 57 "…ventured to reside there.":** William Coates Barrett (quoting Doctor Akins, 1813), *East Coast Port and Other Tales Told Under the Old Town Clock,* Halifax: Imperial Publishing, 1944.

**p. 57 "…such as Toronto and Vancouver.":** Shannon Sutherland, "Bar Starts Trend in Calgary" *Financial Post,* October 20, 1998, p. 22.

**p. 62 Sandra Haar:** Terence Dick, "Not Just for Perverts: Canada's First Co-op Sex Shop," *Broken Pencil* #9, 1999.

**p. 62 Tamara Faith Berger:** Tamara Faith Berger, *Lie with Me,* Toronto: Gutter Press, 2000.

**p. 63 Renata Ramunda:** Renata Ramunda, *Sex Shoppe Tales,* Hamilton: Sex Shoppe Tales.

**p. 64 Simona Choise:** Simona Chiose, *Good Girls Do,* Toronto: ECW Press, 2001.

**p. 73 "…setting up an auto show).":** <www.sfo.com/~csuppes/CFL/misc/index.htm?../Montreal/index.htm>.

**p. 73 "…don't count for much in Alberta either.":** <www.breadnotcircuses.org/kris_olds_p20.html>.

## Food
**p. 82 "…specialize in these drinks.":** Marian Burros, *New York Times,* <www.tourismvancouver.com/docs/media/mediakit/restaurants/quotes.html>.

**p. 83 Jason Dunda:** *Lola* #5, Winter 1999–2000.

**p. 84 Manhattan:** <open.nit.ca/career>.

**p. 84 Kingtston:** <www.paintedladyinn.on.ca/historyKingston.html>.

**p. 84 Quebec City:** <www.yankee-holidays.com/Canadian_Destinations.html>.

**p. 84 Saskatoon:** <www.ccaecanada.org/conference/english/about.html>.

**p. 84 Winnipeg:** <www.scri.sari.ac.uk/ITMI/winnipeg.pdf>.

**p. 84 Manhattan:** <www.nwcb.org/convention2001.asp>.

**p. 86 Rosa Pryor: Rosa Pryor, "Opening Doors:** Vancouver's East End," *Blueprint: Black British Columbian Literature and Orature*, ed. Wayde Compton, Vancouver: Arsenal Pulp Press 2001.

## Shopping

**p. 90 "...billboard spots in Canada has soared by 42%.":** John Heinzl, "Billboards Enjoy Boom Times," *Globe and Mail,* June 16, 1999, p. M1.

**p. 90 "...can live without them.":** Carol Masciola, "Stolen Barbies, Unplayed With," *International Herald Tribune*, October 15, 1992.

**p. 91 The Emperor's New Mall:** Douglas Coupland, *Generation X: Tales for an Accelerated Culture*, New York: St Martin's Press, 1992, p. 71.

**p. 92 "...than wear GAP.":** <alberta.indymedia.org/features/arts_culture>.

**p. 93 Fun-O-Rama interview by Dave:** Cussword, from *Broken Pencil* #1, 1995.

**p. 100 Jason Dunda:** *Lola* #6, Summer 2000.

## Arts and Entertainment

**p. 142 "...will lure the lost viewers back.":** <www.canadacomputes.com/v3/story/1,1017,5476,00.html?tag=133&sb=299>.

**p. 143 "...or sets new lows for sloppy camera work).":** <www.mztv.com/moses.html>.

**p. 143 Moses Znaimer's Laws of TV:** <www.mala.bc.ca/~soules/media212/znaimer.htm>.

**p. 145 "Thanks for the trauma, Waxman.":** <wwwjumptheshark.com/k/kingofkensington.htm>.

**p. 146 "...a package of condoms into the purchase.":** <www.geocities.com/morbidaj/degrassi.htm>.

**p. 147 "...and was aquitted a year later.":** <www.degrassi.ca/Press-Releases/DegrassiCrime.htm>, Degrassi.org/Degrassi Webring <www.degrassi.org>, AJ's Degrassi Universe </www.geocities.com/morbidaj>, Pat Mastroianni (Joey Jeremiah) <www.patmeup.com>.

**p. 148 "...was cancelled by the CBS brass.":** <www.mbcnet.org/archives/etv/T/htmlT/thishourhas/thishourhas.htm>.

**p. 156 Bruce la Bruce:** <www.eye.net/eye/issue/issue_07.16.98/plus/feelings.html>.

**p. 173 "...in all the small towns along the tracks.":** <www.snowcrest.net/bndlstif/canada.html>.

**p. 175 John Nugent:** <www.plugin.org/disarm/archive.htm>.

**p. 184 "...his middle name is misery.":** <www.oacconline.org/oacc01-2.htm>, <www.tv.cbc.ca/witness/elvis/timeline.htm>, <www.canoe.ca/CNEWSLaw0201/25_elvis-sun.html>.

## Real Estate

**p. 186 J.J. Kelso:** J.J. Kelso, "Can Slums be Abolished or Must We Continue to Pay the Penalty?" *Saving the Canadian City*, ed. Paul Rutherford, Toronto: University of Toronto Press, 1974.

**p. 188 Vince Tingley:** Vince Tinguely, *Perfect Waste of Time* #20, July 1997.

**p. 156 "...an increasingly wary public.":** <www.bankruptcycanada.com/leakycondo1.htm>.

**p. 156 "...$2 billion in indirect costs.":** <monopolyinvest2.freeyellow.com/leakycondos.html>.

**p. 156 "...through litigation, bankruptcies, and foreclosures.":** <www.soakedhomes.com>.

**p. 158 "...but so do you.":** <www.celebrationfl.com>.

## Politics

**p. 206 Herbert B. Ames:** Herbert B. Ames, "The Machine in Honest Hands," *Saving the Canadian City*, ed. Paul Rutherford, Toronto: University of Toronto Press, 1974.

**p. 207 "...per unit of service as they grow larger.":** <www.publicpurpose.com/tor-emp.htm>.

**p. 208 Regina Challenges Toronto ...:** <www.saskabush.com/2001/0214/regina_challenges_toronto.html>.

**p. 209 "...could afford the fancy new digs.":** <www.breadnotcircuses.org/kris_olds_p20.html>.

**p. 211 "...appearance of far-off lands.":** *Toronto Star*, July 6, 2002.

**p. 210 World-Class Vancouver:** *Geist* #45, Summer 2002.

**p. 211 James and Robert Simmons:** *Urban Canada*, Toronto: Copp Clark Publishing, 1969, p. 133.

**p. 214 "...most aggressive anti-poverty activist.":** *The National*, CBC-TV, July 21, 2000.

**p. 214 "...driving them up the wall.":** Lynda Hurst, "A Rebel Without Applause: In-Your-Face Activist Makes Enemies Despite His Noble Causes," *Toronto Star*, February 12, 2000.

**p. 214 "...to have any impact on the staff.":** Jim Coyle, "Loblaws Five Case Hinges on Minister's Tunafish Story," *Ottawa Citizen*, March 31, 1996.

## Denizens

**p. 218 Donna Kossey:** <home.pacifier.com/~dkossy/kooksmus.html#lobby>.

**p. 219 "FOR FOOLS AND TRAITORS—NOTHING!":** <www.rickross.com/reference/general/general415.html>.

**p. 220 "...as well as Saints John and Luke.":** <www.nlc-bnc.ca/2/4/h4-3257-e.html>.

**p. 220 The Gentle Swastika:** <www.gentleswastika.com/Introduction.html>.

**p. 220 Friends of the Swastika Declaration of Independence:** <pub48.bravenet.com/guestbook/show.asp?usernum=4096327776>.

**p. 220 Mark Mothertsbaugh:** <www.cyberlink.bc.ca/~manwoman/biography.html>.

**p. 220 ManWoman's paintings:** <www.manwoman.net/art>.

**p. 223 Clystemstra:** Clystemstra, *Spooky Winnipeg*, Winnipeg.

**p. 225 Paul Sullivan:** <www.bconnex.net/~cspcc/daycare/canyup.htm>.

**p. 227 Jason Dunda:** *Lola* #9, Summer 2001.

**p. 231 Gregory Boyd Bell:** <www.eye.net/eye/issue/issue_07.30.98/news_views/media30.html>.

**p. 231 "...during the program's first four days.":** <aspin.asu.edu/hpn/archives/Jul99/0112.html>.

**p. 231 Daniel Cross:** <www.spit.ca>.

**p. 242 Dany Laferrière:** Dany Laferrière, trans. David Homel, *A Drifting Year*, Vancouver: Douglas & McIntyre, 1997.

# Index

intellectuals, 221–223

**K**

Kalynchuk, Valerie Joy, 9–10
khat, 43
*Kids in the Hall*, 145–146
*King of Kensington*, 144–145
kooks, 218–221
Koulakis, Tony (Man of Grease), 84

**L**

Laferrière, Dany, 242
landlords, 186–190
Langlois, Drue, 225–229
Lastman, Mel, 204–205
lifestyle drugs, 42–43
Lindo, Rory, 98–101
literature, 158–168
lofts, 190
*Lola*, 229

**M**

macaroni and cheese, 87–88
Mackenzie King, William Lyon, 219–220
Madame Zee, 218–219
malls, 90–91, 96–98
Mann, Steve, 235
ManWoman, 220
marijuana inspirations. *See* Victoria, Queen of
    England
Martin, Médéric, 203
mating calls. *See* stupid people with loud cars
mayors, 202–205
McCallion, Hazel, 203–204
McGimpsey, David, 9
McIntyre, James, 167–168
McTaggart, 183–184
megacities, 207–208
mental illness, 8–11
metal party, 50
Milgaard, David, 14, 15–16
millionaires, 239–240
Mississauga Anime Shopping Guide, 101
Montreal, 9–10, 56
Montreal Olympics, 73
movies, 148–151
MuchMusic, 142–143
music, 175–184
Music Nazis, 51

**N**

natural disaster, benefits of, 22
newspapers, 138–140
*The Newsroom*, 148
Ninjalicious, 198–200
nostalgia, 19–21

**O**

Olympics, 71–73

organized crime, 12
Ottawa, 4–6

**P**

panhandlers, 231–232
parties, 50–51
Pawelkiewicz, Joanna, 242
phonebashers, 41
*Pocketman*, 220–221
poetry, 163–166
poetry readings, graceful exodus from,
    166–167
prescription drug sites, 42–43
public access cable, 143–144
public art, 173–175
public transit, 27–31
publishers, independent, 168–169
pubs, 56–59
punk, 180–183

**Q**

queer culture, 236–239

**R**

racism, 17–19
radio, 140
Radio-Locator, 140
raw mercantile lust. *See* box stores
recipes, 87–88
record stores, independent, 95–96
regulars, 58
restaurant reviewers, 84–86
restaurants, 84
Richard, Maurice, 69–70
Riel, Louis, 174
Rochdale College, 235–236
rock, 176–177
rollerblades, 31

**S**

Saint John, 206–207
same-sex marriages, 237
school supplies, top ten, 39
scooters, 31
sculpture, 173–175
seediness, 59
sex, 60–64
sex stores, 61–62
sexual liberation, great moments in, 60–61
Simpson, George, 98
skateboarding, 31
sneakers, 100
soccer. *See* football
Sphynx cats, 234
sports, 64–71
squeegee kids, 230–231
St. John's, 206–207
Starbucks, multifarious nature of, 45–46
stupid people with loud cars, 23

suburbanites
    Britney clones, 40–41
    commuters, 36
    matched sets, 92
    night on the town, 23
suburbs, 191–193
Subway Elvis, 183–184
Syed, Shaan, 228

**T**

T&A joints, 58–59
tacos, 88
tax burden legacy. *See* Montreal Olympics
Taylor, Louis D., 203
teenage crime, 14
television, 140–148
*This Hour Has 22 Minutes*, 148
Tim Hortons coffee, need for, 46–47
Toronto Olympic bid, 71–72
traffic, 33–36
TransFair Canada, 46
turntablism, 180
24-hour activity, 87

**U**

UFO sightings, 32–33
urban multicultural menu, 76–84

**V**

Vancouver-Whistler Olympic bid, 73, 210–211
Vaughan, R.M., 238–239
veggie curry, 88
veteran lit, 160–161
Victoria, Queen of England, 6
volleyball, indoor beach, 73–74

**W**

washing machines, beer and vomit in, 50
watering holes, 56–59
Webcams, 47–48
West Edmonton Mall, 96–98
wildlife, 232–234
Wilson, Sharon, 26
window washers, 230
Winnipeggers, vs. public art, 173–175
"world class." *See* inferiority complex
Wrinkly Old Guy, 58

**Y**

Young, Neil, 137
youth subculture, 211–214
yuppies, 224–225

**Z**

zines, 169–172
Znaimer, Moses, 142–14